Cockapoo Training

The Comprehensive Training Guide

Ken Leonard

All rights reserved. No part of this publication may be reproduced, distributed, or transmitted in any form or by any means, including photocopying, recording, downloading from a website or other informational storage, retrieval systems, electronic or mechanical methods, without the prior written permission of the publisher/author.

Disclaimer and Legal Notice

The author has made every effort to ensure the accuracy of the information within this book was correct at time of publication. Whilst the author has tried to keep the information up-to-date and correct, there are no representations or warranties, express or implied, about the completeness, accuracy, reliability, suitability or availability with respect to the information, products, services, or related graphics contained in this publication for any purpose. The author does not assume and hereby disclaims any liability to any party for any loss, damage, or disruption caused by errors or omissions, whether such errors or omissions result from accident, negligence, or any other cause.

The methods described within this publication are the author's prior knowledge and/or personal thoughts and/or opinions and/or experience of the subject. They are not intended to be a definitive set of instructions for this subject. Other methods, instructions, opinions and materials may be available to accomplish the same end result. Again under no circumstance can the author/publisher accept legal responsibility or liability for any loss, damage to property and/or personal injury, arising from any error or omissions from the information contained in this publication or from failure of the reader to correctly and precisely follow any information contained within the publication.

3rd party sources/information:

The author/publisher has no control, and is therefore not responsible for the content, availability or nature of any third party websites or other publications listed herein. Access and use of information of third party websites or other publications, is at your own risk. Any website publication or the information listed within them should not be implied as an endorsement or recommendation by the author/publisher.

The information provided within this publication, is strictly for educational purposes and general informational purposes only. If you wish to apply ideas contained in this publication, you are taking full responsibility for your actions. Therefore, any use of this information is at your own risk.

Additional Disclaimer and Legal Notice information:

You must not in any circumstances:
a) publish, republish, sell, license, sub-license, rent, transfer, broadcast, distribute or redistribute the publication or any part of the publication;
b) edit, modify, adapt or alter the publication or any part of the publication;
c) use of the publication or any part of the publication in any way that is unlawful or in breach of any person's legal rights under any applicable law, or in any way that is offensive, indecent, discriminatory or otherwise objectionable;
d) use of the publication or any part of the publication to compete with us, whether directly or indirectly; or
e) use the publication or any part of the publication for a commercial purpose

(1) No advice

The publication contains information about Cockapoo dogs. The information is not advice, and should not be treated as such. You must not rely on the information in the publication as an alternative to (legal/medical/veterinary/ financial/accountancy or other relevant) advice from an appropriately qualified professional. If you have any specific questions about any (legal/medical /veterinary/financial/accountancy or other relevant) matter you should consult an appropriately qualified professional.

(2) Limited Warranties

We do not warrant or represent that the use of the publication will lead to any particular outcome or result.

(3) Limitations and exclusions of liability

We will not be liable to you in respect of any business losses, including (without limitation) loss of or damage to profits, income, revenue, use, production, anticipated savings, business, contracts, commercial opportunities or goodwill.

We will not be liable to you in respect of any loss or corruption of any data, database, hardware or software. We will not be liable to you in respect of any special, indirect or consequential loss or damage.

(4) Trademarks

Registered and unregistered trademarks or service marks in the publication are the property of their respective owners. Unless stated otherwise, we do not endorse and are not affiliated with any of the holders of any such rights and as such we cannot grant any licence to exercise such rights.

ಊ

Author Note

PLEASE NOTE:

This book contains training information that has previously been reproduced as part of the book "Cockapoo, Comprehensive Care From Puppy to Senior" by the same author, Ken Leonard. The intention of this publication is to offer readers an abridged training version of that book. It is therefore intended for readers who have perhaps already purchased another complete owners manual and who do not wish to purchase another one, but who are now looking for a much more complete, detailed, beginner to advanced training manual.

PLEASE ALSO NOTE:

If you are reading this information as an experienced dog owner, then parts will already be familiar to you. Having said that, the information is intended for everyone and I am sure that even the experienced dog person will find a lot of new facts and information.

It is not my intention to patronise the reader and to tell you how you should read a book. However, unless you are an experienced dog person and are confident enough to skip certain sections, I would highly recommend that you thoroughly read all of the contents before you begin to implement any of the instructions. You may wish to take notes as you go or re-read the book a second time noting important steps to give yourself an action plan.

Also, please note that the use of 'he' or 'him' will be used throughout the text and is simply for ease of reading. It is generally intended to refer to both sexes. It is not meant to indicate a preference by the author of one sex over the other. 'She' or 'her', may also be used specifically where it is more appropriate to indicate the female (bitch) as opposed to the male (dog).

Please also note that throughout the book you will come across website links. At the time of press, the web links were working. However, from time to time, pages get changed, deleted or a supplier goes out of business. If you find these do not work, please go to the route .com or .co.uk web address. Again, the author takes no responsibility for the availability of any of these, when you the reader come to access them.

Table of Contents

Chapter One: 1
Understanding Cockapoos

1.) An overview of The Cockapoo . . . 1

Chapter Two: 5
Necessary Supplies and Equipment Relating to Training

Chapter Three: 7
Preparing for the arrival

1.) Dog-Proofing Your Home 7

2) Toxins To Be Aware of in Your Home.....12

3) Establishing rules before you puppies arrival 13

4) Where Will your Dog Sleep?. 14

5) Setting Up Your Cockapoo's Crate. 14

Chapter Four: 15
Bringing your Cockapoo puppy/adult dog home

1) The First Day Home 15

2) CHECKLIST FOR THE ARRIVAL OF YOUR PUPPY   16
3) DOGS AND CHILDREN 17
7) INTRODUCING YOUR PUPPY TO CHILDREN   19

CHAPTER FIVE: 20
COCKAPOO TOILET TRAINING

1) NECESSARY TOILET TRAINING SUPPLIES . 21
2) GOOD TOILET TRAINING PRACTICE. . . 21
3) TOILET TRAINING ROUTINE 21
4) TOILET TRAINING PROCEDURE INDOORS . 24
5) NIGHT TIME ROUTINE 24
6) CHECK LIST AND SIGNS THAT YOUR PUPPY WILL NEED TO TOILET 25
7) CRATE TRAINING INTRODUCTION. . . . 26
8) ADULT AND RESCUE DOGS 30

CHAPTER SIX: 30
COCKAPOO SOCIALISATION

1) WHY SOCIALISE 30
2) THE 'CRITICAL PERIOD' AND SOCIALISATION   31
3) SOCIALISATION, AND WHO YOUR DOG SHOULD INTERACT WITH 32
4) VACCINATIONS AND SOCIALISATION . . . 34

CHAPTER SEVEN: 35
INITIAL COCKAPOO OBEDIENCE TRAINING

1) HOW YOUR COCKAPOO MAY REACT DURING TRAINING 36
2) POPULAR TRAINING METHODS. 36
3) HOW DOGS LEARN 40
4) OTHER TRAINING CONSIDERATIONS . . . 42
5) INSTINCTS: THE PACK/PREY DRIVE AND TRAINING 42
6) COLLAR/HARNESS & LEASH TRAINING . 43
7) OBEDIENCE TRAINING – TEACHING BASIC COMMANDS 45
8) PHASING OUT FOOD REWARDS 60
9) DISCIPLINE WHILST TRAINING 60
10) PROOFING/GENERALISING BEHAVIORS. . 61

CHAPTER EIGHT: 62
ADVANCED COCKAPOO GUNDOG TRAINING

1) RECOMMENDED ACCESSORIES 62
2) WHISTLE AND HAND SIGNALS 63
3) INTRODUCING GUNSHOT 64
4) ADVANCED 'SIT' COMMAND FOR GUNDOGS 65
5) THE 'STOP' COMMAND 69
6) OFF LEAD RUNS 72
7) THE RETRIEVE (SEND BACK). 73
8) TWO DUMMY SEND BACK 75
9) TWO DUMMY RETRIEVE WITH LEFT, RIGHT AND AWAY HAND SIGNALS) 76
10) THE 'GO BACK' 77
11) THREE DUMMY RETRIEVE 78
12) THE INITIAL BLIND RETRIEVE 79
13) ACTUAL BLIND RETRIEVES 79
14) STEADINESS 81
15) INTRODUCTION TO WATER. 83
16) HOW GUNDOGS HUNT: THE HUNTING CHAIN 84
17) HUNTING/QUARTERING 87
18) OBSTACLE TRAINING. 91
19) FIELD TRIALS AND WORKING TESTS . . 92
20) ESSENTIAL EXERCISE 93

CHAPTER NINE: 95
COCKAPOO BEHAVIOR PROBLEMS

1) DEALING WITH COMMON BEHAVIOR PROBLEMS 95

CHAPTER TEN: 116
WEEK BY WEEK PUPPY DEVELOPMENT & CARE GUIDE: 8 WEEKS OLD TO 1 YEAR AND BEYOND

iv

Chapter One:

Understanding Cockapoos

In this book you will learn beginner to advanced training methods which if implemented correctly will save you time, frustration and ensure you have a happy, healthy, well behaved dog. You will learn what makes the Cockapoo tick and just about everything else you need to know to successfully understand and train your puppy, or adult dog. In order to understand the Cockapoo, you will also be presented with valuable information about the Poodle and Cocker Spaniel parent breeds which will enable you to understand the Cockapoo more completely.

1.) An overview of The Cockapoo

The Cockapoo as it is commonly known, is also known as Cockerpoo, Cock-A-Poo, Cockadoodle (in Sweden), and commonly known in Australia as a Spoodle (Spaniel/Poodle).

The Cockapoo is the result of a crossing between the Poodle and the Cocker Spaniel. However, it is important to note, in case you are not already aware, that the Poodle comes in three sizes; Toy, Miniature and Standard.

In most cases, the Cockapoo is the result of breeding a Cocker Spaniel with a Toy or a Miniature Poodle, but the larger Standard Poodles are also used.

Both the English and American Cocker Spaniels are used and respectively known as either an English or American Cockapoo. However, that isn't to say that only the American Cocker is used in the US and the English in the UK. Breeders in both countries have been known to use either breed. Some breeders and owners also prefer the English Working Cocker Spaniel as opposed to the English or American 'show' Cocker Spaniel.

All of these parent breeds are known for their friendly temperament and charming personalities, so you can expect the Cockapoo to also embody these qualities.

The Cockapoo has the social, family-loving personality of the Poodle as well as some of its intelligence. These characteristics overlap with the friendly, relatively easy going, devoted, people-oriented personality traits for which the Cocker Spaniel is known. It is therefore unsurprising that the Cockapoo is a very social dog that loves to make new friends and that gets along well with children and other pets.

One thing to bare in mind from the outset however, is that the Cockapoo can vary from a moderately active dog to a very active dog. We will go into more detail as we go, but you need to be aware that if a 'working' Cocker Spaniel is used as a parent breed, there is a strong possibility that the Cockapoos produced may have very high energy levels. This obviously means that the dog will require a lot more exercise and training than other Cockapoos. This will not be a problem if you live an active, outdoors lifestyle. But such dogs may prove to be a totally unsuitable choice if you cannot provide opportunities for them to burn off excess energy.

Other than that, Cockapoos are generally very adaptable to a variety of lifestyles. These dogs typically do well with a variety of dog sports because they are smart and trainable.

1

Cockapoo Temperament

Typical characteristics of most Cockapoos include: high levels of intelligence; affection; loyalty; cheerfulness; enthusiasm; playfulness; train-ability; obedience; sociability; friendliness. Again, they excel at most dog sports as well as agility, scent work, trials, hunt tests and make superb assistance/therapy dogs.

Once again, for the most part, the Cockapoo is a friendly and social breed that loves to spend time with family. These dogs are quick to make friends with strangers so they generally do not make good watch dogs or guard dogs, though some develop a tendency to bark.

However, because this breed can have Toy or Miniature Poodle blood, "small dog syndrome" is a risk. Small dog syndrome occurs as a result of the owner indulging the dog's whims and allowing him to get away with things that a larger dog would not be allowed to do. Things like jumping up on people, or barking at strangers. Such Cockapoos will therefore require firm and consistent training to ensure that they do not develop problem behaviors such as chewing, whining, jumping up and barking. As long as you start your puppy with training and socialisation as early as possible you shouldn't have a problem with this.

The 'designer dog'

The Cockapoo is a 'hybrid' or crossbreed/mixed breed. Crossbreed dogs have always been looked down upon by some purists who disapprove of breeding in this way. If however you research any so called "purebreed", you will find a lineage that contains several or in some cases, many crossings with other breeds. Without a doubt there are crossbreeds that are a result of accidental matings and are commonly referred to with derogatory terms such as 'mutt' 'mongrels' and 'Heinz 57'. However, there are fortunately breeders who do follow very careful breeding practices. These reputable breeders will breed from health tested parents in the same way as any reputable breeder of pure bred dogs.

Currently, mixed breed dogs are commonly or fashionably referred to as 'designer dogs'. The term "designer dog" is fairly new, having only popped up during the middle of the 20th century when breeders started to cross purebred Poodles with other purebred breeds.

Like other designer dogs with Poodle parents, the Cockapoo was largely developed in an effort to create a breed with the small size and friendly demeanor of the Cocker Spaniel and the 'hypo-allergenic' coat of the Poodle.

The Cockapoo is actually one of the original and oldest of the so called 'designer dogs'. As well as being a 'designer dog', the Cockapoo is fast becoming one of the most popular canine pets globally.

However, as the Cockapoo is a hybrid, you cannot accurately predict exactly what he will be like in terms of appearance, personality and temperament. Every crossbreed dog will be different depending on the parent breeds used.

The Cockapoo may be a 50/50 mix of Poodle and Cocker Spaniel blood but that does not mean he will adopt an equal measure of traits from both parents. He may display a predominance of physical and personality characteristics from either parent breeds.

But that is one of the things that many Cockapoo owners love about their pets. The fact that each and every Cockapoo is an individual.

A brief history and the furtherance of the breed

Once again, Poodle mixes have been popular since the 20th century with the emergence of one of the first crossbred 'designer dogs', the Labradoodle (Labrador x Poodle). The first litter was said to have been bred by Royal Guide Dog Association of Australia, breeding manager Wally Conron in 1989. The Cockapoo on the other hand was thought to have originated in the U.S.A. during the

1960s, although some suggest earlier than this in the 1950s. However the practice of crossbreeding dogs is by no means a new practice. This being the case, it is possible that the Cockapoo breed has existed for many years.

Since the advent of the designer dog craze, a variety of purebreds have been crossed with the Poodles and other dogs to create hybrids like the Cockapoo. However, no one kennel or breeder is credited with the creation of the Cockapoo breed.

Although there is no 'breed standard', such as those upheld by the AKC and KC UK for purebreds, The Cockapoo Club of America (CCA) are very keen to uphold high levels of standards in breeding Cockapoos. In that respect they strongly insist on breeding unrelated pairs who are selected for high levels of health including health testing as well as excellent temperaments. They are also keen to ensure that there is no intermixing of English and American Cocker Spaniels. Perhaps for obvious reasons the American Cocker Spaniel is considered a popular choice to parent an American Cockapoo. However, the English Cocker Spaniel is more often used mainly because of better health and temperament.

Cockapoo Vital Statistics

In general, the Cockapoo typically stands anywhere between 9 to 20 inches (23 to 50.8 cm) high and weighs anywhere between 10 and 40 pounds or more (4.5 to 18 kg), depending on which parent dogs are used.

In the same way that the Poodle has three recognised sizes, so does the Cockapoo. Respectively these are Toy, Miniature and Maxi. In addition, a 'teacup' variety has emerged, with a similar height to the Toy, but weighing less than the others. Other terminology is also used such as Miniature, Mini Standard and Standard, but again they are used to differentiate the three distinct sizes mentioned.

Teacup Cockapoos are mainly bred in the USA usually weighing less than 6lb and no greater than 10 inches height wise.

The Toy Cockapoo generally weighs no more than 12lb and around 10 inches or less in height. Despite a similar height to the 'teacup', the toy Cockapoo has more bulk body wise.

Miniatures typically weigh less than 20lb and around 14 inches or less in height.

Standard (Maxi) Cockapoo's will usually have a height of at least 15 inches or more and weigh at least 21lb or more.

Although weights and sizes will slightly vary, these ranges will give you an idea of the Cockapoo type in relation to the Poodle type used and the parents specific size.

Breeding terminology: 'F'numbers

As you already know, Cockapoos are basically the result of breeding a Poodle and a Cocker Spaniel. However, breeding practices that breeders employ are not necessarily as simple as that. What are termed 'F' numbers denote how a crossing has taken place. This will be explained as follows.

A first-generation Cockapoo is the result of crossing a purebred Toy, Miniature or Standard Poodle with a purebred Cocker Spaniel (English, American or Working) and is known as an (F1) crossing. In theory this crossing should result in a Cockapoo with 50/50 Poodle and Cocker Spaniel blood. However, as you have already seen, genetically it doesn't always work out as precise as that.

For F1 Cockapoos there will not necessarily be a preference as to which parent breed is the sire or dam. This applies to both the English and American varieties. However, where a smaller sized Cockapoo is required, the dam would more likely be the Cocker Spaniel because of the size difference between the male and female. Conversely, if a larger sized Cockapoo is preferred, a Standard Poodle dam is likely to be paired with a Cocker Spaniel sire. But again, these guidelines are not set in stone and are likely to vary from breeder to breeder. Some would argue that either sex would be suitable, and the size differences would be relatively negligible.

A second-generation (F2) Cockapoo is the result of breeding two first-generation (F1) Cockapoos together. F2 Cockapoos could also have either parent being an F1, but the other parent may be an F1 to F4.

A third-generation (F3) would be the result of breeding two second-generation (F2) Cockapoos together. Again, F3 Cockapoos will use at least one F2 parent, but the other parent could be another F2 or it could be an F3 or an F4.

It is also possible to backcross a first, second, third generation (F1, F2, F3) etc, Cockapoo with a purebred Poodle or Cocker Spaniel. Puppies bred using this method are labeled F1b, F2b etc or first/second generation backcross. However, backcrossing occurs more often with a Poodle for a greater 'hypo-allergenic' effect. Breeds with shorter coats or a low tendency to shed have been considered less of a problem for allergy sufferers.

For more information have a look at the following link:

https://www.aaaai.org/Aaaai/media/MediaLibrary/PDF%20Documents/Libraries/EL-allergies-pets-patient.pdf

Before we delve into the specifics of the parent breeds of the Cockapoo, I first of all wanted to familiarise you with an important general fact about this breed. The important thing to be aware of is that your puppy has a heritage as a Gundog, and will therefore benefit greatly from the Gundog training discipline. This will more than likely prevent any serious behavioral issues as your dog will be engaging in what his ancestors were originally bred for.

You are therefore strongly advised to consider some level of Gundog training, which along with basic obedience training, this book covers in a detailed advanced training section. The instinct to hunt and retrieve will be present in the Cockapoo to differing degrees. Having said that, the dog sports previously mentioned can offer excellent alternative outlets for these active dogs.

What is the difference between a working and show dog?

As you already know, the Cockapoo will be related to a Cocker Spaniel. We have mentioned show types and working types. But what is the difference between the two types? Show types and working types have obvious distinctive differences.

The obvious distinction with a working dog is that it comes from generations of proven working dogs and field trial champions. This will be specifically indicated on the pedigree.

In other words, these dogs will have an excellent natural ability and temperament, making them ideal for the purpose as a working Gundog.

The show dog on the other hand strictly follows the breed standard as laid down by the respective Kennel Clubs.

The breed standards do take into consideration an ideal temperament, but the emphasis is mainly on what the ideal dog should look like for show purposes.

Both types also generally differ in size. For example the Working Spaniels are smaller. Working Cocker Spaniels also differ quite a bit looks wise, generally having shorter ears and less of the distinctive droopy eyed look of the show Cocker. However, the important thing to realise with the Working Cocker Spaniel is the energy level of the dog. Most successful working Cocker Spaniels would need to have the capability to work or run all day. This could prove to be very problematic if the dog does not have the opportunity to burn off excess energy. Quite often such dogs in their frustration resort to problems behaviors such as barking and chewing etc. The show type on the other hand is generally more placid, easy going and less of a live wire.

4

Chapter Two:

Necessary Supplies and Equipment Relating to Training

IMPORTANT: Make sure you have all the equipment and accessories needed BEFORE the puppy or adult dog arrives. Do not leave everything up until the last minute, adding unnecessary stress to your life.

a) Checklist for initial supplies and equipment

- Suitable size dog bed with bedding
- Puppy size collar or harness and lead
- Assortment of soft toys and chew toys
- Poop bags
- Sprays and deodorizers
- Stair/doorway baby gate
- Crate (optional)
- Play pen (optional). Start by looking at items available at your local pet supply.

b) Initial supplies

You will undoubtedly be busy spending as much time as possible with your new puppy when he first comes home, so make sure you have prepared all the items he will need for his arrival

Essential shopping list

You will be looking at one off items such as a crate and ongoing expenses such as food and pet insurance. The following will offer details from the previous list of essentials to get you going. Most towns and cities have a good pet store where you should be able to get most if not all items needed. I personally would get your initial supply, certainly food, from the local pet store before you look at buying perhaps the same items cheaper online.

Treats

Treats will be an important addition as it is advisable to use these for any positive reinforcement training, including early toilet training. Again the breeder may have been offering treats, but if not I suggest asking the advice of you local store as to a good quality food treat that they supply. Certainly do not be tempted with the cheapest you can find. However, my own preference is to make them yourself. It is easy to buy a block or cheese or corned beef for example. Cut them into small cubes of no more than 1 cm square, spread them on a tray and freeze. Once frozen you can then put them in a freezer bag and take out a handful or so for a training session. You could also search the internet or Youtube for [homemade dog treats] to get more ideas. Again, treats are advisable as a training aid, so it is likely you will be using a lot initially. Try to ensure that as well as being nutritious, the treats help to exercise gums and clean the teeth.

Suitable size dog bed with bedding

A soft donut type bed is a good idea, for him to snuggle into. Many breeders and dog owners also recommend a 'vetbed' type product for possible accidents. You don't have to buy the most expensive or luxurious, but make sure it is a reasonably good quality that will withstand regular washes. Washing the bedding can be done once a month or sooner depending on the extent that the puppy is bringing dirt in on its coat. Again go with recommendations from pet stores but it is advisable to not get a dog bed much larger than half their eventual size. You will then need to purchase another suitable for their adult size in several months time.

Again, there are many more choices from hard plastic bucket types to all soft padded base and sides. It is probably more important the choice of bedding, whether you use an old blanket or duvet or again, buy sheets of 'Vetbed', or similar product. When you are house-training your puppy it is certainly best to use an old blanket or a towel, just in case your puppy has an accident. Once your puppy is fully trained, however, you can upgrade to a plush dog bed or a thicker blanket that will be more comfortable. Many people choose to use a temporary box whether cardboard or otherwise and then a proper bed when they are nearing their full grown size in a few months time. The other consideration with a choice of bed is the issue of the puppy chewing anything and everything. In this respect beanbags, foam and wicker baskets can potentially be destroyed in no time. If you opt for a crate, to make it more comfortable, you should line it with a soft blanket or a plush dog bed. You may also wish to purchase a specific crate mat, many of which are water and chew proof.

Lead and collar

A specific puppy lead and collar is recommended initially. But these do not have to be of a high quality or expensive. A young puppy is hardly likely to have the strength to break the cheapest collar or leash. But remember that as they grow you will have to replace them for their adult size. Flat collars are obviously better than traditional choke chains which can cause damage to the neck and throat whilst an over exuberant puppy is first getting used to them. Flat collars can be either leather or nylon webbing and preferably the wider the better again to alleviate any potential force to the throat area. Traditional Whippet collars are often recommended for young puppies as they are much wider and more comfortable than standard flat collars.

Toys

These include toys that you interact with your dog, such as for retrieving, tug toys etc, Kong type toys to stuff with food for added interest, general chew toys and puzzle toys offering mental stimulation.

Chew toys

Chewing is an important and natural activity for dogs at any age and serves a number of very useful purposes. For the young puppy, chewing can relieve the discomfort of teething. At any age the act of chewing releases endorphins, which in turn has a calming effect. Dogs will also chew to cope with boredom or frustration, as well as symptoms associated with separation anxiety. With a wide variety of chew toys it is a very important alternative to floss teeth and exercise gums in the absence of raw meaty bones. They also hopefully provide a distraction and an alternative if you accidentally leave shoes lying around that you would prefer to keep intact. More seriously they provide an alternative to chewing electrical cables which can obviously be dangerous, potentially causing a fire risk, and fatal to the dog if the cables are live. Different dogs, like different toys, so your best bet is to buy several different kinds and let your dog choose which ones he likes best.

Poop bags

Consideration for pedestrians and other dog owners means that any faeces needs to be picked up and properly disposed of. Many local authorities insist on this and non-compliance can lead to a sizeable fine. You can buy disposable poop bags, but do consider cheaper options such as disposable nappy bags for babies or other bags, which are biodegradable.

Sprays and deodorizers

Accidents can and will happen but make sure that the product you use is safe for a dog to be exposed to. A good natural alternative spray cleaner/deodorizer is vinegar. Although obviously not a cleaning agent, an anti chew spray can be effective in keeping a puppy away from items that they may find attractive to chew, but are difficult or impractical to remove from a room, such as part of a wooden chair or other furniture.

Stair/doorway baby gate

Simply restricting your puppy access to a room or part of the house is far easier than trying to train him to keep out. The foot of a stairway is an obvious area that could be hazardous for a puppy to climb. Baby gates are also useful if you need to keep the puppy temporarily confined to one room. They also enable the puppy to see what is going on, rather than having the door shut. This will not make the puppy feel so isolated.

Crate

A crate basically offers a dog a den for them to rest in, safe confinement when travelling by car and a safe place for them to reside when you cannot supervise them. If you use it correctly your dog will not view time spent in the crate as punishment and there is no reason to believe that keeping your dog in a crate for short periods of time is cruel. If you use the crate properly while training your Cockapoo he will come to view it as a place to call his own. He will soon see it as place where he can go to take a nap or to get some time to himself if he wants it. This of course assumes that you leave the door open or remove it. Covering the crate is also a good idea as it makes it more dark and secluded, which many dogs like.

When selecting a crate for your Cockapoo, size is very important. For the purpose of house training, you want to make sure that the crate is not too big. It should be just large enough for your puppy to stand, sit, lie down, and turn around comfortably. Dogs have a natural aversion to soiling their dens. If your puppy's crate is only large enough for him to sleep in, it will be more effective as a house-training tool. When your puppy grows up you can upgrade to a larger crate. As crates can be expensive, you may wish to choose one that will be suitable for the size they will be as an adult. Obviously from a financial point of view you really do not want to be buying a small size for now, then a medium or large etc.

Puppy pen

Once again a puppy pen is a great idea to give them freedom to romp but to also stay out of harm's way. These can be set up indoors or outside in the garden/yard. Your local pet supply should have examples to give you an idea of the size and price.

CHAPTER THREE:

PREPARING FOR THE ARRIVAL

This chapter includes details to help you make your house and garden safe for your puppy or adult dogs arrival. It also provides advice about setting up a crate and establishing house rules. In the following pages, you will find some important steps to take in dog proofing your home:

1.) Dog-Proofing Your Home

Please note, the following will make a number of references to 'puppy proofing', but is intended to indicate both adults and puppies.

Your Cockapoo will want to explore every nook and cranny of his new home. Part of that process involves his teeth. Keep all items that are valuable or dangerous away from him. This particularly includes electrical cables that may be live and therefore risking an electric shock and at worse a fatality. Puppies will not see the value or the danger, so please be aware that it is not your Cockapoo's fault if something gets chewed. Never use harsh corrections. Instead use a firm "No" to indicate your disapproval. However, this needs to take place the moment it happens, otherwise your dog will be left confused as to what you are unhappy about. Then simply replace the item with a chew-able dog toy.

Anywhere within your home that your Cockapoo is allowed to wander needs to be proofed. This is similar to baby proofing your home, and requires you to go down on hands and knees and see what dangers lurk at adult or puppy eye level.

The whole point of this is to get you to think about any potential hazards for your Cockapoo. Remember, they are relying on you as their guardian, in much the same way as a child.

a) Preparing the House

Again, it is very important to keep a young puppy safe from potential dangers. Your dog or puppy will be naturally curious about their new surroundings and will want to explore. You literally need to put yourself in your dogs shoes, getting down on your hands and knees and go through every room to see potential hazards from their vantage point. Plan for restricted areas including staircases, and consider baby gates as it is easy to forget to close doors.

The following presents you with a checklist of possible hazards in and around the house:

» Prevent your Cockapoo from jumping up on any unstable objects such as bookcases.

» Do not allow your Cockapoo access to high decks or ledges, balconies, open windows, or staircases. Instead use baby gates, baby plastic fencing and therefore prevent accidents from happening.

» Keep your doors securely shut and again prevent a potential accident.

» Never slam doors with a Cockapoo puppy in the house. Use doorstops to make sure that the wind does not slam a door in your Cockapoo's face.

» Clear glass doors also pose a danger since your Cockapoo may not see them and run right into one. Use a screen door.

» Make sure any live 'chewable' electrical cables are safely out of reach, either tied up high enough or by cordoning off risky areas

» Fit child locks on any ground level cupboards containing harmful chemicals

» Check that any 'chewable' items shoes etc are out of reach

» If you have an open fire make sure you again restrict access and/or have a fire screen in place

» Be aware of any furniture or furnishing that contains anything toxic, paint or otherwise that a puppy can easily chew and ingest.

» Check for toxic plants, medicines, sharp objects etc.

Potential hazards will include the following:

Electrical cables

A dog and young puppy in particular should not have access to any electrical cables that can be easily chewed. This can obviously lead to a fatality if the cable is live. It can also create a potential fire hazard if a cable is not live, but is chewed through sufficiently to leave internal wiring exposed. If possible keep all cables out of reach, if not, enclose cables with a cable tidy or cable cover. In the case of areas where many cables are gathered, simply prevent access by cordoning off the area. I would not personally want to risk merely using anti chew sprays, which can be used as a general deterrent to a certain extent.

Ornaments

You will obviously not wish to have valuable vases broken, but fragments can retain sharp edges and if mouthed by a puppy could easily cut their mouth or small pieces swallowed. Ornaments should therefore be placed out of reach.

Cupboards

The main hazards here are cupboards at floor level containing chemicals or medications, or glass bottles that can fall out and break if a puppy decides to climb in and explore. But care should also be exercised with similar cupboards higher up which could also contain medications or harmful chemicals that could easily fall out. Your safest option is to fit childproof locks and the instruction to other family members that everyone who needs to access a cupboard, locks it afterwards.

Rubbish/garbage bins

There is no point in attempting to teach a dog to stay out of rubbish bins. If they can find a way in they will do. It is far safer and more practical, if bins are at ground level, to use bins that are either lockable, or fitted with mechanisms, which make the lid difficult if not impossible for the dog to open.

Dog Toilet

This refers to a toileting area that your dog has to use inside your accommodation. In particular, this may be necessary if you live in an apartment where normal house/toilet training is not practical. There is a large choice of commercial dog toilets which you may wish to consider by doing a simple Google search such as [toilet for dogs]. Alternatively, have a dedicated corner preferably on a tiled floor that can easily be cleaned. As with any house-training, a puppy or dog will need to be taught that this is a permissible area to relieve themselves. Hopefully, this will be for emergencies only and they will do all of their toilet business when you take them for a walk, which is another good reason to regularly take them for walks, or employ someone to do this.

House toilet

It is probably best to restrict access here and simply keep the door closed at all times. The main hazard is again the possibility that your dog will get access to cleaning chemicals and may even attempt to drink out of the toilet bowl. At the very least if they accidentally gain access, then get into the habit of keeping the toilet seat down and any chemicals out of reach, preferably locked in a suitable cupboard.

Natural fuel/Gas or electrical fires

Regardless of the type of fire used, make use of a suitable fireguard and particularly with electric fires ensure that there are no cables exposed. Some dogs will want to get as close as possible to a fire and in the case of a log fire, can easily become a burns victim if a log should fall out.

Dog bed

You may have a dedicated dog bed spot, but will still find that your dog likes to lay elsewhere in a room or part of your home. In this respect you may wish to set up beds or bedding in favourite spots. Wherever these sleeping areas are, try to ensure that they are draught free and that they will not be disturbed if people are walking past or opening doors onto them.

Water and food bowls

Most people will locate these in the kitchen, but please make sure the dog has a regular supply of clean fresh water. Also, be aware that in winter when you have the heating on and in hot weather, they will drink much more. This is also likely to affect the regularity of them needing to relieve themselves.

Doors and gaps

These are more considerations when you initially assess your home for hazards. You may need to restrict access to certain rooms and should therefore be vigilant that the doors to those rooms are kept closed. There may also be parts of the room where they do have access, which you also wish to prevent access. This could be gaps in between or behind items of furniture or appliances, which should be blocked off to avoid the dog becoming trapped, or them finding things to chew.

Full-length glass doors and windows

The main hazard in this case is that your dog runs straight into it. Other than boarding the lower part up the only other thing you can do is put stickers on the glass or attach strips of coloured tape across.

Letter box

Chewing is again the issue here if post or newspapers drop through the letter box onto the mat for your dog to find. Simply fit a specific wire basket to catch anything coming through the door.

Stair gate

This effectively restricts their access to dangerous areas or any rooms they need to be restricted from entering. Obviously the top of a stair case is relatively high. As you can imagine, a young puppy climbing up such a stair case, could easily fall down and have a serious accident. A locked stair gate would hopefully prevent this.

Houseplants

Houseplants could be a tempting plaything for any dog who wishes to dig in the soil or attempt to chew a poisonous plant. They can be easily knocked over on the floor and you may be tempted to sit these on a decorative plinth out of reach. Again, they may be out of reach but could be easily knocked to an extent that the pot falls and potentially injures the dog. You may therefore wish to consider keeping these in a restricted access area.

B) A SAFE YARD/GARDEN

The same consideration you give for preparing your home should be given to potential hazards in the garden.

Fences need to be high enough, around 6ft, more so as the puppy gets older, when they may be tempted and able to jump over. There should be no gaps in fences or hedges which a small puppy can easily crawl through. Make sure the gap between a gate and ground level isn't large enough for a puppy to escape.

Ponds should have a surround to keep the puppy out and or covered with wire meshing.

Make sure no garden chemicals, sharp tools etc, are accessible and keep these locked away in your shed.

Ensure your garden does not contain any plants poisonous to dogs.

The garden gate

Most importantly, this needs to be secure and kept locked so a puppy or adult dog cannot simply walk out, potentially onto a busy road. As a matter of routine, check that the gate is locked before you let your dog out. Again, check that there are no gaps where a puppy can squeeze through or wriggle under. As well as the fence, this also needs to be high enough, therefore preventing an older puppy or adult dog from jumping over.

Electrical cables

Similarly to inside your house, these should again be enclosed or kept out of reach to avoid any chewing and potential fatalities.

Ponds and/or swimming pools

Ideally access should be prevented using some form of boundary or sturdy wire mesh covering the pond. If you do not wish to do this, then always supervise especially a young puppy. Older dogs may not be as much of a risk as they will find it easier to climb out of a pond if they fall in, but may not be able to do so with some swimming pools.

Dog toilet area

If say for example you have a bitch and a lawn, you may wish to train her to urinate in a specific area, therefore keeping her off the lawn. Bitches generally leave bleach like patches all over a lawn in places they have urinated. You could therefore encourage the use of a purpose made dog toilet similar to those used for apartments/flats.

Plants

Plants that are poisonous to dogs should be removed. Most if not all dogs like to eat grass and some dogs instinctively know what they can and can't eat. Others will not discriminate and will eat anything. "Plants Potentially Poisonous to Pets." Is also listed in the resources section at the end of the book. The link is as follows:
http://www.humanesociety.org/assets/pdfs/pets/poisonous_plants.pdf

Sheds or storage areas

Storage areas have the same function as cupboards and should be used to keep hazardous chemicals and sharp tools and garden implements out of reach. Sheds and storage areas should therefore be locked. Also get into the habit of closing doors before you leave sheds or storage areas. Any power tools should not be operated with the dog running loose in the garden. Keep your dog inside the house until you have finished cutting the grass or trimming the hedge for example.

Children's play area

It is advisable to keep access restricted here as there may be children's toys lying around that you do not wish destroying. Many people use bark chipping's for play areas, and these will be a temptation for a puppy to chew and ingest, some contain harmful chemicals. There is also the risk that your dog may start using the area as a toilet and consequently your children would be in contact with urine or faeces.

Garden mulch

Always be mindful of what you are using as a mulch, as again if it is possible, your dog will find it. Always use untreated bark chipping's and avoid mulches such as cocoa shells, which may still contain residues of cocoa, which could result in a fatality if ingested. Large pebbles are often recommended to prevent dogs from attempting to walk on flower-beds, as they find it uncomfortable to walk on. They also provide a very useful mulch.

Chemicals

You should carefully read the instructions for chemical sprays for plants, lawn treatments, pest killers such as slug/snail pellets etc, in relation to exposing your dog.

Fence or other boundary

It is highly advisable to ensure the garden is properly secured with a suitable fence or wall that is high enough (6 feet as a minimum but higher for more determined dogs) to discourage them from jumping over. Even if the garden has a natural hedge, dogs can easily find their way through. If there is any possibility of the dog digging under the fence it may be necessary to dig a trench and sink plastic coated wire fencing at least a foot deep to prevent them digging under. A possible alternative is to lay a concrete path or paving slabs around the edge.

Digging area

Digging is usually a symptom of boredom and can be problematic if a dog chooses to excavate your prized flower-beds or even sections of lawn. Digging can also result if a dog wishes to burying something. Sandboxes or a dedicated digging area can be created using a timber board box approximate dimensions of 2ft x 3ft x 6 inches deep or larger if your garden will take it. Once you create a box frame, simply dig a pit 6 to 12 inches deep and fill with either sand or compacted soil.

Shaded area

You may already have a garden table and chairs with an umbrella which a dog will undoubtedly make use of in hot weather when they need to cool off. Trees or large shrubs also offer useful shaded spots. Either way, try and make sure that there are several options available even if you have to create a roofed canopy especially for that purpose. Also be aware that some dogs will lay in the sun longer than is healthy for them which could lead to sun or heat stroke. If there is a risk of this, encourage them to use the shaded areas or as a last resort take them back into the house, particularly when the day is at its hottest. It is often far cooler inside a double glazed house on a hot day, particularly if you can leave windows open at either end to create a draft. You may also wish to make use of a 'magnetic screen' that allows you to leave the back door ajar, but keeps flies and other insects out.

Faeces and urine

Once you start toilet training your dog, you may wish to teach your dog to defecate in a specific area. But most people do not mind as long as it is outside of the house. Either way, as a matter of routine, each day you should check your garden, particularly pathways and other areas regularly used and pick up any faeces. As well as being a nuisance to have to clean it off your shoes if you tread in any, it can also be a health risk. You will also find that you have to disinfect pathways, otherwise you will soon notice a strong stale urine smell. If there is a possibility that your dog will lick any concrete areas, you may be safer spraying vinegar. Otherwise, spraying a diluted disinfectant will kill the smell and keep the area healthy. Most local authorities accept dog faeces as part of their regular bin collections, if not consider the following:

Unless your water authority forbids it, flushing faeces down your own toilet is an option

You may wish to compost it separately if you are not keen on mixing it with other compost you may have. Over time provided it is fully aerated it naturally decomposes and loses its smell.

Specific containers 'dog loo' can be buried in the garden and the faeces added along with an activator which breaks the faeces down.

There are worms that feed specifically on animal waste including Tiger Worms Eisenia fetida also known as "Manure Worms". If you are interested in creating a wormery for the purpose of composting dog faeces, check with a local wormery supplier for suitability and advice.

Plant containers

Provided the plants are non-toxic to dogs, be aware that plastic tubs may be subjected to chewing. Some dogs may not bother the tub or the contents. But if chewing does become an issue, consider stone, terra-cotta or metal. If male dogs are likely to urinate on any potted plants it may be a good idea to buy tall pots or keep these on a raised plinth that will not be easily knocked over if bumped.

2) Toxins To Be Aware of in Your Home

Again, you'll need to watch your Cockapoo puppy very carefully for the first few months to make sure that he does not get into harm's way. If the kitchen is made into the puppy's sleeping area, make sure that all cleaning supplies are removed, locked away or placed elsewhere. Cockapoo pups are curious, and it can take as little as a few minutes for your puppy to get into a poisonous cleaning product.

Possible toxins to be aware of may include the following:

Insecticides; Human medications; Household cleaning products; Foods that we consume that have a toxic effect on dogs such as grapes and chocolates; Rodenticides; Plants; Garden and pool products; Glass, razors, bathroom products; Coins, small batteries and other small objects that may easily be ingested

a) Checking For Toxins in Puppy Toys

Before purchasing toys for your Cockapoo to play with, you'll need to check that they are lead free and cadmium free.

Dog toys that contain DEHP- bis (2-ethylhexl) phthalate have been found to have a huge effect on the reproductive system of rats, even at very low doses.

3) Establishing rules before you puppies arrival

If you have no intention of applying strict or specific house rules, then the following will not concern you too much. If you are particular where your dog will be allowed to venture, or if you are not sure either way, hopefully this will give you a few things to think about.

One of the biggest, if not the biggest problem with 'behavior issues' around the house is a lack of consistent 'house rules'. As with any training the puppy needs to be taught what they can and cannot do and where they can and cannot go. It is therefore advisable to draw up a list of do's and don'ts and make sure that all members of the family stick to this. Dogs are like people in that they like to know where they stand and if things keep changing it is bound to confuse them and leave them frustrated. It is not fair on him when you allow him on the sofa one day but not the next, or let him jump up at you, but shout at him when he does the same to a visitor.

Draw up a list of house rules and make sure everyone sticks to it

The list should include who will be responsible for the dogs care including: feeding, exercise, playtime, house-training, obedience training. Importantly, never let him be without fresh clean water, so everyone needs to check their bowl regularly. Try and be consistent with times that you feed, exercise, play games, train, sleep time etc.

Some people are OK with the dog using the sofa, others are not. It's not the end of the world but again you all have to agree to an all or nothing situation. Couches and other furniture are often the focus of problems where a dog is initially allowed to lie on the couch. He may then object or become hostile when there are attempts to move him. If you have no objection to him lying on the couch with you, it may still be worth training him to only expect this when invited. This will ensure that if problems arise you can soon ask him to leave the couch.

Toilet training is particularly important anyway, but again all family members need to know and follow the routine. Toilet training and crate training will be covered in detail in the chapters that follow.

Be consistent with restricted areas and where they can access (usually this is where ever you spend most time such as the kitchen or lounge). Of course the puppies safety is the most important in terms of keeping him away from potential hazards. In this respect, think about any rooms that you do not wish your dog to enter. House training is often made easier if he is restricted to a limited number of rooms that he could potentially do his toilet business in.

As part of toilet training, and restricted access, many people like to utilise puppy pens. This also allows you to keep the puppy safe when you are not available to supervise them.

Decide whether you wish to crate train the puppy. It will be much fairer on the puppy to start sooner rather than later when the puppy will have perhaps become used to more freedom.

Feeding food at the table encourages begging, and although it is hard to ignore his sad pleadings it is often better to ignore begging. But again, there has to be consistency from all family members.

Similarly, cooking or preparing food can illicit the same problem, so some people prefer to train their dogs to accept it when you are preparing food in the kitchen, they are not permitted in and the door will be closed.

This should go without saying, but reward based, positive reinforcement training involves no shouting or harsh physical punishments. This should not be confined to training sessions but should occur all the time.

Once you have puppy proofed the house, leaving nothing dangerous, poisonous or valuable for the puppy or adult dog to have contact with, everyone should ensure that this is maintained. Therefore nothing should be left around for the puppy to chew or eat.

4) Where Will your Dog Sleep?

Deciding where your puppy will sleep is important. Many people choose to allow their dog on the bed, which is fine. However, it's important to understand separation anxiety if you sleep with your dog, and are allowing him to be with you at all times. Separation anxiety is caused by over-attachment, and sleeping in your bed can be part of the reason for that.

Again this is a decision that you need to decide on and stick to. Many people opt to 'eventually' keep the dog in the kitchen or another room over night. Many also opt to crate train their puppies from day one. Please again remember that this is not punishment and most dogs like their own space. What you may have to do however, is to allow the puppy to be in their crate in or near where you sleep. You should then aim to gradually move the crate closer to where you eventually intend them to sleep. The kitchen is also generally used because most are tiled and therefore easier to clean if any 'toilet accidents' occur over night. The kitchen is also usually the immediate door out into the garden, where you should be encouraging him to do his toilet business during their toilet training and thereafter.

a) The first night

On the first night when you bring your puppy home, I suggest that you don't leave him alone. Imagine how he would feel after being in the warmth of his nesting area with his mother and siblings to be then completely alone. So make a conscious decision to stay in the room where your puppy will be sleeping for a couple of nights. You can also invest in a very specific puppy comforter meant for the first few nights in a new home, they can be warmed in the microwave and some even have heartbeats.

If you have decided that your puppy is going to be eventually sleeping alone, then it's not a good idea to allow him to sleep on you. It would be much better to lie on the couch and have him on the ground beside you. That way you can offer a comforting hand when needed but he will be learning to leave behind the warmth of bodies at bedtime. You can introduce the crate right at the beginning if you prefer, or wait until that first couple of nights are over. Eventually you will be able to leave a happily secure puppy in his sleeping place with ease.

An older dog that will be sleeping in another room in the beginning will probably howl and bark for the first few nights. Do not panic though because this is often due to unsettled feelings rather than severe separation anxiety. It usually wears off when the dog begins to feel secure.

5) Setting Up Your Cockapoo's Crate

Again we will talk more about crate training in a later chapter. For now we are looking to establish a place to keep the crate located on a permanent basis.

Once again, the important thing about introducing your dog, whatever his age, to the crate is to make it a nice place that he finds welcoming. Put a cozy bed, toys and maybe even a stuffed Kong or other activity toy in the crate and allow your dog to sit in there with the door open to begin with.

If you need to have the crate close to you, in order to make your puppy feel secure, then this is fine too. But remember to then gradually move it away later. What some trainers suggest, is that for the first few days when your puppy arrives home, you have the puppy in the puppy crate with you in your bedroom. This will hopefully allow you to hear if the puppy stirs and needs the toilet. What you then do is to gradually move the crate just outside the bedroom door. As the days progress, you can edge the crate further away until it is in your downstairs kitchen or wherever you wish to keep the crate over night. By doing this, the puppy will hardly notice he is no longer sleeping right beside you.

The overall objective is to show your puppy that his crate is a most comfortable bedroom to the point that he chooses it as his resting place, all on his own.

When you do start to close the door of the crate, only do it for a short time. The idea is that your dog never thinks that he is going to be trapped against his will. Never just push the dog in and close the door as this can easily cause a phobia.

Chapter Four:

Bringing your Cockapoo puppy / Adult dog home

This chapter deals with preparations that you may have already done or are yet to do regarding bringing your dog home. It will also offer reminders and checklists to make sure everything is in place. You will also be presented with information about introducing your dog to the rest of the family. Although much of the text states bringing a puppy home, it is also intended to refer to an adult dog.

Please note that the information that follows contains references to "Gundog Training". The reason that Gundog Training is included for a Cockapoo is the obvious connection with the Cocker Spaniel parent breed. In actual fact the Poodle also has a heritage as a working water retriever. In both cases the Cockapoo is perfectly suited to this type of training and would benefit greatly. However, you are not being forced to adopt this type of training. It is therefore included in the separate advanced chapter which you may wish to consider at a later date.

1) The First Day Home

Bringing a new dog home is an exciting and sometimes even a terribly scary time. If you follow the right stages of introduction for the dog though, both into your home and your family, everything should go smoothly.

During this area of the book I will explain how the puppy may be feeling; how you can communicate properly with your new dog and how to make life easy for all of you within this crucial settling in period. One of the most tempting things to do when you bring a new dog home is celebrate their arrival. Everyone comes to meet the new family member and everyone wants to stroke, pick him up, cuddle him etc, particularly if the new arrival is a gorgeous Cockapoo puppy.

When you bring a new puppy home it is important to remember that he will be confused and learning all of the time. That said, if the young dog has a lot of positive, gentle interaction even from day one, it will build his confidence. For this reason the new and young puppy may benefit from some careful visitors. A new adult Cockapoo is a different matter. An older dog will need a quiet time in the home for the first few days. The adult dog will not welcome a stream of visitors on day one. The new dog will likely be scared and nervous. Remember that he will have little understanding about what is happening in his life and the best way you can approach this is keep quiet and allow him to get used to the new environment in his own time.

Similarly the adult dog should be left well alone by family members whilst he is settling in. He can get some positive attention and fuss if he asks for it, but should certainly not be cornered or forced to accept attention. Many canine rescuers have to take dogs back into their care because a problem has occurred on day one or two that could easily have been avoided if the dog was given space and respect to settle into the new home before excited new owners forced their attentions on him.

A dog learns how to react to things, in his life, based upon past experiences. In addition, canine communication is very different to the communication that occurs between people. In actual fact the average new dog owner trying to make friends with a scared Cockapoo by trying to touch him is having the exact opposite effect on their recently arrived dog.

I always ignore a new dog into the home. I barely look at them but offer attention if they ask for it, if they approach you. A very scared dog is allowed to hide where he is happy until he is ready to come out and learn to join in with everyday life in his own time. A crate would be a likely place the dog would wish to retire to. It would also be very helpful to cover the crate with a sheet for even more privacy.

There is something that very few people tell you when they present you with a new dog, whatever age he may be. You may think that you have made a mistake. This is an absolutely normal reaction to such a big change in your life. Whether you have brought home a scared teenage dog, a confident adult Cockapoo or a needy puppy, you may panic before things settle down. With a puppy, you will worry about why he is crying, whether you are feeding him properly, and how you can be sure that he stays happy and healthy. When you bring home an adult dog, he may show separation anxiety, he may bark in the night for a few days and either be very clingy or completely aloof. An adult dog may be so worried that he shows his teeth in the beginning. It's important not to crowd a new dog and everything will settle down quickly. The dog that is left to settle on his own will have no reason to feel threatened.

So all I can say to you is expect accidents, expect upheaval and expect things to change for a short time; then if the dog settles perfectly, far better than you expected, at least you were prepared

2) CHECKLIST FOR THE ARRIVAL OF YOUR PUPPY

Bear in mind an important aspect of gundog training, which should ideally be adhered to from day one. Please do not encourage your dog to bark, whine, whimper etc (in fact these should be discouraged by any dog). It is endearing to have your little puppy to speak like this, but please do not be tempted to encourage this by getting him to speak or ask for food etc. If you encourage this, it will reinforce a desire to bark when he wants something. Although this is something that may not concern you as an average pet owner, for working Gundogs however, this is a cardinal sin as barking scares off game birds and generally causes chaos. For the average pet owner however, barking and whining can be a real problem that can be difficult to correct. As with most problem behaviors that you wish to avoid, the worse thing you can do is acknowledge and encourage it, with words or physical contact. The best thing to do is ignore it, turn your back, and walk away. As long as you do not encourage the puppy to think that the behavior is acceptable. Of course this does not mean that you want to discourage your dog from vocalising and remaining mute. If he barks to go outside to toilet, this is great and should be encouraged. But the point is, he should only be encouraged to bark for specific reasons, not all of the time. Always be aware that you should talk to him and encourage him, when he is doing something desirable. But never encourage barking, whining etc for the sake of it, unless you suspect he is ill. If you fuss him as you should, then fine, but if he starts to get vocal, then stop and ignore the behavior. He will soon learn that he doesn't get rewarded for whining or barking.

Retrieving and carrying things should be encouraged from day one. By all means talk to him with 'good boy/girl' and make a fuss when he is carrying objects, as long as the items are not valuable or dangerous. Swapping should be encouraged for anything you do not wish him to have. This is effectively taking another item, perhaps one of his toys, and offering that to him in exchange. So once you offer the other toy, he will probably drop the one he has and take the one you are offering. Remember to not get into a tug of war match, (he needs to retain a 'soft mouth' in other words holding gently and not gripping tightly or ripping), but gently take hold and say for example, 'leave' or 'give', and gently take it.

We will go into more depth and detail later, but retrieve training is something that should be approached correctly and systematically. Please do not attempt any kind of retrieve/fetch games until you know exactly how to do this. It may seem odd as people have been throwing balls and sticks for dogs to retrieve for years without any noticeable problem. But in terms of gundog training this is a little different and if you are serious about gundog training, please do not try anything without correct instruction first. We will discuss this in the advanced training chapter.

Recall training is also an area that should not be taken for granted, and from day one. For example, it is not advised to call the puppy unless he is already coming back to you. So in the early stages please refrain from calling him randomly, unless again he is looking or coming back to you.

In these preliminary stages, give him all the fuss and attention he needs, but please make sure you follow these basic rules.

3) Dogs and children

a) Dogs and play

Children are naturally inclined to want to play and will probably view a dog as just another plaything.

Dogs also love to play, but will not tolerate being subjected to physical abuse such as having their tail or ears pulled, chasing and teasing them, or being hit.

Please also remember that children can significantly encourage excitement and chaos with a Cockapoo. This can be exacerbated if two children or a group are involved. The puppy will be only too willing to join in with a child who wants to run, play chase games and generally interact with a fun loving Cockapoo. In their excitement however, the puppy, if large enough, could easily knock a young child over, or playfully nip them.

In this case, both need to act in a self controlled manner, as the last thing you want is for the puppy to become over excited and nip a child.

Also be aware that dogs can easily view two young children play fighting as the other child attacking your child and step into a territorial defence mode. Be equally mindful of the fact that other children may also not have been taught correct etiquette around a dog.

b) Teaching respect for dogs

Please be aware of the following, which needs to be conveyed to children who are exposed to your new canine family member:

» Dogs are not toys or playthings and can potentially bite if sufficiently provoked

» The child should never shout, scream, hit, kick, otherwise abuse, or intimidate the dog

» Dogs should be treat with respect and consideration. The dog is not a toy; a young puppy is very fragile.

» The dog should never be teased or chased until the child learns how to safely play games with the dog. Do not allow your child to follow a dog that has tried to move away from the attentions. This is a recipe for disaster because the dog can feel cornered and think he has to resort to aggression simply to be left alone.

» Children should be taught by you demonstrating how to stroke or pet a dog carefully and gently, perhaps demonstrating this with a toy before supervising the child with the dog. Patting a dogs head is often seen as acceptable, but should be discouraged as many dogs do not like it and to the dog it can easily feel like they are being struck. Dogs should be stroked gently on the back, neck and chest and occasionally the head. Children should be taught to not stroke or disturb a dog if they are sleeping or eating.

» The dog should not be encouraged to jump up at the child or anyone for that matter

» Just as you do between two dogs, watch out for resource guarding between dogs and children. Children should not be encouraged to give and take toys or engage in tug of war games with dogs, as this can easily lead to a dog bite. Children tend to grab at toys and food bowls, particularly the little ones. A dog could easily see this behavior as a threat and snap in return. If a dog takes one of your children's toys, the child should be instructed to ask you to get it back, and not attempt this themselves.

» It may be tempting for the child to pick a puppy up, but again there is a risk that the child may drop and injure them, squeeze them too tightly or choke them.

» Always ensure that before eating, the child should be taught to wash their hands if they have been handling a dog.

» Children should not be permitted to take a dog for a walk unsupervised, unless an older child can show that they can safely control a dog that may suddenly take off after a rabbit or squirrel

Children should also be taught respect for other dogs. It is easy for a child having been brought up around a dog to become confident with them and assume all dogs are the same. They should always ask the owner, who will be able to advise if it is safe, before petting their dog. A child should never attempt to approach a strange dog that is not accompanied by an adult, no matter how friendly they seem.

c) Allowing a child to help with caring for the dog

It is important that children should be encouraged to become involved in caring for your dog. However, please do not expect the child to take full responsibility and always check that things have been done if you should give them regular tasks.

Tasks should include all care aspects such as feeding, watering, grooming, going on walks and if old enough holding the lead, acceptable playing, helping with training, letting the dog out to do his toilet business etc.

A rota is a good idea as this will encourage everyone to get involved in all aspects and not get bored with doing the same things all of the time. This also ensures that everyone bonds with the dog and no one becomes the dogs favourite or centre of attention.

d) Keeping children safe

The media is regularly reporting the occurrence of dog bites and this isn't always the so called volatile dangerous breeds such as Pit Bulls and Rottweilers. Dog bites can happen to anyone, but many reported cases have been towards toddlers. Most of these dog attacks also occur in the home.

A young child is unlikely to recognise subtle warning signals until it is too late and some dogs attack without growling. Even when a child has been taught how to correctly interact with a dog they can become complacent or push their luck being excessively rough.

More dog bites occur as a result of a dog being wrestled and roughed about, by a child who has not 'read the rulebook' on canine body language, and the consequent warning signals that dogs give other dogs before they bite. A child may not be aware that a growling dog means, 'go away or I will bite you'.

A mother dog will usually correct or snap at a puppy that play bites a little too hard or becomes otherwise annoying. In a similar way some dogs will growl and then snap at a child or adult that has over stepped the line of this dogs comfort zone.

Therefore, for a dog to safely interact, supervised by an adult, a child should ideally be at a reasonable level of maturity, at least 8 years old, well mannered and having been taught to respect and care for a dog. Once a child has been taught how to correctly interact with a dog they should always be respectful of a dogs potential unpredictability. You should never become complacent and always be mindful that even the most placid, patient, easy going dog should not be left entirely unsupervised with a child of any age.

7) Introducing Your Puppy to Children

Again, Cockapoos are a very social and people-oriented breed and as previously mentioned, they tend to get along well with children. This doesn't mean, however, that you can just put your puppy in a room with your kids and expect everything to be fine. Just as you need to ensure that your puppy is safe in your home, you also need to teach your children how to properly handle the puppy for their own safety.

If you manage your family well and teach an all-round respect, you will be able to integrate the new dog in perfectly. Before you know it, everyone will be great friends.

Follow the tips below to safely introduce your puppy to children:

» Before you bring the puppy home, explain to your children how to properly handle the puppy. Tell them that the puppy is fragile and should be handled with care.

» Tell your children to avoid over-stimulating the puppy. They need to be calm and quiet when handling him so he does not become frightened.

» When it is time to make introductions, have your children sit on the floor in your home and bring the puppy to them.

» Place the puppy on the floor near your children and let the puppy wander up to them when he is ready. Do not let your children grab the puppy.

» Allow your children to calmly pet the puppy on his head and back when he approaches them. You may even give them a few small treats to offer the puppy.

» Let your children pick up the puppy if they are old enough to handle him properly. If the puppy becomes fearful, have them put him carefully back down.

If at any point during your introductions the puppy becomes afraid, you should take him out of the situation and place him in his crate, play pen or sleeping area where he can feel safe. Do not let your children scream or act too excitedly around the puppy until he gets used to them. It will take time for both your children and your puppy to get used to each other and you should supervise all interactions.

Please do remember, that where children are concerned or you already have a few pets, be extra careful of where your attentions go. After all, you want all of your pets to get along with each other, as well as your children. So do not create jealousy by fussing over your new Cockapoo puppy and ignoring your other pets. Share your attention equally between all your pets, so that the relationship starts off well. Much of the future relationship between all of your pets, will depend on what happens during the first few days.

༄

Chapter Five:

Cockapoo Toilet Training

Do you remember the old saying 'rub his nose in it'? For many years this was traditionally how house-training was carried out. Poor dogs! Toilet training a human baby is no easy process and yet unfortunately many puppies are expected to toilet train in next to no time. Toilet training is a relatively easy process provided you are patient, follow a few simple rules and keep to a regular routine.

Once again, if the text refers to a puppy, it is intended to also mean an adult dog. Unless of course the adult dog has already been toilet trained.

Housebreaking a Cockapoo puppy need not be a difficult task. It is simply a case of teaching your dog, as soon as you can, that outside of the house is ideally where he should do his toilet business.

Toilet training for success is a matter of putting everything that you can into those first few days. The more times your puppy gets it right in the beginning the quicker he will learn what you want from him. Cockapoos are generally known to be very clean, so hopefully you will have few if any accidents, and toilet training should take no time at all.

1) Necessary Toilet Training Supplies

For perfect Cockapoo toilet training you won't really need a great deal. Some puppy pads or sheets of newspaper, an odour neutraliser (non ammonia based), and a sharp eye along with a swift movement if you notice your puppy needing to suddenly go.

I say an 'odour neutraliser' because a generic cleaning product is not enough. General cleaning fluids do not necessarily rid the environment of the urine smell, and the dog will always return to a smell when looking for a toilet area. Incidentally, a good natural cleaner/neutraliser is vinegar. It is obviously free from harmful chemicals and can be used as a safe cleaning fluid to generally clean tiled floors, cupboard sides or anywhere else the puppy may come into contact.

2) Good Toilet Training Practice

Get into your mind, the idea that for the next few days, you will be a puppy taxi. This basically involves picking your puppy up and taking him outside at least every half hour to one hour.

It is important to realise that until you can gauge your puppies toilet habits reasonably reliably it is advisable to start at every half an hour. If you are confident, you can extend this to every hour or so.

Similarly it is a good idea to expect to use puppy pads or sheets of newspaper in the beginning. Ultimately once the puppy is toilet trained, he will go outside to toilet every time. However, in the initial stages, expect to have to lay down puppy pads or sheets of newspaper, in case of accidents. These can be gradually phased out, and will be explained later. But do remember that your puppy has a tiny bladder at the moment, and he will not be able to hold it for long. In time, you may only need to put puppy pads down overnight until your dog's bladder and bowel matures.

Please remember that during any training, rewarding correct behavior will ensure the behavior is repeated once the connection is made.

3) Toilet training routine

Hopefully the breeder will have started toilet training the puppy. Whether this is the case or not, start toilet training from day one when the puppy arrives at your house. We have already noted this in the 'bringing your dog home' chapter. However, you are presented here with a step by step procedure. Again, the very first thing you should do the first day you bring your puppy home is to take the puppy to the garden or yard and set the puppy down.

» It doesn't really matter exactly where in the garden or yard this is as long as the puppy urinates or defecates outside of the house.

- » The puppy should be permitted to wander about and hopefully do his toilet business.

- » As soon as the puppy does either toilet business, offer lots of praise and a treat.

- » Once this has occurred take the puppy back into the house.

- » From this moment forward you need to follow a routine and try and stick with it.

It is really your choice, but the most practical place in the house to start toilet training from is the kitchen. This is often the preferred place as most kitchens are adjacent to the yard/garden and they generally have a tiled or at least waterproof floor that is easy to clean.

Choose a convenient spot in the kitchen in close proximity to the door. Lay down the puppy pads or newspaper in an area of approximately 1 meter square. This will act as a focus point for the puppy to always go to if he needs to do any toilet business. As the puppy gets used to the toilet training routine you can then gradually decrease the area to a small square.

The following will give you some idea of a typical routine to follow:

1. Approximately every 1/2 hour, presuming your puppy is somewhere in the house > open the kitchen door and call him > as he gets into the kitchen, step outside so that he follows you.

2. As well as every 1/2 hour or so; follow this routine and take him out after he has eaten, slept, played and had a drink because these are the times he will most likely need to go.

3. As soon as he is outside > close the door behind you and say the word 'toilets' or 'wee wee' or something similar. You may have to repeat this a number of times. The idea is that he associates the act of doing his toilet business with those words. These words should most importantly be used the moment he starts to do his toilet business.

4. It is also very important to 'mark' (acknowledge desirable behavior with 'good/clever boy' or whatever) the moment he pees or defecates > I also prefer to again repeat the word or words 'toilets' or 'wee wee' whilst he is actually peeing. Again it is all a question of associating the act with the words. Always remember in the initial stages of toilet training to reward with lots of praise and a food treat, every time he goes. A reinforced/rewarded behavior will always be repeated.

5. You will need to be with the puppy even if it means standing over him. Therefore be prepared to wait with the puppy for up to 10 minutes or so until he obliges. If you suddenly move away from him there is a strong likelihood he will follow you.

6. You do not have to do this all the time, but just until he is successfully going outside to his toilet area to eliminate.

7. If you find the puppy does not do any toilet business after 10 minutes > take the puppy back inside > but be prepared to repeat this routine from this point, every 10 minutes until he urinates and/or defecates.

8. If he does his toilet business the first time, assume he should be OK for another 1/2 hour from that point (but also note the 'Toilet Training Tim-

ings' section that follows)

9. Again 1/2 an hour later repeat the process.

This might sound like a lot of vigilant watching and waiting, but the puppy will soon get the hang of it. Eventually the puppy will associate him doing his toilet business with going outside to do it and he should wait at the door and bark/ask to go out. He may also excitedly wander to the door indicating that he would like to go out.

Please remember that until your puppy has learned this new behavior/habit, you will need to supervise him at all times. This will only last a short time but will pay off. You should therefore commit yourself to keeping an eye on your puppy around the house, for signs that he may need to go at any moment.

You may see signs such as the following: he may lick his lips, yawn or glance at you. Or if you notice him wandering about, sniffing or circling, anticipate he may need to do his toilet business.

Toilet training; Timings.

A puppy will be around 30 weeks of age before he has matured sufficiently and consequently gained full control of his bladder, and generally be able to hold it for 8 to 10 hours.

Once again, a young puppy will generally need to urinate approximately every half hour to 1 hour whilst he is awake. This is why you are strongly advised to take him out every half hour to make sure you do not risk him having a toilet accident before the hour.

It is a good idea to time when he first toilets and then time every half hour from that point. You may also find however, that when you do take him out 30 minutes later, that he just doesn't want to toilet. But if you can, wait 5 or 10 minutes before coming back in just in case.

However, if after another 10 minutes (40 minutes total), he still hasn't gone, don't wait another half hour as he may be ready to toilet 10 minutes or so later. In this case bring him back in, but carry him back out to his toilet area 10 minutes or so later.

You really just need to be aware of your puppies approximate timings as sometimes he will hold it for an hour another time half an hour.

Or he may even go and leave you thinking it is safe for another half hour, and need to go again after 10 minutes.

What to do to avoid accidental peeing

» Again it is important to keep an eye on your puppy for accidents, or any signs that he may need to toilet.

» If you notice him about to go, don't shout, but in a raised urgent voice, say something like 'outside for toilets', or 'outside for a wee wee' > at the same time quickly move towards the kitchen to encourage him out.

» If you are close enough, scoop him up and take him outside or to the nearest puppy pad.

» Even if your dog has begun to go in the wrong place quickly and quietly pick him up and take him outside. He should stop, the moment you raise your voice.

» Do not make a fuss or get angry with him whilst you do this. As soon as you are outside > put him down and wait as before > periodically repeat, 'toilets' or 'wee wee' > Even if he does a tiny bit, reward him and offer lots of fuss and praise.

» At any time when you are unable to be in the same room, simply leave the puppy in the yard or garden, provided it is safe and secure. This assumes that it is a fine day and you are still at home. It would be very inadvisable to leave the house with your puppy stuck outside alone. An alternative is to utilize a puppy play pen that you have lined with newspaper.

» If you have to leave the house, or during sleep times, a segregated part of the kitchen or again a play pen is also advisable. In such cases make sure that you have his bed, toys, water bowl etc in the area.

The puppy is unlikely to soil his bed, but place paper down to absorb any accidental soiling. Dogs along with other animals have a natural inclination to keep their nest or den clean and will therefore choose to eliminate in designated spots away from their sleeping area.

4) Toilet training procedure indoors

If the previous toilet training exercises are done at frequent intervals throughout the day. The puppy will quickly realise that they are not expected to hold their bladder for long. You will therefore find by sheer repetition that the puppy will quickly learn what is expected and will only ever eliminate outside.

However, when in the house it is probably a good idea to make sure the puppy is with you wherever you are so that you can keep an eye on him and prevent any accidents elsewhere.

It is also advisable to keep any doors closed to avoid him wandering into another room. Alternatively have a training lead (for example 3 to 5 meters long) attached to him and yourself to keep him within a certain radius.

Once you are confident that your puppy knows that he has got to toilet outside, you can start to introduce him to other rooms. Eventually you will have the whole house open to him and not have to worry about shutting any doors.

Remember that if your puppy is finding toilet training difficult you should restrict his access to one room, usually the kitchen, particularly if left alone for an extended period of time.

Clearing soiled puppy pads/newspaper.

You will need to clear away any soiled paper/pads on a daily basis. It will then be necessary to use your vinegar or neutraliser in the general area. You will then want to replenish the area with fresh pads or paper.

An important tip to use in the early stages of toilet training is to leave a piece of the soiled, damp paper. This is particularly important for any initial indoor training. The obvious reason for this relates to scent marking. The dog will naturally return to the area they can smell as scent marked. If you clear the soiled paper and put fresh unscented paper in its place, the pup may not remember where he last went to toilet, or not be able to smell the odour. If you leave a piece of the soiled scented paper, he should instantly recognise this as the place to go. It is important that this only takes place in the very initial stages when you are trying to get the puppy to target the puppy pad. Again, once he is successful at this, the next stage is to move the whole thing outside. But again the scented piece will be useful at that stage. Once he knows were he should toilet, leaving the soiled paper will be unnecessary.

5) Night Time Routine

As you have no doubt now gathered, a puppy does not have a large enough bladder to cope with long periods without having the opportunity to relieve themselves.

For night time toilet training it is therefore necessary to follow additional procedures:

1. Take the puppy out 5 or 10 minutes before you go to bed. Hopefully he will be ready to do his toilet business. Once he is used to this rou-

tine he should be ready to pee at this time.

2. It will be necessary to confine the puppy inside the playpen if you have one > or the kitchen with his bed, accessories and puppy pads/newspaper spread out 1 meter square approx. You cannot realistically expect accidents to not happen initially, so be prepared.

3. Some people prefer to sleep down stairs and move the play pen to where they are so that they can be woken if the puppy starts to whine or restlessly moves about.

4. If you sleep in your normal bed however > it will be necessary to set an alarm 4 to 5 hours after you retire. This assumes that you have left your puppy in the kitchen area.

5. The first day, try 4 hours and hopefully the puppy will not have eliminated and therefore be ready to go when you take him outside. It may seem contradictory that he will need to go every 1/2 hour to an hour during the day, but now you are told 4 hours. The point is that provided the puppy is able to sleep they will probably hold their bladder for longer.

6. If you are successful after a week or so at this time, try 5 hours. However, if at any point you are woken in the early hours, with his short, "asking to go out", bark, or whining, he may need letting outside. Again please don't ignore this, and if it is possible, please do attend to the dog as it will be uncomfortable for him to be expected to hold this until the morning.

7. If after 5 hours he has soiled the play pen or kitchen > move back to 3 or 4 hours for a while.

Ultimately you want him to avoid habitually soiling inside the house. So setting the alarm and getting up mid way through a normal sleep pattern will be a small sacrifice for a month or so. Having said all of that, and I hasten to add I am not necessarily recommending this, but some dog owners simply restrict their dog to the kitchen and leave the dog to it. They simply put paper down, fully expecting the dog to do the toilet business on the paper each night. They then clear this away and disinfect each morning. The choice really is yours as to what you prefer to do.

6) CHECK LIST AND SIGNS THAT YOUR PUPPY WILL NEED TO TOILET

When is a puppy more likely to do their toilet business?

» Mornings and early evening.

» When they first wake up after quite a few hours sleeping, whatever the time of day.

» After drinking and eating.

» When you release him from his crate if and when you get around to crate training.

» When active, chewing a toy, physical exertion, whilst playing a game with another dog or family member can have a similar effect to eating.

If an accident happens, then in future be aware of how long the puppy was playing before they relieved themselves, and take him out for a toilet break, before this time.

» If he starts sniffing or circling, and obviously as soon as 'he' raises his hind leg or 'she' squats.

» He suddenly becomes distracted or preoccupied for no obvious reason, or he wanders from an area he has been playing in for some time.

» If he is inside and he looks towards the door to his toilet area.

As you are now forewarned please accept any toilet accident as an accident that you were not aware of.

There is no point in getting upset or angry with the puppy as they will have no idea why you are shouting, hitting, locking him in his crate or outside or any other punishment. Again, as with all training, a dog will only recognise the very last thing he did as the reason he is being punished or rewarded, not something he did 5 minutes or even 30 seconds ago. If you do not correct him the very moment he does something wrong, he will not get the connection.

You simply need to clean up the mess and try harder next time to pre-empt any future accidents.

Please remember that this is part of his training and he is only doing what comes natural to him until you show him that he should not do his toilet business in the house.

In an 'emergency', if you notice your puppy suddenly squat, or cock his leg, and you are too far away, startle and interrupt him with a loud noise. Hopefully he will not be tempted to carry on with his toilet business. Try to avoid some physical gesture you use for any other command such as clapping your hands or slapping your thigh for a recall command.

You then need to get to him a.s.a.p, scoop him up and take him outside to his toilet area, put him down and wait quietly until he toilets.

If you have made the noise, shouted 'No' or whatever, and he continues peeing, don't be tempted to go into a rant telling him how bad he is. Simply clean up the mess without making a fuss and certainly do not speak or acknowledge this.

The whole point of not getting angry is that you need to avoid the puppy associating urinating or defecating as a bad thing for him to do. It is likely that he will seek somewhere to toilet where and when you aren't present.

7) Crate Training Introduction

Please note: Crate training is something that I would not recommend using in conjunction with toilet training for a young puppy. Many people for various reasons, lock their dogs in a crate overnight. For an adult dog, this may be a practical and feasible option as they can generally hold their bladder overnight. But as you now know, it is not fair to expect a puppy to hold their bladder in the same way.

Although it is necessary to bond with the puppy, it is not desirable for the puppy as well as for the handler to be with each other all of the time. In this respect, interaction and solitude should be carried out in regular short episodes throughout the day. This practice is also an excellent remedy for separation anxiety.

In order to ensure that the puppy does not become dependent and reliant on you every minute of the day, the puppy therefore needs to become accustomed to spending time alone. It can seem cruel to not include the new puppy in family activities at all times. It can certainly be cruel for the puppy to have all of this attention, and then suddenly be left alone for hours. There is no wonder that conditions such as separation anxiety consequently develop.

If he has not been conditioned to sit or lie quietly and patiently, then he is bound to bark or whine in frustration, for your attention. You should therefore ensure that he gets used to spending time alone, and the best tool for this purpose is his crate.

Again, the crate should not be viewed as a cage that he is locked up in. It should be seen as a den or sanctuary, where the puppy can feel safe and secure. Many dogs feel the need for solitude and to have the option for their own space. You will therefore find that many dogs like to hide away either under items of furniture or behind sofas etc.

As with any training, you should build crate training up gradually and repetitively over time. But commence once he has settled in and is happy and confident in his new home.

Start with a couple of minutes of alone time, so he barely realises you are not there, and is confident you will return. Then increase to 5 minutes, then 10 and 15 and so on. Once again, never extend this for longer than 1 hour for toilet training reasons mentioned previously.

By exposing him to alone time in this way, he will develop greater independence and self reliance.

A) INITIAL CRATE TRAINING

Initial crate training should ideally take place in a room where there will be people present.

Prepare the crate with his bed, bedding and toys and leave the door to the crate open. VETBED is often used for whelping and many pups will have been brought up with this. It is very useful as a bed/crate liner as it is very durable and machine washable. Water proof foam, 'chew proof' mattresses specifically for crates, are also a good idea.

1. Put a few food treats at the back of the crate to encourage him to go in > You should let him wander in and out of the crate even if he picks the food up and goes back out again > If he stays there to eat the food then all well and good > Sooner or later he will associate going into the crate as a rewarding experience. As with any training > when he successfully goes into the crate to get the food > offer lots of praise.

2. As soon as you start this routine also add the words 'on your bed' or 'in your crate', or simply 'bed' or 'crate'. Say these in an enthusiastic , encouraging tone of voice. These words will then become the 'command' words for when you need him to go into the crate at bed time or any other reason.

3. Once he has become accustomed to spending time in the crate with the door open, start closing the door behind him for very short periods. So the routine would be (i) have the door open and drop a few food treats to the back (ii) at the same time, call him in with the command word you have chosen (iii) as soon as he goes into the crate to get the food, praise him and quietly close the door behind him (iv) Once he has eaten the food and comes back to the door of the crate > pause a few seconds, providing he remains quiet and doesn't whine or start barking > open the door again. Please remember to only let him out if he is quiet. If he whines, wait until he stops before again opening the door. He will soon realise that by not whining, he is let out of the crate (v) as soon as he comes out of the crate, offer lots of praise.

Please also be aware that if he does start to whine he may persist and this could be for 10 minutes or so. If this is the case you will need to choose a moment, when he is quiet and quickly open the crate. It is very important that you do not give in and let him out while he is whining. You need to time it so that he isn't whining when you open the door otherwise he will think he just needs to whine to be let out. It may seem very cruel to ignore him like this, but as long as you stay in the room with him, he should soon stop, at which point you open the door and give him lots of praise.

Cockapoo Toilet Training

Do not view crate training as a traumatic experience that you should avoid doing just because he is whining or crying. He will resist most things that he does not like and will very quickly get used to the idea. It is no different to him pawing and rolling about on the floor to get his collar off. If you give in to his crying, he will cry every time.

B) Extending Crate Time During The Day.

On a night for example, your puppy will settle down for a lot longer period than during the day. It is also obviously dark, quiet and no one around to give him attention. But do not expect him to be happy to stay locked in a crate when he is wanting interaction during the day.

» When you start extending his crate training, close the door as before. Now as soon as he is waiting to be let out, wait for 2 seconds or a slow count of 'one and two and', then open the door as long as he has remained quiet.

» During the first day aim to do this about 10 to 15 times.

» Now repeat this procedure, increasing the time by 1 second each time.

» So when you have repeated this at 2 seconds up-to 15 times, increase to 3 seconds for another 10 to 15 times, and so on.

» You can also extend his time in the crate with the door closed by feeding him his meals in the crate. As you can imagine, he will at least be preoccupied for as long as it takes him to eat the meal. Again, place his food bowl in the back of the crate so he has to go all the way in to eat. At first leave the door open. However, once your puppy is comfortable eating his meals in the crate, you can start to close the door while he is in it. Open the door again as soon as he is finished eating. As before, each time you feed your puppy in the crate, leave the door closed a few minutes longer after he has finished eating, until your puppy remains in the crate for 10 minutes after eating.

» After extending his time in the crate with you present, start to leave him in the crate whilst you leave the room. So once he has finished his meal and is waiting at the door, leave the room for a few seconds, then return and let him out. Each time you do this extend by a couple of seconds until you get to 1 minute, then 2 minutes, 3, 4, and so on. Again, If he starts whining or crying, you may have increased the duration of your absence too quickly.

This kind of repetition will very gradually condition the puppy to accepting the crate and he will soon settle without any problem. There is no real time limit as to how long this will take, as again you should only increase the time when he is not whining and asking to come out.

One additional point to note when you take him out of the crate each time, is to get into the habit of taking him or calling him to his toilet area. Remember that this is a time that dogs typically wish to do their toilet business.

This is important as you do not want him to get into the habit at some point of coming straight out of the crate and doing his toilet business within the house.

Please also remember to never leave your puppy alone in the crate for extended periods during the day.

Once again, refrain from extending crate training beyond an hour until he is at least 6 months of age. By this time you may have successfully managed to condition him to accepting being in the crate for a few hours. You could now attempt extending this over night.

c) Crate Training During The Night

It is assumed that at this stage he will be accustomed to being locked in the crate for an extended period of time. Again, this should have been carried out in the previous initial crate training.

The important thing is that with correct crate training your puppy will soon get used to the fact that night time is for sleeping. All the attention and activity of the day comes to a halt for everyone not just him. The first time is likely to be as hard as it gets for him and he may well start whining, crying or howling for attention. Again please remember to only let him out once he has stopped whining.

There are a number of items you can use to make this a lot easier and more bearable for him. Draping a blanket over the crate is a good idea as this can make it more of a cozy den for him. A lot of dog trainers swear by comforters such as a ticking clock, radio or TV left on low volume. A heat source, heat pad, hot water bottle and lots of cuddly toys are other good comforters as these are thought to replicate his litter mates. However, if a heat source is used this should not make him too warm. Also be careful that whatever you use is safe for him, ensuring that he can neither bite through an object nor burn himself.

Remember that most young puppies will not last 6 hrs without needing to toilet.

As before for his initial toilet training, there is no easy way around this. You are again strongly recommended to make the sacrifice of getting up early for a few weeks, to let the puppy do his toilet business.

As for the initial toilet training, for crate training this will again ideally mean setting your alarm for 4 or 5 hours time after you go to bed, then getting up to let him out to toilet.

This should be approached differently to his initial toilet training. You can expect the odd toilet accident initially, but it is not fair to leave him locked in a crate, having to hold it for any length of time. You are taking a big risk that the puppy will have to toilet overnight and if not allowed to empty their bowels, are likely to mess up their crate and get into the habit of doing so again.

If when you come down he has messed up his crate then you will need to set the alarm 30 minutes to an hour earlier.

It will make it a lot easier if you realise that as the weeks and months pass, this need will get less and less until they can go a full eight or nine hours without having to toilet.

d) The procedure when your alarm goes off:

Take him out of the crate and call him to his normal toilet area, where he should relieve himself as soon as he gets outside > Give him lots of praise if he does > but wait with him if he doesn't, before he hopefully eventually relieves himself.

Once he has done his toilet business > bring him straight back in and put him in his crate and then leave him again while you go back to bed.

e) Crate training accidents

Once again, most breeds or individual dogs are unlikely to mess or do their toilet business where they sleep, unless they are locked in a crate for hours without the opportunity to relieve themselves.

An obvious reason for eliminating away from the den is to lessen the chances of spreading disease through harmful bacteria, parasites, organisms etc. Eliminating away from the den is also commonly practiced for many wild animals as this prevents potential predators picking up scents in or around the den.

So please do not blame your dog for any accident in the crate as it is most probably because he has been in the crate too long and he simply couldn't hold it.

Do not keep him in the crate for any longer than you know he can comfortably manage. Always give him the opportunity to toilet outside before putting him in the crate.

Be aware that he may have had a big drink of water before going in the crate. You may therefore need to prevent access to water an hour or so before you retire to bed. For obvious reasons, if he has water available all of the time, he is more likely to drink and therefore need to go. If it is particularly warm over night, then allow a reasonable amount of water in the crate.

Talk to your vet if you suspect urinating is happening more frequently than normal as he may have some sort of infection or disease.

If you are starting to feel frustrated that this training is taking too long, please just be patient. At any point, please do not be tempted to keep the puppy outside in a garage or kennel, even for a double coated breed who are traditionally able to withstand reasonably cold temperatures. It will be too much for a young puppy if there is a drop in temperature. Not to mention the fact that the puppy will be frightened, anxious etc and is likely to whine and cry.

8) Adult and rescue dogs

Older dogs can have housebreaking problems based on a few different things. If a dog has never lived indoors or never been house-trained, then he may assume it is natural to do his toilet business anywhere, including indoors. This is not his fault as he hasn't been toilet trained, nor taught the social etiquettes that we live by. You should therefore apply the steps above in the same way to show the dog what you want. It may take longer, but you should get there eventually, so be patient.

When you bring a rescued Cockapoo home, it's important to expect at least a couple of accidents, regardless of whether he has been toilet trained or not, simply because he or she will be confused and nervous.

a) Scent Marking

» Male dogs may scent mark in the new home if they are un-neutered or particularly nervous.

» Scent marking is the dog's way of showing other dogs that he is there, and can be a nervous reaction or a hormonal response.

» Castration can help with the male dog that scent marks, but is not a definite solution as it can cause further insecurity in some worried dogs. It is worth speaking to your vet if you are having a problem like this.

b) Elderly Dogs

Dogs can lose control of their bladder with old age. This is a sad situation and one which we have to adapt to because we love our dogs. The vet can prescribe specific treatments for leaking and may need to check out your dog's overall health, if this is an issue.

Many older dogs fail to make it through the night in the last months/years without needing to go out. Again, the best solution is to put down plenty of newspaper for him to go on. Cleaning this up in the morning is a small sacrifice to pay, as you need to make things as easy and comfortable for them as possible.

Chapter Six:

Cockapoo Socialisation

1) Why socialise

Please note: socialisation should continue as soon as the puppy comes to you at 8 weeks old. However, it is considered that the 'critical period' for socialisation is from 3 to 4 weeks of age to approximately 12 to 16 weeks old. What this means is that if you leave socialisation later than this, he will start to develop a wariness and at worse fear, towards certain things and people. Before this 12 to 16 week period, he will be happy to accept most things presented to him. The puppy that has been thoroughly socialised from a few weeks to 12-16 weeks will be confident, sociable and friendly and will remain that way.

There are so many dogs in rescue shelters and homes that simply do not know how to react in social situations. This is because they have never learned what to do in the company of other dogs, children and crowded areas or around other animals.

However, stop for a moment and think of street dogs in Europe and similar places. You never see them fighting do you? They manage to get on with no tension and certainly no aggression. They never bark at cars or people.

The street dogs never seem to worry too much about their surroundings. Which points to the fact that there must be a specific reason for the behavior. You guessed it, the reason for poorly socialised dogs is us humans, more specifically the restrictions we impose on them.

We leash them up, stop them interacting, panic when another dog comes towards them and often keep them well away from social situations altogether. Then when a puppy gets to a few months old we complain about their social behavior.

It is possible to grasp back some social skills with an older dog, after the 'critical period' has elapsed. Yet the dog that isn't positively socialised as a puppy, will never really be completely relaxed in new circumstances. However, do not worry too much, as exposure to fearful situations will eventually lead any dog to be less fearful.

Positive socialisation should incorporate everything that you possibly can into a dog's everyday life as early as possible. Not only that though, every experience should be positive.

A good socialisation schedule will include positive experiences of and with;

As many dogs as possible; Buses; Cars; Children; Domestic animals; Farmed animals; People of all ages; Push chairs; Sounds such as recorded thunder and fireworks; The groomer (if you are to use a professional); Trains or trams; Unusual looking people (those wearing hats and unusual clothing); The veterinary surgery; Wildlife etc etc. In other words, just about anything your dog is likely to come into contact with.

Socialisation locations include:

Car rides or bus rides if you take the bus; Visits to local parks; Country walks; Trips to the seaside

As you are likely to walk your dog, he will get regular daily exposure to traffic, other dogs and people etc. But try and go at different times and change routes so that you are not seeing the same things.

2) THE 'CRITICAL PERIOD' AND SOCIALISATION

A) PUPPY DEVELOPMENT AND EARLY SOCIALISATION

So what exactly is the 'critical period' and why is this important?

During a puppies early weeks, they are very much aware of sounds for example, which is why it is so important that they are exposed to all household sounds, and therefore become desensitised and unafraid. Any new sound as well as sight when this becomes applicable, is likely to frighten the puppy at first, until they realise there is nothing to fear.

It is also very important that the puppy receives adequate socialisation with the mother and litter mates during weeks 4 to 8 of its life, otherwise there is a risk of them being dog aggressive, fearful and generally anti social.

The brain of a puppy is growing right up to about 5 months. However, the importance of social interaction continues up to 12 months of age. Again this is why it is very important to continue his socialisation when he comes to live with you.

As previously mentioned, what is known as the 'critical period' occurs in a puppies development roughly between 3 to 16 weeks of age. During this period, the puppy is at its most impressionable and easily influenced.

Famous studies carried out by Scott and Fuller and documented in their book (Genetics And The Social Behavior Of The Dog; 1965) highlighted the 'critical period' and established a number of very important findings:

Among their many experiments they discovered that puppies that had no human contact up to 7 weeks of age, were then exposed to humans and took 2 days before they attempted to make contact.

In a different experiment, puppies were deprived of human contact for 14 weeks. After this period contact with humans began and resulted in the dogs showing extreme fear of humans. The puppies consequently behaved like wild animals.

Although the experiments were conducted with limited individual cases, the results were a startling indication of how important socialising was and is during those early stages.

If you therefore assume that the critical period of 3 weeks to 16 weeks has to be adhered to, then we have to hope that the breeder has started the socialisation from 3 weeks, which is why you should always question them about this. It then gives the new owner another 6 to 8 weeks to continue this vital socialisation, assuming your puppy is 8 to 10 weeks old when he arrives.

Again, many behavior problems are cited as a direct result of failure to provide adequate early socialisation during the critical period. The consequence of this is that thousands of dogs are euthanised every year globally.

3) Socialisation, and who your dog should interact with

Socialisation isn't something you teach a puppy as such, as they effectively teach themselves. But we need to facilitate this by exposing them to a wide variety of experiences and environmental stimuli.

Although socialisation is a vital component of a puppies development, you should guard against flooding the puppy too soon with stimuli likely to frighten him. In the initial stages, large groups either at a park or obedience class are likely to overwhelm and become a stressful, fearful experience for him. In such situations, you may notice him display signs of obvious unease such as a fearful look, his tail between his legs, or calming signals such as yawning or licking his lips. So gradually expose him to stimuli and desensitise him gradually, rather than throwing him in at the deep end. For example a trip to the park should be at a time when you know there will only be a few people about rather than crowds of people and dog walkers.

At first, aim to socialise him a few times per week and if he reacts in any kind of adverse fearful way, take him out of the situation. However if possible, allow the pup time to investigate and go toward the stimuli in their own time.

You certainly want to avoid any kind of negative impact on the puppy as this could easily have a lasting effect and be difficult to cure. Some early experiences known as imprinting become fixed and in some cases this is irreversible and remains with the dog for life.

As the puppy gets older and his confidence grows, he will be less intimidated. You should then increase his exposure to different dog types, sizes, ages, temperaments and larger groups etc.

Also, please do not make the mistake of thinking that your dog only needs to be exposed to experiences in your immediate environment. Take him to different locations and expose him to different people, animals, vehicles etc.

It really is important that he experiences as many unusual places, people etc as possible, to ensure he is comfortable and unaffected by any eventuality. In fact whenever you go anywhere at all, if it is practical and safe to do so, take your puppy with you.

A) SOCIALISING WITH OTHER DOGS

Your dog ultimately will need to learn canine manners from other dogs. In turn this teaches him good behavior, social skills and etiquette. Early exposure to lots of different dogs, ages, sexes, breeds etc is vital. However, he will need to learn that although he may well be the happy go lucky breed that he is, who wants to play, not every dog or breed will share his point of view. Your Cockapoo will need to be exposed to some dogs that are unfriendly or show hostility. It is a mistake to only allow your puppy to interact with dogs they know, and you know to be friendly. This only gives a false sense of security as the friendly, familiar dogs will no doubt tolerate his exuberant behavior, which may not be tolerated by dogs that wish to be left alone. Being exposed to relatively unfriendly, aloof dogs will also teach and hopefully prevent him from bounding up to strange, potentially hostile dogs in the future. Such occasions could possibly initiate a dog fight or attack. However, do make sure that the owner of any strange dog that you introduce your dog to, has theirs on a lead and can control and prevent their dog from attacking your puppy, should they attempt this. Ultimately, the under socialised puppy who hasn't experienced lots of different dogs, will possibly fail to read the signals to back off, and again an unintentional fight or attack could occur.

B) PLAY AND INTERACTION WITH OTHER DOGS

Most adult dogs in general have a desire to play and interact with other adult dogs. Although adult dogs do play, the type of play is not the typical rough and tumble, chasing etc that puppies engage in, but more subtle forms of engagement.

As adults and puppies play differently, an over exuberant puppy can get into trouble with a less tolerant adult who is no doubt easily annoyed at such immature behavior.

An adult however, will be more forgiving with a puppy than with another adult, and will teach the puppy appropriate social skills.

For a puppy, play is also vital regardless of the breed as they learn important social boundaries such as bite inhibition and respect for other dogs etc. In the litter for example, puppies will let other puppies know if they are not happy with certain rough play.

But again, quite often puppies will be far more boisterous than adults and under socialised puppies can grow up thinking this type of behavior is perfectly acceptable. It is therefore important that well socialised and experienced adult dogs are available to correct inappropriate behavior from a puppy.

Also be aware that the temperament and age of other dogs can have an effect on a young puppy. An older, larger juvenile puppy is likely to be too strong and rough for a young puppy.

This can lead to your puppy developing a defensive and perhaps aggressive approach to other dogs. It is therefore advisable in the initial stages at least, to try and allow interaction with other puppies of similar ages and temperaments.

The problem with adult Sporting/Gundog types however, is that many of them behave like puppies and juveniles even once they mature, and again get into trouble with less understanding, tolerant non Sporting/Gundog type adults.

Terriers and other breeds for example, who were bred to be independent and solitary in their working and interacting generally have a reduced desire to play and interact beyond puppyhood. They can therefore be intolerant and hostile of breeds such as the Cockapoo who still wants to play and interact as if they are still puppies.

c) Problems that can occur during play

Do be aware that if your dog is associating with, or being made to associate with incompatible, domineering breeds, perhaps in a class situation or dog park, they may have a negative experience and possibly pick up unacceptable social behavior.

Many Cockapoos, again because of their friendly playful natures can also become victims and can easily learn to fear certain bullying dogs.

Dogs being pack animals tend to create a pack association when they get together with other dogs. It isn't about any kind of 'alpha dynamic', but a general status, 'pecking order', or hierarchy is established, which isn't necessarily fixed and can therefore change from moment to moment.

Unfortunately what can happen if a group of unknown dogs get together, rather than give and take play occurring, a pack can be formed and bullying or chasing a weaker perceived dog can take place. It therefore becomes more like the prey/hunt instinct taking over which is not pleasant, desirable, social behavior.

Be aware of such dogs, and in such cases your puppy may be better off spending quality time with you alone exercising, playing fetch or training, without having to endure such dogs. Again, if any such interactions ever become hostile, simply pick your puppy up and take him away from the situation.

d) Socialising with people

Dogs generally being social animals, like to interact with each other as well as receiving social interaction, attention, love and affection from us, their human guardians. Interaction with people typically teaches them their place amongst humans, and how to behave around the house.

Kennel bred, puppy mill dogs rarely get to see anyone other than the person who handles or feeds them. As well as limited human interactions, they are also largely isolated from interacting with too many other dogs.

Such dangerous neglect can result in a puppy that grows into adulthood either timid, fearful, hostile, aggressive and potentially dangerous toward other dogs and humans.

When greeting people, perhaps other dog walkers, always ask them if your dog can greet their dog. It is probably best to ask any strangers if they could keep their distance at first and then gradually introduce each other. Also asking them to perhaps crouch down and encourage the puppy or offer tasty treats. This will all help to positively reinforce the experience.

Children that are unfamiliar to the puppy can also pose a similar problem as they can be more unpredictable making sudden spontaneous movements likely to make a puppy frightened or wary.

Always pre-empt if an adult or child appears overbearing, perhaps if they attempt to pick the puppy up, which may shock the puppy. But don't make a fuss yourself if you have to intervene. The puppy can easily associate your reaction as confirmation that this is something to be feared.

4) Vaccinations and socialisation

Veterinarians have for many years advised puppy owners to restrict a puppies access to other dogs and areas frequented by dogs until approximately 16 weeks of age when they should have completed their immunisation programme. The main reason for this is the serious risk to the puppy of contracting one of the deadly diseases such as Distemper or Parvo Virus, which the inoculations are supposed to protect them against.

Canine behaviorists conversely assert that if a puppy does not obtain sufficient socialisation during the 'critical socialisation period', then you risk behavior and temperament problems developing which can be difficult to correct.

They also argue that there are far fewer puppies catching one of the deadly diseases, as opposed to the many that develop serious behavioral issues, resulting in needless annual euthanisations. Consequently owners either embark on behavior management courses or give the dog up to a rescue organisation where the dog again potentially faces being euthanised.

It has furthermore been asserted that the death rate of puppies contracting the aforementioned diseases is considered to be significantly low, even when the puppies are socialised in areas of potential risk during the inoculation period.

As you can see, it is an obvious dilemma that on the one hand the puppy needs to meet as many different people and dogs as possible during their 'critical socialisation period' but on the other, certain opinions assert they should not leave the house to do so.

So what is the answer to this obvious dilemma?

Once again it is fair to state that there will always be a certain risk of a puppy contracting a disease. Obviously the risk factor is greatly lessened if the puppy remains indoors, but again their socialisation will suffer.

a) Minimising the risks:

In general you are strongly advised to not take risks at this critical period and if possible only allow dog to dog contact with animals that you know have been fully vaccinated or are at the same stage of vaccination as your puppy (at least one, preferably two vaccination jabs).

If you know other vaccinated dog owners that will allow you to visit them and allow your puppy time to play and interact with their dog, then so much the better.

As meeting many different people is vital it may be necessary to rely on as many people as possible visiting your home. For a busy household, this will probably not pose a problem. But if visitors are infrequent, you will probably have to be a little bit more proactive, by inviting people round for that purpose.

You can also consider organised puppy classes with owners in a similar position to yourself. Dedicated puppy groups do exist and give puppies the chance to socialise with other puppies who are between the 8 and 16 week critical period and also going through their immunisation programme.

You would be well advised to check your area for such a puppy group to ensure your puppy is at least mingling with other puppies and owners.

b) Taking the puppy outdoors:

It is also recommended that whilst a puppy is going through his vaccinations, during his 'critical' socialisation stage, should you decide to take him outdoors, that you carry him, particularly in areas where other dogs are known to frequent. Ideally you should avoid areas where other dogs are known to urinate or defecate, as again this could pose a potential disease risk.

» You are certainly strongly advised not to allow him to wander about on public ground where other dogs have frequented, even if there are no other dogs present.

» He will of course be unable to sniff or scent mark himself but at least he will be exposed to traffic noises and sites that will ensure he does not develop abnormal phobias.

» If you do meet other dog walkers, do not allow the puppy to come into direct contact with their dog.

Chapter Seven:

Initial Cockapoo Obedience Training

In this next chapter we will cover specific step by step obedience training methods for your Cockapoo.

The text here and elsewhere refers to 'gundog training'. Although the Cockapoo is not a traditional gundog as such, as you know, the parent breeds are. In this respect as previously mentioned, you are strongly advised to recognise the benefits that gundog training will provide your Cockapoo. If gundog training is mentioned, it is also therefore intended to refer to your Cockapoo also.

The intention here is to offer basic obedience such as 'sit', 'stay', 'down' etc. The next chapter will deal with more advanced training. This advanced training typically represents the type of training a working gundog would go through and which is becoming increasingly popular with many ordinary dog owners. If you are only interested in basic obedience then this chapter will be all you need. The advance training will cover aspects of gundog training including: basic and advanced retrieve; exposure to gunshot; introduction to water; quartering; hunting in the field etc.

All of this may hold no interest for you. However, I would strongly advise you to consider teaching your dog the 'stop' command. It is similar to the 'down' command which we will cover here, but goes into much more depth and detail. For many gundog trainers, the 'stop' command is THE most important command you can teach your dog. When properly taught it should reliably stop your dog instantly, wherever he is or whatever he is doing, and this may be in an emergency. It does however involve using a relatively inexpensive whistle, which is very simple to use. Details of which will be given in the Advanced chapter, section on whistles. Recall training is also very important, and although basic training involves some sort of recall or 'come' command, it will be covered here. It will however be included with instructions again including the whistle; but you can follow the exercise without using the whistle quite easily by simply omitting the whistle part.

Please note that the text throughout the chapter will also be interspersed with information for working Gundogs. Don't be put off by this if you are only interested in a well behaved, well mannered house dog. It it is merely intended to put into context the traditional, and in some cases, current purpose of the breed.

In addition to receiving step-by-step instructions for training your Cockapoo dog, you will also learn the basics about different training methods and canine learning theory.

IMPORTANT: Please read through this chapter to familiarise yourself with certain training procedures that should be initiated when your puppy comes to live with you. These include preliminary 'recall' and 'heel' etc.

1) How your Cockapoo may react during training

The Cockapoo is a very intelligent breed that typically responds well to training but he can sometimes be easily distracted. Some Cockapoos also have a bit of an independent streak. This can result in him being stubborn when he does not want to do something. This wilful attitude has been noted in working dogs whilst hunting when they can suddenly decide to do their own thing (hunt for themselves)and ignore you. However, their single mindedness can prove to be a major advantage when they are in pursuit of certain bird scents, which other dogs would miss, relentlessly pursuing it. Please remember that it is important that you are patient, firm and consistent during training sessions. For the best success, you should plan to keep your training sessions short and fun so that your Cockapoo gets something out of them each time.

2) Popular Training Methods

When it comes to training your Cockapoo, other than traditional gundog training, you may come across a variety of different training methods. Traditional punishment-based methods are unfortunately still used by some trainers, gundog or otherwise. Thankfully this has been superseded to a large extent by modern positive reinforcement methods which can also include clicker training. In this section you will receive an overview of popular training methods in use today.

A.) Positive-Reinforcement Training

One of the most popular training methods used by trainers today is positive reinforcement. This type of training involves 'operant conditioning' (we will cover this shortly), in which the dog learns to associate an action with a consequence. In this case, the term consequence does not refer to something bad, it is just something that happens as a result of something else. In other words cause and effect. The goal of positive reinforcement training is to encourage your dog to WANT to do what YOU want him to do.

The basics of positive reinforcement training are simple; you teach the dog that if he follows your commands he will be rewarded. For example, you teach your dog to respond to the word "Sit" by creating an association for him with the word 'sit', and the action of him sitting down. In order to teach him to associate the command with the action, you reward him with a treat each time he sits on command. It generally only takes a few repetitions for dogs to learn to respond to commands because food rewards are highly motivational for most dogs. It's a simple concept, but it can go wrong very easily. Don't worry too much for now as the procedure will be explained as we go. Timing is very important in order to get the dog to associate a cue word with what you want him to do.

Once again, the key to successful positive reinforcement-based training sessions is to keep them short and fun. If the dog enjoys the training, he will be more likely to retain what he has learned. It is also important that you make the connection between the command and the desired response very clear to your dog. If he doesn't understand what you want him to do, he will become confused. It is also important to pair the reward immediately with the desired response. This helps your dog to make the connection more quickly and it motivates him to repeat the desired behavior.

B) Positive-Reinforcement Training; The Gundog Training Perspective.

There seems to be much confusion about when is the best age to begin gundog

37

training. The traditionalists have always believed this as being between 6 and 10 months of age. In some cases the opinion is that the dog should be older than this. This begs the question, what is the reason behind leaving it this late. The usual reasons revolve around building and developing confidence as well as a strong hunting/retrieving drive, and that early training would hinder the development of those qualities.

Adherents of positive reinforcement training, argue that the hunting drive will not be hindered providing the puppy has ample exposure and freedom to hunt and explore for themselves. It is furthermore argued that merely teaching the puppy basic obedience such as sit, stay and heel work is unlikely to eradicate the puppies natural in-built desire to hunt.

It is fair to agree to a certain extent the view of traditional trainers that not all dogs are the same and a particularly sensitive individual could significantly lose the desire or instinct to hunt or retrieve if 'too much' repetitive gundog training such as retrieving is given too early. Again the traditional view makes a valid point where the natural instinct to hunt may be hampered, at worse lost as the dog will be always watching the handler or afraid to make a mistake.

The view is that the dog should be allowed to hunt, but to take directions or guided, if needed or should the dog go wrong. The overall objective is that the trained dog will be confident and keen to work and hunt, but be disciplined and equally keen to please the handler.

But again, if we look at the way traditional gundog training has in the past, and still is being administered, we can see additionally why the puppy was left to their own devises until the 6 to 9 month mark, when 'serious' training started. Confidence is the big issue here, as the puppy had to become spirited bordering on troublesome. The so called 'breaking' would then begin. Traditionally, breaking would involve punishment tactics such as hitting, slapping, scruff shaking etc.

These are not even considered appropriate methods by many traditional trainers now, but 'snapping' the choke chain back, is still common practice. A young, impressionable, vulnerable puppy can be severely affected rendering them intimidated, frightened and wary with such training. The older dog is considered tougher mentally and physically, and able to accept this without it affecting them too much.

Traditional trainers quite rightly assert that their training is completed much quicker. However, if a fundamental reason for delaying traditional training is because of the corrections and aversive methods, then positive reinforcement which doesn't involve aversive methods, can and should logically be started much earlier. It is also fair to state that non aversive methods take longer in comparison, because of the 'proofing'(this is basically the dog carrying out an action in a variety of different 'distracting' locations and under different circumstances), necessary to get the dogs doing what we need them to do. It is also worth pointing out that much of the hunting training will only commence after the puppy has spent a considerable amount of time mastering basic obedience 'sit', 'stay' etc.

Another important thing to note here is that a lot of the traditional training view point focuses on dogs that were not meant to be kept in the house but in kennels. If you live a busy family life, then the puppy will need to contend with behaving and keeping out of mischief or even danger. A traditional dog kept in kennels will be relatively safe and not have much more than their play time and daily exercise, which is all bound to occur away from the house. If you live in an urban area, then there is a strong likelihood that lead walking will be necessary. The flip side is, if you live in the country side, where apart from keeping a dog on the lead if they exercise where livestock are present, lead work will probably be only necessary on shoots or field trials. In other words much of the obedience training needed to keep the house dog well behaved is deemed unnecessary for a dog living in kennels.

For the family dog, things are so much more complicated. We have to keep a balance between, on the one hand allowing the puppy to happily grow and develop. On the other hand, we have to maintain order in the house, where everyone lives safely and harmoniously. In other words it is necessary that the puppy fits in with our lifestyle, and behaves.

For the traditional gundog trainer they can easily leave obedience training such as heelwork much later in the dogs education. But for a family who needs a dog to have manners and to behave in the house as well as on the lead out walking in public places, obedience training has to start at an early age.

However, dogs are not mind readers and therefore need to be shown what to do to achieve this.

In order to make the positive reinforcement approach work, you ideally expose and encourage the dog to freely hunt and explore by themselves in the initial puppy stages. You also start the basic obedience training at the same time. The key however, is to keep these obedience sessions entirely separate from their 'free time' explorations. You therefore ensure that there are no negative associations whilst they are pleasing themselves exploring and hunting. However, it is important to state here that where any free running is allowed, this should take place in a safe relatively enclosed area, or a long training leash should be attached.

Please remember to not rush the initial puppy training. Always keep the sessions short as their initial attention span is quite short. In other words they will be easily distracted and it will be a mistake to force them into doing disciplined training when they would rather be playing. The whole point of any training is that the puppy keeps a high confidence level by being given the opportunity to succeed at every step, and never set up to fail.

c) Punishment-Based Training

Punishment-based training is not as harsh as the word suggests. It is not exactly the opposite of positive reinforcement training, but it is very different. Whilst positive reinforcement training is about encouraging your dog to repeat a desired behaviour, punishment-based training is about discouraging your dog from performing an unwanted behaviour. The goal of punishment-based training is to teach your dog that a certain action results in a negative consequence and thus the dog will choose not to perform that behaviour in the future. Traditionally, punishment would unfortunately be in the form of physical acts likely to cause pain to the dog. Fortunately things have evolved to the extent that punishment now involves ignoring the behaviour or withholding a treat or praise.

The limitation with punishment-based training methods is that they are generally only effective in teaching your dog to stop doing something rather than teaching him to respond to a certain command. It is also important to note that punishment-based training can have a negative impact on your relationship with your dog. Even though your dog may stop performing the unwanted behaviour, it may not be because you taught him that the behaviour is undesirable. He will likely only associate the behaviour with him having done something wrong, when he ideally wants to please you.

Again, a typical example of this 'punishment' approach is that you simply ignore an undesirable behaviour. With normal positive reinforcement you reward good behavior that you have asked for. If the dog then jumps up or starts barking at you, you simply ignore the behavior by not acknowledging it by not speaking, touching or turning away from the dog.

Traditional punishment-based training approaches in the past would involve aversive techniques that would result in the dog learning not to perform the undesirable behavior. The dog would also learn to be fearful of you and in some cases aggressive. If you know

Initial Cockapoo Obedience Training

anything about dog behavior, you may already know that in most cases, aggression is born of fear. Even the most even-tempered dog can become aggressive if he is afraid. If you use traditional punishment-based training methods you not only risk teaching your dog to fear you, but there is also the possibility that he will become aggressive with you, or someone else, at some point in the future.

Note: I would like to point out here, that you should NEVER, under any circumstances hit your dog. It is not only cruel, but an unnecessary action on your part. If you are ever having recurring behavioral issues with your dog, you should either seek an alternative approach or in extreme cases, seek the help of a professional dog trainer/behaviorist.

D.) Clicker Training

Clicker training is a type of positive reinforcement training. With this type of training you use a small clicker device to help your dog form an association with a command and the desired behavior. Because this is the most difficult part of positive reinforcement training, clicker training is often a very quick and effective training method. To use this method you follow the same procedures as you would for positive reinforcement training but you click the clicker as soon as your dog performs the desired behavior and then give him the reward. Once your dog identifies the desired behavior you then stop using the clicker so he does not become dependent on it.

A quick idea of how this works is to firstly get your dog associating the clicker with getting a reward, usually food. So for example you throw down a piece of food. As soon as the dog picks it up, you click with the clicker. You repeat this a number of times. Very quickly the dog starts to associate whatever he does with hearing a click and getting a food reward. So once he hears a click he knows food will follow. You proceed with this by next using a command word such as 'sit'. As dogs naturally sit anyway you can quickly capture the action of sitting with a click. Timing is essential here, so as soon as the action of sitting is performed you click. Once you have repeated this a number of times you add in the cue word 'sit'. Say the word 'sit' just before he sits. As he starts to sit, click, then give him the food reward. There is more to it than that, but that is basically how this works and how you proceed with other commands.

If you want to get a visual idea of how clicker training works, there are some excellent videos on Youtube, you may wish to check out. Just type clicker training and take your pick. If you are interested in much more detailed information about clicker training, books by Karen Pryor are usually recommended, although I am sure others are useful also.

Fortunately clicker training has become popular for gundog training. There are a couple of useful books that use a clicker training approach. If you are interested, search Amazon books using the search term [gundog clicker training]

E) Training Recommendations

As you have probably gathered by now the only method I can recommend is some form of positive reinforcement training. Whether you opt for the method taught in this chapter or choose a clicker training approach, is entirely your choice. As the Cockapoo is considered to be a sensitive gentle personality, you are certainly not recommended to use any harsh treatments. Cockapoos are a very intelligent breed so they typically pick things up fairly quickly. Using a clicker may help you to speed up your training sessions once you learn how to use the clicker effectively.

3) How dogs learn

The problem for the Cockapoo is that aspects of their natural instinctive behavior can get them into trouble with our civilised, ordered lifestyles. How they naturally act is then deemed as being a 'problem behavior' which we are expected to train out of them, or at least to suppress to an extent. The answer is not to attempt to mould them into humans, but to work with their natural instincts and tendencies and teach them acceptable behavior that will make them well behaved members of the family.

For a start, although for centuries dogs have successfully adapted to living side by side with humans, they are still dogs who think and act very differently. They do not perceive things the same way, cannot reason, solve problems, learn or communicate in quite the same way as humans. We therefore need to understand how they do learn and then teach them how to be well behaved, to keep them safe and us happy.

A) How dogs learn: 'learning theory'

Before we get into the actual training, it is important to point out the learning theory behind how dogs learn. Modern dog training and how puppies learn are governed by two main types of learning. These scientific theories are operant conditioning and classical conditioning.

Classical conditioning; most famously relates to Russian scientist Ivan Pavlov's experiments which became commonly known as 'Pavlov's dogs'. The experiments basically studied how dogs salivated when hearing the sound of a bell ringing. This would indicate to the dog that food was about to be given. It worked to the extent that the very act of the bell ringing would initiate the dogs to start drooling in anticipation that food would soon follow.

In modern dog training, words or sounds are used to gain the same effect. Clicker training that uses food as a reward has exactly the same effect. The sound of a click indicates to the dog that they are about to receive a food reward. The idea is to use something that the dog finds highly valuable, such as food, and use this to motivate and train them, consequently getting the dog to do what we want.

Operant conditioning; involves 'punishment' and 'reinforcement' to make changes in behavior.

Punishment; is not, or certainly should be nothing to do with pain, violence or any harsh treatment. Punishment in this sense is something unpleasant to the dog that ensures that a certain behavior is not repeated. Examples include sudden loud noises, smells, bright lights, being ignored or isolated. As previously noted, ignoring a behavior is usually recommended as this simply and clearly indicates to the dog that they do not get rewarded if they repeat a particular behavior.

The difficulty is finding the trigger that works for the individual puppy. A firework may terrify one dog, but have absolutely no effect on another. Obviously many Gundogs are un-phased by gunfire or at least conditioned to be that way.

A young impressionable puppy who is reliant on you for his safety and welfare, should never be exposed to any form of punishment. If in an emergency you have to scoop the puppy up away from danger, then fine. This is likely to shock and frighten the puppy, but you have to potentially save the puppies life, so such a drastic act is necessary. Under normal circumstances, any kind of harsh treatment, even an angry voice or tap on the nose can have a long term detrimental effect on your relationship and bonding with the puppy. The last thing you need is for the puppy to be wary or at worse, fearful of you. Modern dog training usually avoids, and finds most aspects of punishment unnecessary.

Reinforcement; or 'positive reinforcement', is the opposite to punishment and therefore the most acceptable method in use. Again, the idea is that the puppy initiates a desirable act and is rewarded, or the act is reinforced to ensure the puppy repeats it. Reinforcers or rewards include; toys, food, games, attention, kind words of encouragement etc.

There are grey areas whereby puppies are rewarded unintentionally by us. Usually this occurs with attention we give them for undesirable behavior. For example, the dog jumps up and we handle the dog to push it down. We may think that this rebuke is

Initial Cockapoo Obedience Training

showing the dog our dissatisfaction, but to the dog he may still view this as attention that he craves and therefore is rewarded. In this case it would have been better to ignore the dog (a subtle form of punishment), best executed by physically turning away from him as he jumps, and importantly not speaking either. In essence the puppy will soon learn the difference between when we are happy with them, they are rewarded, and when we are not, the behavior is ignored and they are not rewarded.

There is a very subtle example that relates specifically to the Gundog, which is a successful retrieve. gundog puppies will naturally wish to pick things up and bring them to you. You will naturally be delighted by this and will offer lots of praise and encouragement. A subtle problem could occur if the puppy drops the object. You could easily do one of two detrimental things. You either inadvertently praise them as they are coming back to you and at the same time they drop the object. The puppy can easily view the dropping of the object as praise worthy. A working gundog should never be trained to drop an object as they are coming back to you. This is particularly important as they may drop an injured bird, that would otherwise die a slow and painful death. The other problem is that you could get angry and make the puppy feel the act of retrieving is a bad thing. Again the best course of action is to ignore a specific mistake and never reward it.

Four learning stages

Learning basically takes place in four stages as follows: Acquisition; Practice; Proofing; Repetition.

» New knowledge "acquisition" (you teach sit a number of times so that when he hears the word sit he automatically sits)

» Practicing the knowledge to become better (you repeat this to solidify the new behavior)

» Apply this to other situations (proofing/generalising). (You increase the level of difficulty by practicing in different locations with added distractions). This is important as he learns to listen to you and carry out an action wherever you are and who ever is present. Please see the section on proofing/generalising at the end of the chapter. Proofing is also very similar to socialisation, learned earlier. Please note that if sufficient socialisation has not taken place, then proofing will be a lot more difficult to achieve.

» Repetitively practicing this new behavior all the time, not just in class or during training sessions.

B) Points to bear in mind for successful learning:

The puppy is always rewarded for desirable behavior, and never rewarded for undesirable behavior.

Avoid acts of 'self rewarding', such as wilfully chasing, taking food from the table or out of bins. In other words, second guess the puppy and keep them away from any such temptations.

Again, please be aware that positive reinforcement should be practiced all the time and not just on the training field. Many potential problem behaviors could develop without you realising this.

4) Other training considerations

A) The independence phase

As your puppy grows in confidence, he will naturally become more independent and start to explore for himself. There is no definitive age that this will happen as some develop this after several months whereas others take over a year. Being part Gundog, you will notice his instinctive hunting behavior start to develop. He will focus on following scent trails, which will mean he is not clinging to your heals. But you will need to ensure he doesn't get carried away and goes too far. So recall will be important at this stage and he should be encouraged to return to you when you call. If he seems to ignore you, it is probably because he is getting lost in the moment. Provided you are in a safe area away from danger such as a busy road, then there is probably no need to panic or worry unduly. If you are concerned about giving too much freedom in this way, please do attach a long 10 meter or so training lead, or a retractable leash. What is important is that he learns to enjoy his independence from you. This freedom is what the traditional gundog trainers deem as being necessary for their effectiveness as a working hunting dog. However, it is also necessary to strike a balance between them doing their own thing, but you being in control when the need arises.

5) Instincts: The pack/prey drive and training

Before we get started on training your Cockapoo; the following will give you a brief insight into what drives him as well as the need to work with their instinctive drives to successfully train him.

How any dog behaves instinctively may not be acceptable to the family needing a well behaved dog.

Because Sporting/Gundogs or dogs such as the Cockapoo are hard-wired to react to game or prey, a first time encounter may elicit a host of behavior such as becoming excitable by barking, quivering, lunging at the leash etc. Depending on the breed, they may even instinctively react by pointing or stalking. This is merely dogs being dogs and nothing at all abnormal. However, in order for the dog to behave and not take off chasing the bird or whatever, we need to train self control.

We are not looking to extinguish this instinct or suppress their interest, but to teach them to change their normal instinctive reaction. It is therefore far better to understand their natural reactions and work with that rather than making the dog do something they do not have an instinctive desire or inclination to do.

This does not mean that we should allow them to react as they normally would without our guidance. We are not wanting to make them unhappy or spoil their fun, but to keep them safe from danger.

So, although dogs such as the Cockapoo have a very sociable people oriented side to them, otherwise known as a 'pack drive', you also need to be aware that they additionally have a very strong 'prey drive'.

The prey drive or any other drive is triggered by what the dog instinctively feels the need to do at any given moment. He can be happily walking by your side in 'pack drive' perhaps nudging you for attention one moment. The next moment he sees a rabbit or a bird and switches into 'prey drive' and all attention on you vanishes as he is compelled to chase after the rabbit.

Drives

Triggering the pack drive is needed to reliably control the prey drive which causes problems such as chasing and generally ignoring commands. We develop pack drive by generally engaging him with training, play, bonding, interacting, touching, praising him etc.

The difficulty with drives however is that with most dogs, but not all, the pack drive is much harder for us to trigger than their prey drive. The prey drive is certainly harder to over-ride once triggered. Fortunately for us, Gundog types have a relatively strong 'pack drive'. But again this needs to be encouraged to maintain a reliable self control. Play can be used very effectively in working between pack and prey drive. Games involving us, the dog and a chase element offer a good example.

Incidentally food is part of their prey drive. This is primarily why in primitive terms wolves, feral dogs or similar hunt or scavenge. It is therefore unsurprising that food can be such as powerful motivating factor when teaching or wishing to control a dog.

INITIAL COCKAPOO OBEDIENCE TRAINING

In order to effectively prevent the dog from reacting to anything likely to trigger the prey drive, this self control has to be taught. You only have to see how a well trained gundog has to behave on a shooting field to see how effective gundog training is and has to be. However, this training takes time and does not happen over night. So be patient with the following training steps.

6) Collar/Harness & Leash Training

a) A word on the hazards of using collars in the field

It is extremely important that when out in a field environment where there is cover such as hedges, collars of any type should never be worn by your Cockapoo, puppy or adult. A dog can very easily pass through hedges and get snagged quite severely and sometimes with fatal consequences. Chord choke type leads are always recommended for this purpose. The choke lead, being all in one, simply passes on and off the dog as required.

b) Walking Equipment (Collar or harness and leash)

Dog walking equipment should be introduced carefully, particularly to a puppy, and only the kindest collars or harness types should be used.

A harness for a young puppy is generally better than a collar, as it redistributes the weight of his body and naturally, immediately stops him pulling on the leash. However, please note that once the dog matures and grows stronger, his pulling power will be greater and a harness can make him difficult to control, or more difficult than utilising a collar.

Puppies are far easier to control on walks when wearing a harness and there is no nasty pulling and coughing, as often happens on a standard collar and leash.

If you intend to use a collar however, initially use a small leather or man-made collar suitable for a puppy.

When you put his puppy collar on, do make sure that it is not too tight. You should quite easily be able to slip two fingers under the collar. It is up to you whether or not you allow him to wear the collar around the house on a daily basis. Please however remember that he will be growing day by day so it is important to check that you can still slip two fingers under the collar, every other day.

Most puppies do not like having to wear a collar, but this is something you should apply within a few days of his arrival.

In the early stages he will do everything to get the collar off. So simply accept that this is not cruel and wait for the scratching and head shaking etc to stop once he gets used to it.

Basically when you first introduce a Cockapoo puppy, or older dog, to a collar or harness make it a nice and positive event. Pop it onto the dog and play for a while, then remove it again whilst the dog is still happy. After doing this a few times, add the leash and allow the dog to trail it behind in the house or garden.

Putting the collar or harness on

As with any new training you can always sweeten the experience with a treat.

» Some people simply put the collar on and leave the puppy to get used to wearing it for an hour or so.

» Or if you prefer, you can do this in 5 or 10 minute stages by first putting the collar on > offering a treat > leave him five or ten minutes > take it off and repeat several times.

» Remember to give him lots of praise whilst he is accepting the collar, but ignore any protestations

» You can then take it off and leave him a few minutes so that he knows the collar is no longer on.

» You then put the collar back on, once again offer a treat, but this time leave him with the collar on for an hour or so.

» You next attach the leash to the collar and allow him to wander around with the lead trailing.

» Again leaving this on for 30 minutes to an hour, so that he gets used to it.

» All of this should be done supervised as it could be dangerous for the pup if the lead in particular gets caught and potentially cause a choking.

» Once your puppy seems happy wearing the collar and leash, he should be ready to go for a walk.

c) INITIAL WALK

Obviously we are not training the puppy to walk, but introducing him to the restriction imposed by applying the collar or harness and leash.

The following training steps are to help you prevent pulling on the leash. They are simply to make your Cockapoo walking experiences happy and relaxed forever.

The steps may take longer if the dog has learned to grab the leash in his mouth or fight against the tension, but if you persevere they will still work.

You will have more success with this if you start the training with few if any distractions. It is therefore best to utilise your yard, garden or a large room.

Training Steps;

1. With your dog on his leash, walk a couple of steps and if the leash stays slack say 'good boy/girl' > offer lots of praise and a treat. Please note that a slack leash is what we want and it is only that which should be rewarded.

4. If the leash becomes tight at any point, do not acknowledge this by speaking or offering any kind of reward. He needs to realise and associate that when he pulls on the leash he does not receive a reward.

5. If the leash goes tight you may need to change direction a few times to initiate a slack leash. If your puppy does not follow immediately you may have to stop and call him by saying 'this way' or using his name, perhaps slapping your thigh as you do. I also find that by simply stopping, thus breaking the sequence of him pulling, is often enough to make him realise he shouldn't pull. Try and avoid suddenly stopping without him realising and yanking him to a stop. Give him chance to stop, by calling him.

6. As soon as any tension vanishes from the leash, again say 'good boy/girl' > offer lots of praise and a treat. In other words we are 'marking' the desired behavior with praise and a treat.

Be patient with this and please don't get into the habit that some 'impatient people' seem to do, and pull the poor dog back with enough force to pull him over. The dog is keen and excited to be out walking and sniffing about. Given the chance he wants to go off and do his own thing. So again, please be patient and considerate.

Repeat and practice this several times, rewarding a slack leash each time. You should soon notice he gets into the habit of not pulling, but instead walking nicely.

Teaching a Cockapoo to walk easily on a leash will probably take 3 to 6 training sessions in a quiet area. It will then need practice (proofing) in various areas, gradually increas-

Initial Cockapoo Obedience Training

ing distractions, to become flawless behavior. This will eventually require exposure to roads and busy traffic. You will need to get to a point of teaching him to sit and wait at the road side until it is safe to cross.

7) Obedience Training – Teaching Basic Commands

Whilst your puppy may not be able to comprehend complex commands right away, you should be able to start basic obedience training at a fairly young age. Although we will cover other aspects of training here, however, there are five main commands which form the basics of obedience training; Sit, Down, Come, Stay and Heel. In this section you will receive step-by-step instructions for teaching your Cockapoo these five basic commands.

However, before we get started with those basic training commands I want to firstly remind/introduce you to a couple of useful preliminary aspects of his training. In the initial stages of training, please make the training sessions relatively short. Ten or Fifteen minutes of good concentrated practice should be fine initially. When you feel he is keen to carry on, extend these lessons. Or practice these commands frequently at odd times around the house, rather than appoint one session for a designated time. The idea is that you can use the training at a moments notice when required anyway.

Just to recap, to be successful with this training, you need to clearly communicate to your dog when he has successfully completed an action.

Again we will illustrate this by using a previous example of clicker training. Clicker training as you know is based on issuing a click at the precise moment the dog performs desired behavior. If the dog has been clicker trained, they will know that when they hear a click they have (a) performed acceptable behavior that we want and (b) they are about to be rewarded for it.

The principal works the same without the clicker when we say 'good' or 'good boy/girl'. When the dog hears that word or words again he knows he has performed behavior that we are happy with and he is about to be rewarded.

What we are effectively doing is 'marking' the behavior with a click or a praise word 'good'.

a) Sit

Again for the dog that sits naturally, it is simple to capture or mark the behavior with a click (or "good boy/girl"). It is also possible to easily lure the act, so that the dog is in the sit position.

This is a position that comes so naturally to a dog that most Cockapoo dogs, as they are so naturally intelligent, will pop into the sit position if you show them something that they want.

All you now have to do is teach him to sit on command.

Please note that 'sit' is also taught in the advanced gundog chapter utilising additional steps to take. If you only wish to teach your dog the basic sit presented here, it will not affect your dog also learning the advance sit work later. The basics of sit presented here will be needed for that anyway.

However, the sit exercise in the next chapter is taught in conjunction with a whistle command and hand signal. What you will find is that teaching your dog using a whistle command, gives you more control and flexibility. The sit taught here uses a verbal sit command which can be limiting if you need to stop your dog at a distance. For this reason I would strongly urge you to read the section on 'sit' in the next chapter and consider incorporating that from the beginning of your dogs training.

To teach your dog to sit on command, follow these steps:

Please note that the following assumes that the dog is already standing. If not, then it may be necessary to lure him into a stand. You can do this by using the treat to draw him into a stand by moving it away from him, then acting quickly with the following steps: Incidentally luring can also be carried out by simply bringing your hand, without a food treat, to his nose and then drawing it away. This is very effective when a dog does not understand a verbal command to move in a certain direction. You therefore use your hand to indicate the direction you want him to take.

1. Kneel in front of your Cockapoo and hold a small treat in your dominant hand > Pinch the treat between your thumb and forefinger so your puppy can see it, but can't take it.

2. Hold the treat directly in front of your Cockapoo's nose and give him a second to smell it.

3. Immediately move the treat slightly away from your puppies nose, towards you and upwards > then move it away from you > towards the back of your dog's head. This again is a technique known as leading or luring, in that you lead your dog to perform the required action.

4. Your dog should lift his nose to follow the treat and, in doing so, his bottom should lower to the floor

5. The moment that he starts to sit > say the cue word 'sit'. You are effectively marking his action of sitting with the cue word 'sit'.

6. As soon as your dog's bottom hits the ground, praise him excitedly with 'good boy/girl' to let him know he has performed desirable behavior > finally give him the treat as his reward.

7. Repeat this sequence (1) to (6) several times until your puppy gets the hang of it.

8. Now when you get to step (5) say the cue word 'sit' as soon as he starts to sit, but for step (6) start delaying when you praise him and give him the treat. In this way he will retain focus for longer.

9. Now instead of repeating the sequence (1) to (6) > walk away from your dog and hopefully he will follow > before he gets chance to sit, say the cue word 'sit' , leaving out the luring part.

10. Hopefully he will sit down > if he sits praise him and give him the treat.

11. Now practice (9) & (10) a number of times.

By proceeding this way you are getting him to sit simply by using the cue word 'sit' . This is ideally what you want to achieve. So you now should not have to lure with the food anymore, but simply say 'sit' and he should sit.

Teaching a Cockapoo to sit in this way will probably take 1 to 3 training sessions in a quiet area then it will need practice in various areas. Gradually increase distractions, to become a flawless command. Again Please see the section on proofing/generalising at the end of the chapter for examples of increasing distractions.

Another useful way of practicing the sit command is as follows:

Early 'Sit' conditioning

A useful method to ease in the idea of the sit command for your puppy is as follows:

1. During feeding, you take the food bowl with food and whilst the pup is excitedly moving and bouncing about waiting for you to place the bowl down, simply hold the bowl until he becomes calm and stops.

2. At this point there is a strong likelihood that he will sit > As soon as he starts to sit > say the cue word 'sit'.

3. As his bottom touches the floor > mark him actually sitting with a verbal 'good boy/girl'.

4. Wait a couple of seconds and place the bowl down, the food being his reward.

It would be useful to attempt this every feeding time from day one, as soon as he comes to live with you.

b) Down

Once you have taught your Cockapoo to sit, teaching him to lie down is the next logical step.

The down command is not a requirement for a traditionally trained Gundog. However, the down command has similar benefits to the sit command in terms of controlling your dog. It can have a number of benefits including, stopping him in his tracks, telling him to drop at distance in an emergency, if for example he is approaching a road with busy traffic. It can also settle him down when visitors come to the home, if he is getting over excited or is about to jump up on someone.

The easiest way to teach a dog the down position initially is to lure the position. After a few successful attempts, he will be offering to get into the position very quickly if he thinks you have something he may want.

For this exercise it doesn't matter if he is standing or sitting to start, as long as he is not already lying down.

To teach your dog to lie down on command, follow these steps:

1. Kneel in front of your Cockapoo and hold a small treat in your dominant hand > Pinch the treat between your thumb and forefinger so your puppy can see it.
2. Hold the treat directly in front of your Cockapoo's nose and give him a second to smell it.
3. Give your puppy the "Sit" command and wait for him to comply. Unless of course he is already seated, or again standing.
4. Once your puppy sits > immediately move the treat quickly down to the floor in between your puppy's front paws > Make sure that you keep hold of the treat for the time being. Do not let him take the treat. He may be tempted to raise up to a sit or stand position, or even do a grab and run.
5. Again it is best to place the treat on the floor within his reach in between his front legs. If you place the treat in the right position, you generally find that he will crouch down into a beg position as he follows the treat.
6. As soon as he starts to assume the down position say the cue word "Down", or "Lie Down" > Again it is important to say the word as he is carrying out the act > He will then begin to associate the cue word 'down' with the action of lying down.
7. Your puppy should now hopefully be assuming the lying down position as he attempts to take the treat > The instant he is actually lying down > again mark this with a click if you are using a clicker > or praise him excitedly with 'good boy/girl' and let him take the treat. It is important that he remains in the down position before you offer praise and allow him to take the treat. The other problem you may find is if his rear end remains raised. You will find steps to take for this following these steps. If your puppy stands up instead of lying down, calmly return to the beginning and repeat the sequence (1) to (7). The important thing is to not acknowledge this with praise or giving him the treat. Again, you do not want him thinking that the down is him assuming a beg position.
8. If he carries out the correct action, repeat this sequence (1) to (7) several times until your puppy gets the hang of it and is successfully carrying out the 'down' action each time.
9. Now instead of repeating the sequence (1) to (7) > walk away from your dog and hopefully he will follow

> before he gets chance to do anything, say the cue word 'down'. This will obviously skip the 'sit' command. Hopefully he will start to assume the lying down position. If he does and as soon as he is lying down, offer lots of praise and give him the treat.
10. Now practice step (9) a number of times.

When Things Go Wrong

There are some extra options for the dog that is simply not getting the idea. You can sit on a chair and lure your Cockapoo under your outstretched leg.

1. Sit on a chair that is high enough so that you can sit comfortably and stretch your leg out, placing your heel to the floor, your outstretched leg at an angle to the floor.
2. Depending on which side your dog is on > hold a treat with which ever hand will be comfortable to tempt him through the triangular gap
3. He should hopefully be 'lured' and start to crawl under your leg > Again as soon as he starts to assume the down position say the cue word 'down'.
4. Hold the treat to the floor > As soon as he is in the down position offer lots of praise and let him take the treat.
5. Practice steps (1) to (4) until he is successfully repeating this.
6. Now as before, stand up and walk away from your dog and hopefully he will follow > before he gets chance to do anything, say the cue word 'down'. Hopefully he will start to assume the lying down position on his own. If he does and as soon as he is lying down offer lots of praise and give him the treat.
7. Be patient here, and be prepared to repeat steps (1) to (6) a number of times. But if after countless attempts, nothing seems to be working then try the following: As you go through the sequence above, if his back end is sticking up in a beg position, gently apply some pressure to his hips. As you gently push down say the words, 'down' or 'lie down'. Again, as soon as he does it, and doesn't immediately get up, click or praise to mark the behavior and reward.

Teaching a Cockapoo to lie down will usually take 3 to 6 short training sessions in a quiet area. You will then need to practice in various areas, gradually increasing distractions, to become a flawless command. Please see the section on proofing/generalising at the end of the chapter for advice on distractions.

c) Come/ Recall

For basic obedience, teaching your dog to come to you when called is incredibly important. Say, for instance, that you open the front door of your house one day and your Cockapoo rushes out before you can stop him. Your dog does not understand the danger of a busy street but if you have taught him to come to you when called, you can save him from that danger. In an emergency situation, your 'down', 'stop' or the 'stay' command can be vital. Using either one of those will hopefully stop him in his tracks. You can then call him back and away from any danger.

The Cockapoo needs to be taught to come back when called as soon as possible and in careful stages.

Most dogs can either be very responsive to recall or happy to leave you standing all day, calling his name in vain, whilst he chases rabbits or squirrels around the park.

Recall training can be broken down into easy steps. The exact same approach is taken when teaching recall as when teaching anything else to the dog. You always set the dog up to succeed; never allow room for failure; therefore building his confidence high.

With recall you need to make certain that your dog sees you as the most interesting and attractive prospect in the area. If you are red

49

faced and shouting his name with frustration he is less likely to want to come back. He will naturally think you are angry with him.

There are some very specific habits that you can procure when teaching recall;

Please do remember that Cockapoos do have a reputation to take off after rabbits, and some without adequate recall training, can run away. Always be on your guard to potentially hazardous areas (busy roads etc) and therefore avoid accidents. I once had a situation with an Irish Setter that took off across a field, after she had picked up the scent of something. I literally shouted my head off and fortunately she came to her senses and came running back. Dogs can easily give chase to rabbits and if you are near a road there is a chance the rabbit may cross, along with your dog. Please pre-empt and avoid this from happening. If in doubt, keep your dog on a long 5 or 10 meter training type lead.

If you get a situation as described above, never punish your dog when he gets to you. Always be welcoming and friendly, no matter how frustrated you are, or he may not come back at all next time.

Early recall training

Recall training, or what many trainers refer to as 'come', is simply getting your puppy to come to you when called.

In the early stages of puppy recall however, a puppy is not always keen to obey in this way. As your puppy grows in confidence he will go from being under your feet all day, to wanting to wander off, explore and generally do his own thing.

What you therefore need to do, is to condition or encourage the puppy to come back to you at random times around the house or garden.

This is only early stages training and works by getting the puppies attention, coaxing him to come to you, and as he is running back, use the recall word, (and for gundog training purposes, the whistle and hand signal also).

It cannot be stressed enough how beneficial it will be to start using the recall cue word, whistle command and hand signal, at this early stage. He will therefore get used to associating these commands with coming back to you, in the very early stages, and make further training so much easier.

Before we start, please be aware of a few useful pointers as follows:

» Unless in an emergency, try and avoid running after your puppy. This can often lead to a chase game which all puppies love, and he is likely to carry on running away anyway.

» The exception to this is if he is running towards an open gate or open field onto a road. Once again you need to pre-empt this and take measures to initially train him in an enclosed or a secure area.

» Also be aware that he may try and engage you in a chase game, by coming up to you and then darting away.

» If you continue with advanced gundog training, when you get into retrieving dummies, if this behavior were not ignored, he may do the same with the object, which again should not be encouraged.

Early recall exercise

Once again in the initial stages, this is best started in your yard, garden or other safe enclosed space with limited to no distractions

Again you will be using the cue word, whistle command and hand signal as follows:

Cockapoo Training

As a reminder there is a small section in the Advanced training section giving advice about purchasing a whistle. Again it is highly recommended to make use of one. They are also cheap to buy and use. You dont necessarily need to purchase from a specialist supplier but can easily and cheaply pick them up on Ebay or Amazon.

» The whistle command should be several short pips/toots (pip, pip, pip, pip) = come back/recall

» The cue word should be something like 'come' or 'here'

» The recall hand signal to use is to throw your arms wide (ideally this is holding your arms straight out, at around a 90 degree angle to your body (approximately parallel to the ground); palms facing towards the dog)

1. Lets assume your puppy is wandering around your garden, sniffing and exploring > Allow the puppy to wander and explore for a few minutes.
2. Whilst he is busy sniffing and investigating, in other words not paying any attention to you > make a funny noise, high pitched or whatever, or call his name to get his attention
3. As soon as he looks towards you, suddenly move or jog in the opposite direction > The puppy should soon notice you disappearing and start chasing you > If not then pat your thigh or use a hand clap to encourage this > If you are using a whistle command, it is best to put the whistle in your mouth at this stage before the next steps. The whistle should be on a lanyard around your neck, as you will need to drop this from your mouth to give the verbal cue.
4. Keep checking back unless you decide to jog backwards > As soon as he starts moving towards you, blow several short pips/toots (pip, pip, pip, pip) on the whistle > almost simultaneous to this, throw your hands wide for the hand signal > drop the whistle from your mouth > issue the command word 'come', 'here' or whichever cue word you have chosen to mark the behavior of him being recalled. As with the other training exercises, you have waited until he starts the action. You then 'mark' the behavior with the verbal, whistle and hand signals.
5. Always try and let your puppy catch you, so either slow down and stop or fall to the floor, which the puppy will love as he tries to lick your face.
6. It is important that you only use the cue word; whistle signal and hand gesture, IF he is already coming back to you. That way he immediately associates the command with the action of coming to you.
7. When he gets back to you, reward him by giving him lots of praise and perhaps a piece of food.
8. Repeat steps (1) to (6) several more times.
9. Practice this procedure for two or three weeks, each day.
10. After you have practiced this for a few weeks, test his response to one of either the recall command 'here', the whistle command or hand signal > Practice each one on its own a number of times > then alternate each one randomly. It should only take him a week or so to get the hang of this, but practice every day until he is coming back to you as soon as you issue the command word 'here'.
11. Only when the recall command is solid and reliable, use the whistle or vocal cue, when he is not looking at you.

51

Initial Cockapoo Obedience Training

12. Around the house at random moments, call him or blow the whistle > This is a big step forward as this is effectively formal recall training > In other words, you are wanting him to come back to you as soon as you give the whistle, recall word, or hand signal if he is looking at you > If this does not happen then proceed as follows.
13. If at any point the puppy starts to blatantly ignore you use the correction word 'No' or 'Ah ah', to get his attention > Be careful with your tone of voice here, as you do not want to frighten the puppy.
14. Once you have the puppies attention, repeat either or all of the recall commands > As he will not have heard this correction up until now, you may have to coax him by kneeling down and offering lots of encouragement.
15. Again, if he successfully comes back to you offer lots of praise.
16. Keep practicing this every day, and again don't just practice on the training field. Practice recalling and praising him around the house and garden.

Rapid recall

You should only practice this once he is successfully and reliably coming back to you with the initial recall.

This exercise gets the puppy used to responding immediately and with speed. It should therefore condition a quicker response.

He simply responds to the whistle, verbal cue or hand signal > returns at speed > is immediately sent off > you then repeat.

The easiest way of approaching this exercise is to use pieces of food that you throw away in order to send him away, then recall him.

1. Recall your puppy to you (whistle, verbal cue or hand signal) > as soon as he gets close to you > throw a piece of food as far as you can in any direction which the dog should race after
2. Once he has picked up the food and as soon as he looks at you > issue the recall command, (whistle, verbal cue or hand signal) > It is important to time the recall command, as soon as he has picked up the food and is about to return. In other words you will see that his intention is to pick the food up and return to you.
3. Again as soon as he gets close to you > throw a piece of food as far as you can throw it, but this time in the opposite direction > repeat this several times.
4. Once he has the hang of this > throw the food shorter distances for a more rapid recall.
5. Now repeat the exercise in different areas/locations and with gradually added distractions

It is important to use the food as a strong incentive and physical object to chase. You could use a dummy or favourite toy, but until he is practiced retrieving a dummy you may not be as successful with a rapid recall.

A few pointers to bear in mind

In the initial stages, only use the recall command when he is either looking at you, or actually coming back to you. Once he has learned to associate the recall command with the action of coming back to you, you will of course be able to simply blow the whistle, or use the cue word. This is ultimately the whole point and objective, in order for you to use it in emergencies or when he is preoccupied doing something else such as chasing a scent or rabbit. Using the hand signal will obviously only work if he is actually looking at you.

Don't make this a chore, but get into the habit of repeating the recall a number of times each day. Soon it will become a really ingrained habit and you will have taught the puppy recall as part of a game and not regimented formal training.

If he runs away and then comes running back, always offer lots of praise for him coming back and never punish the act of him running away. Even though you know he initially went wrong by running away, an act that you do not want, the last thing he did was to come back to you, which is what you want.

Remember that it is necessary to teach a young dog an effective recall in as many different environments and with as many varying distractions as possible, in order to make it reliable.

Failure on the dogs part to respond to a recall can include the following:

» The stimulus of sighted or scented prey outweighs the desire to come back to you.

» The dog has not been exposed to sufficient environmental experiences and has therefore not been sufficiently desensitised to the stimuli.

» Incorrect or insufficient reinforcement/reward (it is important to always reward correct behavior and that you get the timings correct)

» Teaching the recall has only occurred initially and has not been maintained regularly.

Once again the 'recall' is particularly important for breeds with a strong prey drive such as Gundogs.

It is hard for dogs who are highly driven to hunt, to suddenly be expected to stop hunting and return to you. The recall therefore needs to be seen by the dog as part of him hunting. This is the reason many gundog trainers start recall 'conditioning' in the very early stages. In other words he should ideally associate it as part of a fun hunting game. Not some boring discipline that takes him away from doing what he would rather be doing.

If you do advance into high stimulation situations (live game; pheasants, rabbits etc) it is important to use the long line for the dogs safety.

Please note that the reliable recall can take many weeks or months to achieve.

D) EARLY RETRIEVE

The following is intended to give the puppy a basic introduction to retrieving an object. He will later on be introduced to formal retrieving, which is best practiced once he has learned other commands such as stop, sit, recall etc.

Please first of all be aware that although many gundog breeds, instinctively pick up and retrieve items, they do not always realise that you want them to return the object to your hand. It is therefore advisable to start at relatively short distances and then build up. This will ensure that he gets into the habit of retrieving to hand at all times. If left untrained the dog may run off with the object or drop it before he gets back to you.

Early retrieve exercise

This exercise can be practiced along with the early 'recall' in your house or garden. However, please be aware that in the initial stages, giving the puppy too much space can encourage him to wander off. It is therefore advisable to initially practice in a narrow area such as a hallway or any long narrow lane, even if you have to construct something yourself.

The first dummy you use should be lighter than the 1lb dummies you may be using if you move further into dummy work with advance training. A simple dummy can be made very easily using an old sock stuffed with rags, tied off at the open end.

1. Have your puppy on a training lead or retractible so that he gets used to this and you can control him should he wish to attempt to run off with the dummy.
2. Firstly encourage your puppy to come to you and let him inspect the

dummy > Once he shows sufficient interest, toss the dummy a few feet > say something like, 'go fetch' > he will hopefully run and pick the dummy up > the moment he picks it up > excitedly offer praise and encourage him to bring it back, by calling his name.
3. If he doesn't want to bring the dummy back to you > encourage him by saying the words 'here' or 'come', and move away from him > hopefully he will follow.
4. When he gets back to you, hopefully with the dummy > praise him and gently take the dummy > use the command word 'give' or 'leave' at the same time.
5. If he refuses to leave > you may have to hold the dummy with one hand and gently prise open his jaws with the other > all the while saying 'leave'. As soon as he lets go, offer lots of praise.
6. Do not be tempted to engage in a tug of war as he will hold on tighter and this may encourage him to rip the dummy.
7. Repeat the exercise 5 or 6 more times. Aim to practice each day and gradually increase the distance by 1 foot or so each time.

However, as with all early training, do not over do this, as it can soon lose its fun factor for the puppy and become a chore that he gets bored of and resents doing.

Progress can be made with the dummy by throwing longer distances, then hiding the dummy for him to find or throwing into long grass etc.

As the puppy gets older, the dummy should be made appropriately larger until he reaches adulthood, and the dummy resembles in weight and size a large bird such as a pheasant or goose.

Tennis balls are also an excellent training tool that are easy to throw and of the right size for most dogs to pick up easily.

If he has successfully picked up the dummy, brought it back when called, and handed this over to you, you will have taken a big step in his training.

It is important however, that he doesn't get into the habit of dropping the dummy. He therefore needs to be taught that he must hold onto it until you take it. Again it is not imperative that you insist on this if you have no interest in gundog competitions etc, but it is still good practice and discipline.

A working gundog that got into the habit of dropping the dummy in practice is likely to do this in the field. The whole point of field work is that the dog retrieves a bird that is shot. It is equally important that they also retrieve an injured bird that would otherwise suffer and possibly have a slow death.

It is also important for these training exercises, that the dummy is not seen as his plaything that he can wander off and start chewing.

The action of the retrieve therefore needs to be made very clear. When you instruct him to retrieve, in this case a dummy, he needs to go to fetch it, pick it up and bring it back to you.

We will go into more advanced retrieves in the next chapter 'Advanced gundog Training'

E) STAY

After you have taught your dog to come to you on command, the next logical step is to teach him to stay or wait until you call him.

When teaching the stay command it is not important what his starting position is. The important thing is that he stays where he is until you recall him back to you. But for the purposes of this exercise we will use the 'sit' command, but again he could be standing or lying down.

To teach your dog to stay on command, follow these steps:

1. Kneel in front of your Cockapoo and hold a small treat in your dominant hand > pinch the treat between your thumb and forefinger so your puppy

can see it.
2. Hold the treat directly in front of your Cockapoo's nose and give him a second to smell it.
3. Give your puppy the "Sit" command and wait for him to comply.
4. Now say "Stay" in a firm, even tone and hold your palm up towards the dog (similar to the stop signal a traffic policeman would give) > now take a step or two backward away from your puppy. You have issued the 'stay' command, but this assumes he has remained seated, or his 'action' is to stay whilst you issue the verbal 'stay'.
5. Pause for a second then walk back up to your puppy > provided he stays, click or praise to mark the fact that he has stayed put > reward him with a treat.
6. Repeat steps (1) to (5) several times, rewarding your puppy each time he stays.
7. Each time you practice this, aim to increase the distance between you and your dog. You can measure this in paces if you like, so two steps to four, then eight and so on. So start him in the sit position as before and say 'stay', holding your hand up to him > I usually keep repeating the 'stay' cue word as I walk backward > Once you have walked back quite a few paces > stop and pause as long as you feel he is concentrating > Then walk back > praise and give him the treat as before.

Once he is successfully remaining in a stay position you can increase the level of difficulty with the following exercises:

The stay is a very important behavior that not only teaches steadiness and control, but also allows you to increase the 'stay' command at a distance; add distractions that may prompt him to move from the 'stay'; increase the duration in terms of how long he stays for; he stays regardless of where the handler moves to.

Those four aspects should be taught in order to increase a reliable stay, so do not merely add distance and duration, but also distractions and where you move to.

Duration and distance relate to one another because as you increase the distance, i.e. walking away, you are taking time so adding duration.

But you can add duration being close to the dog by pausing.

'Stay' in relation to orientation

1. Start the exercise with your dog in a sit position with you standing in front of your dog.
2. Say 'stay' and hold your palm up towards the dog (again similar to the stop signal a traffic policeman would give)
3. Take one step back with either foot but keep the other foot rooted to that spot. In other words you are pivoting on the one foot and not moving away as such > Return to the start position > Mark the behavior with a verbal 'good' or click > Offer a treat and as soon as he takes it > hold your palm up in the stay signal > Say 'stay'
4. Now take one step to your right > again pivoting and not actually moving away > Return to the start position > Mark the behavior with a verbal 'good' or click > Offer a treat and again as soon as he takes it > hold your palm up in the stay signal > Say 'stay'
5. Take one step to your left > again pivoting and not actually moving away > Return to the start position > Mark the behavior with a verbal 'good' or click > Offer a treat > Say 'stay'
6. Take one step back, but this time slowly walk all the way around the dog returning to the start position > Mark the behavior with a verbal

'good' or click > Offer a treat
7. Repeat steps (1) to (5) but increase to 2 steps then 3 and so on.
8. If the dog moves at any point as you increase the steps, take a step back until you can increase the distance again. Make sure the dog can successfully repeat each step at least twice before moving on.

This will be a lot for your dog to do in one go so have a break in between sessions or concentrate on moving backwards facing your dog before adding the orientations of going all the way around.

Some dogs are very sensitive to the slightest body language movement. Therefore be aware of how you are moving if you are having problems with a dog that moves as soon as you do. In this case, move much slower.

Walking around the dog

Once you are successful moving left, right and back at a distance, then attempt to walk around the dog at distance. For this you will need to get your dog to stay as you walk away. Then start walking around him

Start moving around from the left then the right. At this stage you may have moved away ten steps or more.

However, if the dog moves when you walk around, again you may have to go back to the beginning making one step movements and increase the steps again.

You may even have to hold your palm close to the dogs nose and as you move around keep your hand there prompting the dog to stay.

Further 'Stay'

You simply advance here with both generalising (i.e. proofing, as described at the end of the chapter) in different locations and adding distance.

Once the stay is accomplished at a set distance test this with the distraction of walking around him in a circle.

1. Start in front of the dog at a certain distance.
2. Give the stay command and walk in a circle over to the dogs right side.
3. Now walk back and over to the dogs left side.
4. Next again walk over to the dogs right but continue walking all the way around.
5. Once you are back in front walk over to the dogs left side all the way around and back to face the dog.
6. Now increase the distance several feet more and repeat (1) to (5).

Add levels of distraction by not facing front but having your back to the dog or side on. Walk faster > break into a slight jog > jump up and down on the spot > do star jumps etc.

Practice a stay as you do some chore or activity around the house. The idea here is that you give the stay command but do not pay the dog any attention.

Also remember to practice the above exercises with him standing or lying down.

You will next need to be in a location where wildlife likely to trigger the prey instinct, will be present. For this you will need to work with a long training lead or retractable, attached for his safety in case he decides to give chase. You should then build up the distance gradually.

Practice any or all of the stay exercises so far covered.

Distraction

Distractions should be anything that the dog has an impulse to move towards. Initially distractions can be anything in the immediate surroundings.

However, a good item to start with would be a favourite toy. You simply get your dog to stay > you walk a few steps away > place the toy on the ground > walk back to the dog > provided they have remained in place > give lots of praise and fuss.

Additional Examples similar to those highlighted in the proofing section, should be used until you can reliably get him to stay when other dogs or wildlife are likely to appear, prompting his instinctive desire to chase.

Please remember that any time he moves or attempts to give chase, you should firmly say 'stay'. If he ignores you and goes anyway, start the exercise again. Do not offer a treat or praise. Don't shout at him, get angry or attempt to go after him (he will only be able to go as far as the training leash any way).

F) HEEL

Teaching a Cockapoo to heel is easy. Or it should be if you have been using this initially when you started his general walk training earlier.

The ultimate objective of 'heeling' is to train the puppy to walk at your side, under control, without the use of a lead. For the average pet owner who walks their dog on the pavement, perhaps near a busy road, you would need the peace of mind, that your dog is safe from danger. Obviously a collar would need to be worn and lead attached. In certain countries such as the UK, it is a legal requirement that when walking on a public highway a dog must be attached to a leash at all times.

A lot of trainers teach walking to heel with him on a leash first, then off leash in a safe area. The traditionally trained gundog in particular needs a level of heel control whereby they effectively heel, but without a collar and lead. As previously noted, Gundogs on a shooting field should never be allowed to run loose or hunt, wearing any kind of collar. Again, this is purely for the safety of the dog as he could easily get caught when flushing in thick undergrowth. This could cause a serious injury to the dog, at worse the dog could become snagged and possibly choke. Once again, all in one slip leads are generally used, which can be easily removed. These are also a very good piece of walking equipment, even for the average dog walker.

Initial 'heel' conditioning

From the day your puppy arrives, you are strongly advised to encourage him to walk beside you around the house or in the yard or garden.

1. Pat your leg, encouraging him to you with words such as 'here [his name]', or 'come on' etc, which should have him coming to your left or right side.
2. When he comes to you and stays to 'heel' at your side > say the cue word 'heel' > remember to give him lots of praise and perhaps the occasional treat.
3. After a number of repetitions like this, just use the cue word 'heel', when you want him to come to your side.

Incidentally, for gundog purposes, which side you walk your dog at heel has usually been dependent on whether you shoot right or left handed. So if you were to shoot a gun with your right hand for safety and practical reasons you would heel your dog on your left, and vice versa.

Having said that quite a number of gundog people prefer to train their dogs to walk on either side. This obviously gives you flexibility to choose depending on your circumstances. Perhaps walking near a main road and wishing to keep your dog safe to the inner side of the path. It is also useful if you walk two dogs either side of you.

So bearing this in mind, do not feel restricted to which side he should walk to heel. Certain competition rules insist that a dog must heel on one side or another. It is for this reason that I prefer to teach a dog to heel on both sides which leaves you with the freedom to choose.

'Heel' training:

It is important that you have the loop of the lead through whichever is your preferred lead hand, so it hangs on your wrist. Unless you intend to practice with both sides in which case you will use both hands anyway. Your puppy should then be on the opposite side to that. So if you hold the loop of the lead in your right hand, have the dog walk at your left side and vice versa. This is more for control and

Initial Cockapoo Obedience Training

safety of your puppy in these initial stages. With the other hand, in this case your left, grip the lead, so that it is relatively close to your dog, again giving you greater control. This will also act as a guide or restraint to let your puppy know where you want him, should your puppy surge forward or hang back.

When you are teaching a dog to walk to heel it is important that you focus on the position of the dog and not on the leash.

It is also advisable to use a short lead in the initial stages of heeling to prevent the dog from surging ahead or lagging behind, which can obviously happen with a long training lead. Once he is reliably heeling at your side you can slacken the lead but be prepared to verbally keep him in check.

To keep pulling or jerking the dog back from a tense leash, to a slack one, whilst stating the command to heel is not really what we want to be doing. This can turn into a form of harsh training, which we want to avoid.

You should proceed with official 'heel' training as follows:

You can do the exercise with or without a lead, but only do this without a lead if you are in an enclosed yard or field away from a busy road or other distractions.

1. Call him to you and get him to sit directly in front of you. Attach his leash if you are leading him, if not then carry on to step (3).
2. Hold a treat to his nose, as before so that he can sniff or lick, but not take it.
3. Now lure him around the back of your legs to your left or right side > So whilst holding the treat in front of him, draw this to your left or right side which he should follow > The moment he is beside your leg, say the cue word 'heel' > Once he is beside your leg, hold him there with the treat to his nose, but do not allow him to take it. This might seem long winded. But the idea is to get him to associate the cue word 'heel' with the action of coming to, or being at your side.
4. Or for simplicity you may prefer to start the puppy in a sit position > get him to stay > then you move to either the right or left hand side of the dog.
5. Now that you are in this position, with your puppy beside your right or left leg > Please make sure that you hold the treat near your leg and not out in front.
6. With the treat held to his nose start to walk forward > as soon as you move, he should follow the treat and remain at your side > again the moment he starts to walk at your side say the cue word 'heel'.
7. Keep repeating 'heel' periodically as you walk, as long as he is actually 'heeling' at your side.
8. When you have walked a few paces > give him the treat and offer lots of praise.
9. Repeat steps from (6) to (8) with another treat and gradually increase the level of difficulty by walking further and withholding the treat for longer each time. But remember in these initial stages to have the treat in your hand, held to his nose, whilst you walk.

In the initial stages you will find that you have to crouch down to reach your puppies nose. But eventually do this standing up. So again show him the treat and move forward > but this time stand up > quickly draw the treat away > and walk a few paces > all the while saying 'heel' > when he has successfully walked with you several paces > bend down and give him the treat, offering lots of praise.

Again repeat step (9) but keep increasing the distance you walk before giving him the treat and praising him.

Corrections

If at any point he tries to jump up to grab at the treat, you probably have the treat too high.

You will need to bend just enough to keep it at his nose and just remember this will only be for a short while until he gets used to the 'heel'. You should then be able to stand upright as you walk.

You will also reach the point where you can stop the treats, or just give the treat when you finish. Or you may prefer to not use treats at all, but simply use your hand to lure/lead him as you walk. The food however, usually gives him more of an incentive to follow you.

If once you are no longer luring him with the treat, he gets distracted and starts moving away or in front, do an about turn and walk in the opposite direction. You may have to pat your leg and again say 'heel' or 'this way'.

Once again, if your puppy continues to pull at the leash, you may need to stop and stand still until your pup understands that he's not going anywhere until he listens. Once your puppy understands that he only receives praise when he begins to respond appropriately, it will only take a few days before he's walking right next to you without pulling on the lead.

Once he is successfully carrying out the 'heel' in a straight line, I would suggest walking in zig zags, 90 and 180 degree turns. This is more or less what happens in agility training and dog shows. The dog follows precise paths at your side. This will also help if you find your puppy gradually starts walking ahead and eventually pulling at the lead.

Also try altering the speed at which you walk, walking normally then exaggeratedly faster or slower than normal.

This is usually the method recommended for a dog that pulls, as the walk becomes unpredictable for a dog that would otherwise surge straight ahead.

Whilst on a leash, if he moves ahead or lags behind, once he reaches the end of the short leash, it will stop him going further.

Eventually however, you should get to a point where he can heel like this without the lead. But be prepared for him to move ahead or behind once you remove the leash. In this case if he fails to respond to your heel command and wanders off, an effective remedy is to blow the stop whistle. But obviously this will only work if he has practiced the stop command before hand. Again, the 'stop' will be covered later. Once you have issued the stop command, which hopefully stops him instantly > praise him for stopping > walk to where he is, stand next to him and wait for 20 or 30 seconds > then continue with the heel.

Pausing before continuing, will ensure that the dog doesn't associate you stopping him as punishment > commence heeling with the leash applied.

Teaching a Cockapoo to walk nicely at heel will probably take 4 to 6 training sessions in a quiet area.

Further 'heeling'

Once the basic 'heel' command is being successfully carried out, it is just a question of proofing or generalising the heeling with added distractions and in different locations. Also remember that once your dog learns to heel he will get plenty of practice during normal lead walking exercise. In this respect you should not have to keep repeating the 'heel' cue, but only if he moves away from you.

With most of the advanced work it is important to start testing distractions that will trigger their prey instinct such as rabbits or birds.

In other words it is important to take him to locations where such wildlife will be present.

At this point you will need to begin with your dog on a leash but work up to being off leash.

But as usual attach a loose safety line.

G) 'STAND'

The 'stand' command is beneficial when you need your dog to stay where he is, but the sit or down would not be as suitable.

Situations where the stand will be particularly useful would be when you need him to stand and stay when grooming, visiting your vet, bathing or drying him.

Initial Cockapoo Obedience Training

In those cases you need to be able to get all around him.

What it means is that you can ask him to stand rather than have to physically lift him into that position.

To get him to stand, you will also need him to stay.

1. Start in either the sit or down position > but obviously not already standing.
2. Kneel in front of him with your treat as before and slowly move the treat away from his nose towards you > You may have to stand and move away.
3. Hopefully he will follow you by standing > the very moment he initiates the action of standing, say the word 'stand' > pause a moment and say 'stay' > again pause a moment and provided he has successfully stood still > praise him and give him the treat.
4. Practice and repeat steps (1) to (3) a number of times.
5. If at any point he attempts to move out of position simply issue the 'stay' command. If he completely ignores you, repeat steps (1) to (3) again as many times as necessary.

Your objective is to be able to issue the 'stand' command and hopefully he will 'stand' and 'stay'

A good way to practice this is, once he is in the stand position is to start to massage or stroke him, all the while saying, 'stand'. Also start practicing this when you groom him. Praise him if he stands for a while. You can also hold him if he moves or raise his back end, or lure him forward, if he tries to sit. Again say stand when he stands, and praise as before. It is useful to imagine everything a groomer or vet may need to do. So lift his paws one at a time and stroke each leg etc.

8) Phasing Out Food Rewards

Food is a highly motivating reward for dogs. But you do not want your Cockapoo to become dependent on a food reward indefinitely to perform the desired behavior. Once your puppy starts to respond consistently with the right behavior, when you give him a command, you should start phasing out the treats. Start by only rewarding your puppy every second time. Then cut it back to every third time and so on. Even though you are phasing out the food rewards you still need to praise your puppy so he knows that you are pleased with him. You may even choose to substitute a food reward for a toy and give your puppy a brief play session with the toy as a reward instead of the treat. Do not feel guilty that your poor dog is looking sad, disappointed and bewildered by no longer receiving his treat. All dogs are only too happy to please their owner, and he will soon get used to no longer getting the treat every time. Of course you are free to treat your dog occasionally. But you are doing his long time health no favours by constantly giving him treats. Also please be aware that there are dog trainers who do not use treats at all and successfully train happy dogs.

9) Discipline Whilst Training

We have now talked a lot about positive reinforcement training as opposed to any punishment based methods. I always advocate a firm but fair approach and dislike the idea of 'disciplining' a dog. But it is worth clarifying your approach to training. Most dogs behave perfectly well and respect you as their carer. Some dogs however, can have a wilful personality and they will sometimes test you and misbehave. Again, I would never advocate hitting a dog nor would I advocate being a strict disciplinarian for the sake of it. But if your puppy does appear to be developing wilful disobedience, the following will be worth bearing in mind.

Remember a well behaved adult is the result of a correctly trained puppy, given firm basic training.

Your dog will respect you when you are firm but fair, and when you say 'No', they should know this by your tone of voice. You obviously do not want to become a sergeant major, barking commands. But if say for example, you tell your dog to stay or wait and he starts to move before you have given the word, then tell him in a slightly disapproving voice, 'No'. Some trainers like to use a short, sharp 'Ah Ah'.

Do not feel bad, or feel that you are being cruel and do not forget that this training could potentially save your dogs life in an emergency situation. In this respect, I would not advise shouting at your dog whilst generally training your puppy. However, if you are in an emergency situation shouting may be the only way to shock or frighten your puppy into realising something is seriously wrong. If you shout all the time, he will probably see this as normal, and be unable or unlikely to differentiate when something is seriously wrong.

Sometimes he will need to know that he is doing wrong with a firm 'No' or 'Ah ah'. It will be even more satisfying to him, when you shower him with praise. Also remember some personalities need and respect someone who they take as a strong leader. Again, without wishing to get into a debate about 'alpha dog' training, dogs generally respect you when you are firm but fair or assume the role of leader.

10) PROOFING/GENERALISING BEHAVIORS

Initial learning should take place in a single distraction free room or area such as your back yard or garden

Advantages of a yard or garden include:

» Limited distractions and plant cover, which could harbour wildlife even in your garden.

» Limited wild animals as they are likely to stay away whilst you are present

Once behaviors are learned in a distraction free area it is necessary to generalise different locations including the following if these have not already been used:

Kitchen; Other rooms in the house; Driveway; Front yard or garden; The previously mentioned locations with other people present; Whilst out walking (again go at different times, so they get used to it when things are quiet and busy with lots of other dog walkers.); With you taking up different positions sitting down, standing in different areas, lying on the floor; Standing in front of the dog; Standing at the side of the dog; Standing with your back to the dog

When moving on and adding levels of difficulty to exercises it is important to increase or improve on the following if they are appropriate:

Increase the distance; Increase the duration; Add and increase distractions; Change directions

In all cases take note of how fast the dog complies as an indication to whether he is ready to move on or whether you have moved on too fast

Public areas:

Once behaviors are learned and proofed in familiar places, it is necessary to practice and 'generalise' the behaviors in unfamiliar surroundings, for example:

A recreation area; Public fenced park; Sports field; A field or park where some wild animals and other dog walkers may be present.

It is very important to always apply a long training leash until your dog is demonstrating a reliable 'stop' and 'recall'.

Exposure to different locations and countryside.

After you have trained and proofed in the previous areas it will be time to expose him to terrain and countryside where game and

Advanced Cockapoo Training

other wildlife are present.

Exposing the dog to a variety of terrain obviously depends on where you live and whether you are able or willing to travel to a variety of locations.

Such locations should ideally include the following:

Flat land fields; Hilly ground; Crop fields if you have permission; Wooded/Forest areas; Marshland; Hedgerows; Walls; Fences; Dykes; Ditches; Ponds; Lakes; Streams; Rivers etc etc.

Please note; initially dogs should only be exposed to water with a gradual slope such as a shallow pond rather than a shear drop.

With experience you can graduate to seaside beaches, lakes etc.

However, check that there are no potential hazards and consider the dogs safety by fitting a life-jacket.

Chapter Eight:

Advanced Cockapoo Training

This chapter will follow on from the previous chapter. Most of this section contains new exercises specific to gundog training. However, there is an extended section which relates to the 'sit' command previously taught, if you wish to expand on this. Once again, most of this will only interest you if you wish to expand your training or are interested in gundog training. But as mentioned in the previous chapter, if you have no interest in anything else in the chapter, the one exercise I would seriously consider here is the 'stop' command.

However, many of the exercises presented here will give you far greater control of your dog than basic training can offer. It is for this reason that I would urge you to consider continuing and practicing the exercises in this chapter.

1) Recommended Accessories

The following is a list of every accessory you are likely to need if you are serious about Advanced gundog training. However, you do not need to rush out and buy every single item. This section is intended to give you some guidance of recommended accessories you may need at some point. However, please read the chapter which will highlight items you are likely to need now such as the whistle, a selection of dummies, slip lead, training leads etc. Other items such as dummy launchers are useful but not vital items.

Quality release clip collar: Flat buckle collars are also recommended for training as opposed to traditional choke chains etc. These are more for pavement walking and not if you take your dog out into the country side.

Slip lead: Equipment needed for training a gundog is not dissimilar to any other dog with the exception of the slip lead/collar. These effectively act as an all in one lead and collar and are essential when hunting where hedges and thick undergrowth is present. For obvious reasons a dog can easily become entangled and choke, so the slip collar allows you to quickly remove the collar for off lead hunting and quickly apply it again when the dog returns.

Normal 5 or 6ft lead for general leash walking.

A 30 foot approx (10 meter approx) minimum check cord and/or a similar length retractable leash. Although a 15 foot approx (5 meter approx) can be used initially: These are an invaluable training aid as it allows full control, easy correction and greatly lessens the chances of things going wrong.

If you have to use the check cord to stop your dog in an emergency be aware that grabbing the cord may cause friction burns on your hand/hands.

For obvious reasons therefore you are advised to wear gloves or at least a glove on the hand you will be grabbing the rope with. http://www.Gundogsupply.com/

Standard harness to be used with long check cord leash. This will be safer for the puppy, in case he takes off running and you have to suddenly stop him.

Whistle: One of the Acme 210 to 212 whistle range are recommended and choose one only rather several different pitches. Acme 210½ or 211½ gundog whistles are quite popular

It is also not recommended to buy a hand crafted bone type which are difficult to replace with the exact same tone that a plastic one will have.

Waterproofs: For wet weather, dark brown, green or black waterproofs are recommended as are rubber boots or wellingtons.

A suitable **dummy for a puppy:** A light dummy for a puppy (Again, some people will use an old sock stuffed with cloth rags)

Larger **one pound canvas dummy**

Optional **3lb and 6lb** canvas dummies

A floating **rubber dummy** to retrieve from water

The colour of the dummies should ideally be white, black or some variation of, although green are common.

The fluorescent orange type you would think would be the most visible but are actually more difficult for dogs to see, particularly against green or brown (grass or soil)

Tennis balls of different sizes if possible

Toys with different squeaks

Soft toys resembling ducks, pheasants or other animals, preferably with floppy parts

Chew toys, plastic gnarl bones (never give your dog cooked bones, as they are known to splinter, causing internal problems), other soft toys etc. These act as additional reward/reinforce/motivators.

A **clicker** unless you use a verbal marker and suitable reward treats.

Water bottle and water dish for a drink when on a remote location.

First aid kit for you and your dog.

A compass and map for navigating unfamiliar terrain.

A shoulder bag or rucksack to carry dummies, toys, leads etc (some people prefer traditional game bags for this)

Other accessories can be used which are not vital in the early training stages, but may come in use later:

Tracking collars which provide GPS and indicate when your dog is moving and when they are on point.

Bird calls including duck, quail, pheasant etc.

Rabbit fur covered dummy.

Marker poles for blind retrieves.

Dead Fowl Trainer or **Dokken** used for retrieving, which resemble ducks, pheasants etc, usually with a hinged head to replicate the weight and movement of the real thing.

Dried game bird wings.

Optional **dummy launcher** for longer distances: A dummy launcher is not vital, but will be something well worth considering for advanced gundog training. They are recommended for advanced retrieves over long distances both over land and into and across water. These have the dual purpose of simulating gun fire, the blank cartridge to launch the dummy, and also the capability to propel a dummy a lot further than you could throw it).

Starter pistol to expose the dog to gunfire if you intend to shoot.

A variety of **bird scents** to apply to dummies. Bird scent for the dummies are a very useful training aid.

2) Whistle and hand signals

Traditionally gundog hunting/shooting has involved the use of signals or cues to be given by whistle, hand or body language. This has been of particular benefit when a dog is working at distance. Obviously for training and when in close proximity to the dog, some verbal cues will be necessary.

In addition, game are able to hear anything above a whisper, even at long distances, so talking and verbal cues have typically been discouraged.

Whistle commands

Whistle commands are generally limited to three basic cues as follows:

» A single whistle blast for a second or two duration (this varies between trainers; some use a single, short, sharp toot; others use one long whistle blast of several seconds duration) = stop/sit, look at me, Pay attention, wait for the next command. This is particularly applied to any Gundog, but for HPR training where a dog has to work at distance it is beneficial when you wish the dog to slow down to a stop and also to remain steady when on point.

» Several short pips/toots (pip, pip, pip, pip) = come back/recall.

» Two short pips (pip, pip) = to change direction, for example getting the dog to turn in left or right when quartering.

Practice these before you use them and remember that consistency is vital, otherwise the dog will be confused about what he is being asked to do.

As the previous chapter has noted, whistle commands are advised from the early stages of training. Take any opportunity to use the whistle, for example if during early training the puppy suddenly comes running back to you, blow the recall whistle.

Eventually you can discontinue with the vocal command once he recognises what is required and simply use whistle commands.

3) Introducing gunshot

Please note: The exercise is introduced early in this chapter, as it is generally considered beneficial to introduce a puppy at an early age.

For the gundog owner with no interest in shooting, field trials etc, then this exercise will not really be necessary. However, if you are likely to compete in field trials or some other capacity, then the following will give you a basic overview.

The objective of familiarising a gundog puppy to gunshot is to effectively desensitise them. In other words the puppy needs to be unaffected by the sound of a gun going off. For obvious reasons if the dog is frightened by gun fire, which is possible as a lot of dogs fear fireworks etc, then it will not be suitable in the shooting field.

Exposure to gunshot:

This can be started when the puppy is around 8 weeks old but the same routine can be carried out with an older puppy or adult.

1. With a starter pistol or a dummy launcher, have a friend go to one end of a field with a starter pistol.
2. Whilst you preoccupy the puppy with a game or allowing the puppy to play with other dogs and generally becoming comfortable sniffing or playing, signal to your friend to fire a shot.
3. The puppy will probably look up but hopefully not recoil with fear.
4. Get your friend to come ¾ of the way in, again taking a shot whilst you play with the puppy.
5. Get them to come half way, then ¼ way.
6. At first it will be advisable to attach the 30 foot check cord or retractable leash for safety purposes in case the puppy takes off running.

You do not have to repeat this until later in his training.

If at any stage the dog or puppy shows fear then do not proceed coming closer until they are again comfortable at remote distances.

Another advantage of exposing your dog to gun shot, which again will only be of interest for anyone intending to pursue game shooting or field trials, is that the dog needs to be trained to 'drop to shot'.

Dropping to shot simply means that the dog stops and sits upon hearing gunshot. It is therefore necessary for him to first of all fully learn stopping to the whistle (the 'stop' command). You then proceed as follows:
1. Get a friend to help you with this as they will need to fire a shot some distance away. This can be either a starter pistol, dummy launcher or shot gun.
2. Go through the exercise for stopping to whistle, a single short whistle blast = stop/sit.
3. As soon as you have blown the whistle > simultaneously signal to your friend who should then immediately fire a shot.
4. Provided the dog has previously been exposed to gunshot they should not be fazed and by proceeding like this, will quickly associate gunshot with stopping or dropping.
5. Repeat this several more times, then try firing the shot only, whistle the stop whistle, which hopefully they will stop and sit to.

Practice this as many times as necessary until you are only firing the shot to indicate they have to stop and sit.

However, please be aware that if you intend to enter your dog for field trials teaching the dog to 'drop to shot' will cause problems when retrieving. For the purposes of field trials a dog is expected to complete a retrieve when gunshot is fired.

4) ADVANCED 'SIT' COMMAND FOR GUNDOGS

The following is intended to extend the basic obedience training 'sit' previously covered

Basic 'sit'

Please note: the basic 'sit' command covered in the previous chapter, is often best combined with the 'sit to one side' command, but not vital if you add this later on. It is however, considered easier to combine the two at the same time. The implications of this are that the dog becomes conditioned to only sitting in front facing you, and becomes confused if expected to now sit at one side. However, it should only take a little bit longer to add sitting to the side as well.

For gundog purposes, the 'sit' is often used in conjunction with the 'recall' and the 'stop', but is used to good effect as a general control command.

Again, sitting down is natural for any dog, but is a key immobilizer along with the 'stop' command for a Sporting/Gundog type. This often needs to be carried out at an instant regardless of distractions, such as birds flying by or rabbits bolting from nearby undergrowth. So as well as being an important obedience command, the sit is a very useful control mechanism.

You will have occasions when you need to stop him in his tracks, such as he is about to go rushing off somewhere, or he is jumping up at you or other people or anything you do not want him to do. You can second guess an impulse that he is about to do something and stop him. You can therefore arrest him in his tracks, simply by getting him to sit wherever he is. It is for such reasons that it is taught as part of the 'stop command'

It can also be used to anchor the dog when putting a collar and lead on, examining him, to politely greet someone etc. As previously noted, for the initial training, use a room in your house or the back yard/garden without any distractions. Quite often it is necessary to seemingly go back to basics, even though he may have progressed in training to an advance level. A new exercise or version, will need to be taught, practiced and proofed, as if it is the very first thing you have taught him.

Incidentally, the traditional gundog terminology for the 'sit' command, particularly spaniels, has always been 'hup'. If you suspect you may wish to advance your gundog training, or are contemplating shooting at some point, then 'hup' may be preferable to 'sit'. But its not the end of the world if you have trained with the word sit, and you continue using that.

Sitting to a whistle and hand signal

As you have seen in the previous chapter, many general dog trainers teach the sit command simply by luring the dog into a sit > issuing a verbal 'sit' cue > marking the behavior with a click or verbal 'good' > and finally a reward to reinforce the behavior. Gundog trainers generally follow that procedure also, but add a whistle and hand signal. The significance of this is that done correctly, you can get your dog to stop, sit and stay at a distance without having to shout 'sit'.

I would therefore strongly suggest incorporating using the whistle and hand signal from the beginning. This will therefore condition the dog to associate the whistle, hand and verbal signal with the 'sit'.

Incidentally, the hand signal for the sit command will be carried out in two different ways, depending on how close you are to your dog. When you wish to signal to him at a distance, hold the palm facing away from you vertical, but at an approximate 45° angle to the ground in a similar way to a policeman stopping traffic. You will obviously notice that this is slightly different but similar to the 'stay' hand signal previously taught. You will also no doubt note that the important objective of the 'stay' and 'sit' is to get the dog to stop. So if he thinks you are asking him to stay, then in fact we are. So there is no need to worry about whether this will confuse him.

When in close proximity, for example when he is next to you, hold your palm parallel to the ground, about chest height, as if signalling a down command, or pressing the palm towards the ground.

You are also likely to use variations of the two hand signals together. Firstly using the traffic police hand signal to stop or stay the dog and a variation from that where you tilt your hand from vertical to parallel, to get him to sit.

Remember, the whistle is simply a single whistle blast for a second or two duration. So the sequence would be as follows:

Please read through the following, and fully familiarise yourself with the procedure before you begin. It may look complicated at first, but it is quite an easy procedure once you know what to do. It is important to break it down like this so that you can see the mechanics of it and how the dog will best learn the command.

Getting A Dog To Sit In Front Of You

Among other reasons, the front sit is necessary if you want him to deliver an object that they have retrieved. The objective is therefore to get the dog to sit in front of you from the recall.

Please note: You will recognise similar steps for the 'sit' from the previous chapter. However, as previously mentioned, additional elements of the whistle and hand signal are included.

For this exercise you will need a clicker if you use one; a few pieces of food and your whistle.

1. Prepare yourself with a piece of food in your dominant hand > your whistle should be around your neck for easy access > Pinch the treat between your thumb and forefinger so your puppy will be able to see it.
2. Recall your dog with which ever cue word you have chosen ('come', 'here' etc) > and as he gets towards you place your whistle in your mouth > hold out your food hand to your dogs nose, making sure he cannot take it > give him a second to smell it > if necessary Kneel in front of him
3. Pull your hand towards you and up to a level six inches or so above the dogs nose so that he is forced to look up > The dog should start to sit at this point.
4. Please note that if the dog lunges forward or upwards in an attempt to grab the food, you have probably lured the dog too far in either direction > You will soon know where you can place your hands in relation to your dog so that the dog simply looks up and sits.
5. If he doesn't sit at this point it may be necessary to 'lure' him as we did in the previous chapter > again holding the treat a few inches away from his nose so that he doesn't grab it > simply move the treat away from you, over and towards the back of your dog's head > as he looks up and follows the food he should naturally sit.
6. The moment the dog starts to sit, either at step (3) or (5) > blow the whistle (single short blast) > drop the whistle out your mouth > use the hand signal previously described (palm facing down towards the ground) > say the cue word 'sit' > [those three steps need to happen all at the same time, or as near as without pausing] > again it is important to only say the cue word as the dog is actually carrying out the action of sitting > It is also important to say the word once to mark him actually sitting > Not before when he is standing or coming to you, or after when he is taking the food > Otherwise he may associate the word sit with coming to you or taking the food.
7. The very moment the dogs rear hits the ground, click with your clicker or praise him excitedly with good boy/girl; this effectively marks the 'sit' behavior > and finally reward/reinforce with the food.

So to summarise the 'sit' procedure up to this point:

» As he starts to sit > blow the whistle > use the hand signal > say the cue word 'sit'; all almost simultaneously.

» Once he has actually sat down > mark the 'sit' > give the food reward/reinforcer.

Repeat steps (1) to (7) as many times as necessary until the response is conditioned/habitual. Remember to start from the beginning at any stage if either you or the dog goes wrong.

It is doubtful, but again, if after all this, you find that he doesn't seem to be getting the idea you can apply gentle pressure to the top of his hips

» again, as he starts to sit > blow the whistle > use the hand signal > say the cue word 'sit' > and once again, the very moment his rear hits the ground > click with your clicker or praise him excitedly with good boy/girl; effectively marking the 'sit' behavior > and finally reward/reinforce with the food.

It is important to note that you can delay giving him the food reward by several seconds or so. However, it is very important that you only blow the whistle; use the hand signal; and issue the command, as he is going through the motions of actually sitting. Additionally it is equally important that you correctly time 'marking' the sit the very moment he is actually seated, not before or after.

So the full sequence should be as follows:

» You lure him with food, your hand close to the dogs nose pulling your hand far enough up and away from him to induce a sit.

» As he starts to sit you a) blow the whistle b) use the hand signal c) say the cue word 'sit', as close together as possible.

» As soon as he is actually seated, mark the sit with a click or "good boy/girl". The verbal cue word or click to marks the action.

» You then give him the food reward to let him know that the act of sitting and the associated cue word 'sit', has resulted in the reward. The food acting as a stimulus/reward/reinforcement.

» After a number of repetitions you shouldn't need the luring, but simply issue the whistle, hand and verbal signal. Eventually you should be able to get to the point where only the whistle is needed.

Corrections if things go wrong

He may start to walk backwards as you raise the treat in front of him and over his head. This usually happens if you move it too fast and he assumes you are moving forwards and he needs to catch up. If this happens, simply move the treat at a slower pace, so that he watches it rather than feels the need to move.

He may also try to jump up and grab the treat which usually happens if you are offering the treat out of his immediate reach, in other words, too high. In this case make sure the treat is close enough, not too close and not too far away. You will soon know once you practice a few times.

Sitting At One Side

This is an alternative to him sitting in front and will be used when he is walking to heel and you need him to stop and sit at your side. It is also generally used in obedience trial competitions.

Please see the explanation previously at the beginning of the sit instruction.

This is usually carried out with the dog on the left hand side and the food given with the right hand, but there is nothing stopping you reversing this. I would strongly advise practising both left and right for reasons of flexibility.

1. Start this with your dog in a standing position, as taught in the previous chapter (eventually you will practise this walking to heel) > move over to the dogs right, so that you are both facing forward with the dog at your left leg.

2. If your dog attempts to sit in anticipation, simply lure him to a stand with your hand with the food held to his nose and walk him forward into a stand.

3. You should now have your hand with the food in front of the dogs nose with him standing > Now raise your hand up 6 inches or so above the

Cockapoo Training

dogs head usually at the tip of his nose, not too far back or forward.

4. Hopefully the dog will start to sit > if not as for the sit alternative > draw the hand back over the dogs head so that he follows it with his eyes and drops into a sit.
5. Now follow the previous 'front sit' steps (6) and (7) and any of the recommended adjustments if necessary.
6. Repeat steps (1) to (5) as many times as necessary.

Ideally, alternate this with the normal 'sit' in front, above so that the dog does not get stuck with one command only and remains flexible.

Eventually you will notice that your dog doesn't need a verbal cue but simply reads your hand signal and or whistle. He will even start to drop into a sit as soon as you stop moving and simply stand there. Obedience trials have sometimes carried rules whereby the use of hand signals and cue words are not permitted and the dog sits accordingly when you stop.

Moving on

Once you have practiced the above steps:

[luring him > blowing the whistle > hand signal > verbally saying 'sit' as he starts to sit > then marking the 'sit' with a click or 'good';]

try the steps without luring, but simply saying 'sit', or just the hand signal or the whistle. In other words, adding the cue word 'sit' before the dog actually sits. Do the same using only the hand signal or the whistle.

It is at this point that you should phase out giving a food treat every time, but give him lots of praise for a successful sit.

Also be careful not to reward a sit unless you have asked for a sit, blown the whistle or used the hand signal. Otherwise the dog will start to sit when they feel like it, not when you need them to.

It is good practice to test the sit at speed. For this you will need to ask for a sit, blow the whistle or hand signal > marker word 'good' > treat > repeat > ask for the sit/whistle/hand signal and so on.

See how many you can get through in a minute.

Further 'Sit'

The sit at this point has been carried out when the dog has been in close proximity, either in front or one side of you. You ideally need your dog to sit regardless of where you are and where he is. In other words when you issue the sit command the dog needs to stop and sit where ever they are. If you do not teach them and practice this, what happens is that they associate the sit command with coming back to you, then sitting.

So as above, ask your puppy to stay where they are, walk a few paces and then call him to you > Alternate using either the verbal cue, hand signal or whistle > gradually increase the distance each time

Experiment using either the verbal cue, hand signal or whistle, but issue these before the puppy gets back to you. You will practice more of this in the 'stop'. But it is important to note that he should not get used to only sitting at your feet every time, but wherever you decide to stop him.

You also need to further develop the 'sit' by generalising and proofing which should occur for example when: heeling, again whilst you move away or around, sitting down, laying on the floor etc. So you give the cue word 'sit' once you are lying or sitting down. The locations should also change and gradually introduce more distractions such as more people or dogs etc. However, be prepared for your dog to come back to you to sit. Which is why it usually works better in conjunction with the 'stop' command.

It is obviously advisable to not reinforce/ acknowledge, if he does come back to you to sit. Simply ignore it and offer lots of praise and a treat when he does sit and stay at distance. Make sure that this is solid, well practiced and that the dog is successfully completing each sit most of the time before moving on.

You next need to add distance and distractions. As before it is simply a matter of starting at the reliable distance you were at for the further sit and gradually increase the distance by a few feet.

If the dog breaks the position then go back a few steps and build up again.

5) The 'Stop' Command

The 'stop' is probably THE most important command you can teach ANY dog. However, it is a vital component in successfully controlling the Gundog.

Please note: The 'sit', 'stay' and 'heel' commands should already have been taught before you can successfully apply the 'stop' command.

The 'stop' command is technically applied as part of a recall for training purposes. But instead of the dog returning to you, you get him to stop immediately at a mid point or any where else on their way back to you. Ultimately the stop should be taught not only as part of a recall but also if he is going away or to either side.

When properly trained, the stop command will ensure your dog will instantly stop wherever he is and wait for the next instruction. The 'stop' is an extension to him coming back and sitting at your feet. In this case he should stop and sit where he is the moment you blow the stop whistle, usually at a distance.

However, whilst out walking your dog, in an emergency situation it is useful to apply this to stop them in their tracks. They could be heading off away from you, perhaps towards a dangerous busy road.

It is also sometimes used to redirect the dog that is heading the wrong way on a 'directed retrieve' or 'send back'. It is therefore easier to stop them, then send them a different way. Redirecting is often applied as part of a hunt/quartering.

Initial 'stop command' training

The stop command actually means 'stop', 'sit' and 'stay' but should be used as an isolated command. It is useful to begin to teach this as part of the 'heel' command as follows:

For this exercise use your normal walking leash attached to his collar:

1. Give the 'heel' command and start walking your puppy to heel > suddenly stop > issue a verbal command 'stop sit' > at the same time give one single whistle blast/toot on the whistle as well as a hand signal as follows: palm held flat, thumb to the chest, palm facing down and parallel to the ground. You will notice this is similar to the 'sit' command hand signal. Obviously you want him to sit, and it is your action (body language) of suddenly stopping which hopefully conveys that yes you want him to sit, but also stop.

2. Hopefully whilst heeling, your puppy will keep to your side and stop when you stop suddenly. If he stops and sits then offer lots of praise. If he stops but doesn't sit keep still but give the verbal, hand and whistle signals > if necessary, repeat the verbal, hand and whistle cues, as many times as needed until he sits. However, don't be tempted to say 'sit'. You ideally need him to associate this as a new command which again is 'stop/sit'. This may seem contradictory, as he has been taught the same signals for the previous sit. However, the difference now is that you are in motion and he should get used to travelling any distance and needs to get used to stopping and sitting on cue.

3. Again move forward > giving the 'heel' command > then suddenly stop > issuing the commands as above > and lots of praise if he is

successful
4. Repeat this several times for this session at different distances along the walk.

Over the next few days repeat this training then after a few days like this, try without the verbal command and just issue the whistle and hand gesture. If this doesn't work at this point, issue the verbal command as well but keep trying with just a hand gesture and whistle.

Try to get to a point where you are just issuing the whistle and he will hopefully stop and sit as soon as you give one short whistle toot/blast.

Once he stops and sits to these commands > the next time he stops and sits, don't speak but carry on walking to test if he stays seated > If not, do not worry as the next step is the 'stop/stay'

'Stop/stay command'

This follows on from the initial stopping whilst heeling. It involves getting him to stop and then stay as you walk away about 10 feet or so, then get him to come to you with several short pips of the whistle.

For this exercise you will need to use your long training leash or retractable leash attached to his collar

1. Walk your puppy at heel as before > suddenly stop > issue a verbal command 'stop/sit' > at the same time give one single short whistle blast/toot on the whistle as well as the hand signal, palm held flat, thumb to the chest, palm facing down and parallel to the ground.
2. This time, with the puppy hopefully sitting at your side > step in front of him > issue the 'stay' command > and then step back about 10 feet (3 meters approx) or so. (Repeat the stay command, if he makes a move; if necessary move back a shorter distance)
3. Stop a moment > give the 'recall' (verbal = 'come' or 'here'; whistle = several short toots; hand signal = hands thrown wide) command > when he gets back to you offer lots of praise
4. Repeat steps (1) to (3) several times for this session > gradually increase the distance between you and your dog.

Again, over the next few days repeat this training then after a few days like this try without the verbal command and just issue the whistle and hand gesture. If this doesn't work at this point, issue the verbal command 'stop/sit/stay' as well but keep trying with just a hand gesture and whistle.

Try to get to a point where you are just issuing the whistle and he will hopefully stop, sit and stay as soon as you give one single short whistle blast/toot on the whistle.

Also aim to get to a point where you are just issuing the cue word 'stop', rather than stop/ sit/stay and the single short whistle blast/toot.

Then practice everything so far with just the single short whistle blast/toot

If at any point he is not responding with just the single short whistle blast/toot, include the verbal cues and hand signals if necessary. But always be aiming to phase out everything except the the single short whistle blast/toot

Please be patient here as it may take quite a few sessions for him to get the idea.

The Full 'Stop' Command: using the whistle and hand signal:

For this exercise you will again need to use your long training leash or retractable leash attached to his collar:

1. Walk your puppy at heel as before > suddenly stop > issue a verbal command 'stop/sit' > at the same time give one single short whistle blast/toot on the whistle as well as the hand signal, palm held flat, thumb to the chest, palm facing down and parallel to the ground.
2. Again, with the puppy hopefully now sitting at your side > step in front of

him > issue the 'stay' command > and then step back about 10 feet (3 meters approx) or so. (Repeat the stay command, if he makes a move)

3. Give the 'recall' command, but about halfway give the 'stop' command. Hopefully by this stage, this should simply be the single short whistle blast/toot. But again, if necessary use the verbal cue and hand signal if needed.
4. If he stops straight away then immediately walk up to him and give him lots of praise. This will be a big successful step.
5. However, if he does not get this and comes straight back to you, it is recommended that you take him back to the very spot you issued the stop command and again get him to sit and repeat from (1). Do not make a fuss, or say anything, just simply give the 'heel' command and walk him back > ask him to sit and stay, while you again walk back to your start position.
6. Proceed from (3) to (5). If again he doesn't immediately stop and sit, but seems determined to come right back, try saying 'No' or 'Ah ah', and hold up your palm 'stay' hand signal, which will hopefully stop him in his tracks.
7. You will need to repeat from (1) as many times as necessary until he stops immediately you give the whistle command, mid way through the recall.

As before, increase the distance and vary at what point you stop him. Eventually you will be at the end of the training lead. Hopefully at this point he will be well practiced, and you can attempt this by releasing the leash.

Again, do not get frustrated or angry with him, if he ignores the command to stop and comes back to you without stopping. Simply start the procedure again and do not be tempted to either offer praise and certainly do not shout at him.

Once he gets it right, excitedly offer praise so he knows at that point he has succeeded.

Once again, the 'stop' command is a very important aspect of the whole training process and you are therefore advised to continue with this until he is reliably carrying this out every time.

However, be aware that some dogs will be well behaved when they know they are attached to a leash but ignore all commands and run riot when you release them. In this case in the initial stages of the stop command you are strongly advised to keep your dog on a long training leash. If once you release him, he is misbehaving and ignoring you, try the following:

1. Attach your long training lead and your shorter walking leash.
2. Release the shorter one so that he knows you have released him but keep the longer one attached.
3. Continue as usual with the stop command and if he ignores you and races off, he will come to an abrupt stop when he reaches the end of the training leash.
4. Hopefully this will be sufficient to let him know that you are giving him freedom but he cannot run off and ignore you.

It is also very important to practice being unpredictable with commands. Always vary when you issue the stop signal and for how long you stop him, before sending him to continue with the retrieve. If you always stop him at the same point he will easily anticipate stopping at a particular point rather than waiting and listening for your command. If you are not careful he could start to make his own mind up about when to stop and you suddenly have disobedience.

6) OFF LEAD RUNS

Once he has learned a reliable 'stop', 'sit', 'heel' and 'recall', you can introduce off lead runs whether in the countryside or a large field.

The idea here is to allow him to freely wander for short distances exploring, but to also keep him in check by calling him back to heel and getting him to stop and sit periodically. You are therefore utilising and testing everything that he has learned up to this point. This will effectively train him to realise that although he runs free and hunts, he also has to respond to commands from you when necessary.

Failure to do this would probably see him pleasing himself, possibly running riot or worse still give chase and risk a road accident or other accident rushing into rough cover.

Off lead running

Some trainers recommend allowing their dog off lead running, scenting, hunting in a separate location to where you train them. The idea is that they associate the two locations for specific purposes rather than allowing them a free run on the same field and then expect them to concentrate and focus on training. The same would apply for shooting terrain where they would be expected to focus on your direction rather than pleasing themselves.

Regardless of his behavior outdoors though, this breed really needs a free run every day in order to be truly healthy.

Even the very best behaved pet that is happy to settle in the home, whether he has been for a run or not, will suffer if he isn't given the opportunity to stretch his muscles. A bored Cockapoo dog can easily become depressed, destructive or even aggressive.

Owners give many reasons for not giving a Cockapoo the free run that he needs, most of the reasons are fear in one way or another. The main concern is that the dog owner is scared of their pet running away and never coming back.

However, always be mindful of where you let them free run. It is always important that where there is livestock grazing pastures, you keep your dog on a leash. In some cases this is a legal requirement. Land or livestock owners also sometimes have the legal right to shoot a dog they suspect is attacking their animals. In this respect, you should always ask permission from the land owner.

7) THE RETRIEVE (SEND BACK)

The basic retrieve (also known as 'the send back')

This retrieve work moves on from the initial retrieve exercise covered in the previous chapter 'Initial Obedience Training'.

This is the basic marked retrieve that involves you throwing a dummy and ensuring that your puppy does not go and 'fetch', until instructed to do so.

You will need a 1lb training dummy, or something similar, to hand for this next exercise.

If you are using a retractable training lead for this make sure that the lock is on. Or if you have a normal long training lead, make sure that you hold on to enough of the lead so that your puppy cannot leave your side. The reason for this is as soon as you throw the dummy the puppy will possibly try and run to retrieve it.

Again, we only want the puppy to fetch this when instructed to do so. Start this exercise as follows:

1. Walk with your puppy at heel, to a part of a field in a safe area that is relatively close to a fence or hedge > blow the stop/sit whistle and use the hand signal for sit. Your puppy should now be seated next to you, both facing the same way.
2. With your puppy at your side, again make sure that he cannot run off by either having the retractable on a lock or holding a normal training lead close to you.

3. Throw the dummy a couple of meters, no more than three meters (10ft approx) away from you.
4. If he tries to move, the leash will stop him running off > but again blow the stop/sit whistle and use the hand signal for sit > You may have to repeat this a few times until he settles.
5. Once settled, make sure you release the lock on the retractable or let go of the normal training lead, but keep the loop around your wrist.
6. Provided your puppy is at your side > sweep your hand towards the dummy, pointing forward, bending at the knee if necessary > give the verbal command 'go back', or 'back' (some trainers use phrases such as 'get on' here, but I prefer to use the get on when sending left or right, and 'go back' when sending him back). > Be prepared to repeat the 'go back' command if he is not sure what to do and again encourage him with the pointing forward. Make sure you are allowing him slack from the leash > Hopefully at this point he will run up to the dummy > pick it up > and bring it back to you. He cannot run away with the dummy as you have him attached to the lead.
7. If he doesn't immediately bring it back use the recall command. So immediately follow the verbal command 'here' > with several short pips/toots of the whistle > and throw your hands wide for the hand signal > Repeat this as many times as needed until he brings it back to you.
8. As soon as he returns with the dummy make a big fuss of him > and if he offers you the dummy > take it. If he holds onto it whilst you fuss him > then that is fine at this stage. Let him hold the dummy > then gently take hold of the dummy and say 'leave'.
9. Again, avoid encouraging him in a tug of war game > As soon as he lets you, gently take the dummy from him > again give him lots of fuss and praise > But if he drops the dummy at this stage > do not acknowledge this with any verbal rebuke such as a 'No' > But certainly do not praise him, as he may think this is acceptable to drop the dummy and get into the habit of doing this every time.

Moving on

Eventually you need to get to the stage where you are doing the heel, the recall, the sit/stay and the retrieve all without the use of a collar and lead. However, for the time being it will be safer to increase the training lead length to 5 meters then 10 then 15 and so on. At which point after a while your dog will have had sufficient practice that he can be trusted and relied upon to respond 100% to these commands.

When you do eventually remove the lead do this gradually.

1. So for example mid way through your session > walk him to heel > as you walk try and unclip him without him noticing and carry on the heel work.
2. After a few minutes > clip the lead back on > and carry on the session with the lead.
3. Then each day increase the time off the lead until you have been doing this for a week or so.

If in any doubt, when you do the training without a leash, always work in an enclosed paddock or field well away from traffic.

Please bear in mind the following pointers for all of the following retrieves:

When starting with the retrieve it is important to get the puppies focus before you send them for a retrieve. In other words we need him to be looking at us before we send him off. This may require waiting until he gives us eye contract.

Any time he deviates from the exercise, command him to stop/sit, before moving on.

If at any point in the training things seem to be getting out of hand, stop the retrieve training for 5 or 10 minutes, and practice some other exercises. Then start again with the retrieve work.

He may not understand what is expected of him the very first time you throw the dummy to retrieve. If this happens, simply walk up to the dummy, call your puppy to you and get him to sit. Now throw the dummy, but this time throw it half the distance previously, and go through the retrieve routine again. If the puppy picks up the dummy but refuses to come back with it, blow the stop whistle.

As long as he is still holding the dummy, call him to you with the recall, 'here' command, again hopefully he will come back. As usual, if he successfully brings the dummy back to you, give him lots of praise.

8) Two dummy send back

Once he is successfully retrieving the dummy for the previous exercise it is time to move on to sending him out for two dummies.

It is important that the 2 dummies are at least approximately 30 feet (9 meters approx) apart. If they are too close there is a temptation for him to go to one then the other, rather than just concentrating on bringing you one at a time, before you send him off again.

To start with, you can throw these an approximate distance of 5 meters from yourself. But for longer distances you will either have to place these at some distance either walking the dog at heel to a spot, getting him to stay while you walk to a suitable spot to drop the dummy, then do the same for the other. Use a dummy launcher if you have one, or get a friend to place them while you wait with your dog seated at your side.

Choose an open field in a safe area that does not have too much grass growth.

Once again, use the training leash for this, (it is best to use a training leash of at least 10 meters, preferably 15 meters, to allow plenty of slack) and allow plenty of slack. Bear in mind that he will be going out approximately 5 meters to each dummy, so allow him slack of at least 7 or 8 meters. As a reminder it is often more practical to carry the training leash separately and walk him to heel with a slip lead

1. Again, walk with your puppy at heel, to a part of a field in a safe area that is relatively close to a fence or hedge > blow the stop/sit whistle, with hand signal > he should be seated by your side, both of you facing towards the direction you will be throwing the dummies
2. Issue the 'stay' command > take his slip lead off and attached the training leash > making sure that you unravel enough slack of about 7 meters > throw one dummy diagonally to your left about 15 feet (4.5 meters approx). The dummy should therefore not be to your immediate left, but forward and towards your left, ahead of you at an approximate 45 degree angle > pause a few seconds > throw a second to your right, again 15 feet (4.5 meters approx) diagonally > so that the two dummies are approximately 30 feet (9 meters approx) apart.
3. Again with your dog at your side > sweep your hand pointing towards the last dummy that you threw > your arm should be parallel to the ground > bending at the knee if necessary > give the verbal command 'go back', or 'back'
4. He should run out and retrieve the first dummy > as soon as he gets back to you, take the dummy > give him a treat/offer lots of praise
5. Again, if he doesn't return immediately follow the previous basic retrieve instructions (8) to recall him
6. Get him to sit at your side > Now sweep your hand as for (3) pointing towards the second dummy >

Advanced Cockapoo Training

bending at the knee if necessary > give the verbal command 'go back', or 'back'.

7. He should run out and retrieve the second dummy > again as soon as he gets back to you, take the dummy > give him a treat/offer lots of praise
8. Repeat steps (1) to (7) throwing the dummies further each time, until as above you have to place, launch, or have a friend place them. By the time you reach the full extent of the training leash with you holding it, it will be necessary to trust him by not holding it. However, keep it attached but allow him to drag it. If he does take off, it should be possible for you to run and catch up with the leash if not the dog. At this point make sure it is safe to do so, and there are no distractions present that will tempt him to take off.

Repetition of the send out command and pointing to the dummies is a very important aspect of gundog work. This gets him relying on you indicating/pointing to on object which he cannot himself see, in other words the 'blind retrieve', which will follow.

9) Two dummy retrieve with Left, right and away hand signals)

The following exercises will require the use of left/right hand signals. This is a similar exercise to the two dummy send back. However, this time you are positioned at a distance in front of the dog. The dummies are also placed to the dogs immediate left and right. The idea is that the dog runs out immediately to his left and returns the dummy to you. You then walk him back to his start position and send him for the second dummy.

The following will briefly describe the hand signals and how to apply them:

Verbal cue

For either the left or right, issue the verbal command 'get on'. Again some trainers use 'seek on' particularly when sending left or right whilst the dog is 'quartering'.

Whistle cue

Again the whistle cue to send him left or right is two short pips/toots on the whistle 'pip, pip'. It is important to introduce it here as this will be his cue for when he eventually 'quarters'. Quartering will be explained in more detail later, but it basically involves the dog hunting or moving in a zig zag pattern going left to right and moving forward.

Hand signals

Hand signals used for directional cues should be clear and direct.

To send the dog to his left, your right arm needs to go out parallel to the ground, to your immediate right. This obviously assumes that your dog is facing you. Your body should slightly lean that way also so it will be necessary to bend at the knee. To send him to his right, your left arm should be thrust out similarly horizontally to your left, again leaning your body the same way.

Hopefully you will be at a stage in his training where he has practiced retrieves quite a number of times. He is therefore less likely to run off with the dummy, and so a training leash should be unnecessary.

However, if you do experience problems, it is advisable to attach a long training lead; 10 meters will be OK initially, but 15 and 20 meters will be needed as you progress. Again use the point previously mentioned about keeping the leash attached but without you holding it. Again, letting him drag this so that you can more easily catch it if necessary.

This exercise is best practiced with your dog close to a fence or hedge. The advantage of this is that he will have an obvious line to run parallel to, rather than a wide open space where he may be tempted go off course.

1. Again, walk your dog to a part of a field in a safe area that is relatively close to a fence or hedge > heel him around so that you both have your backs to the fence/hedge > blow the

stop/sit whistle > ask him to stay > he should stay seated whilst you carry on walking forward, away from the hedge > walk about 10ft (3 meters approx) away > stop and turn to face him > (if he carries on walking with you, you should immediately stop > blow the single short whistle blast > and walk him back to the start position > again getting him to sit and asking him to stay).
2. Once you are facing him 10ft (3 meters approx) away > throw the first dummy about 20ft or so (6 meters approx) to your right or left, roughly in line with his immediate right or left > now pause several seconds before throwing the second in the opposite direction roughly the same distance.
3. Please bear in mind that most dogs will naturally wish to retrieve the last dummy you threw out: At this point it is advisable to put your whistle in your mouth ready to give the 2 toot/pip cue > Pause again before giving a left or right hand signal for the last dummy you threw (again use the previous description for hand signals) > at the same time give two short pips/toots on the whistle 'pip, pip' and the 'get on' command [again all three should be done simultaneously] > sending him in the direction pointed, to pick up and retrieve the dummy back to you. Again, if he does not respond to you pointing left or right with the 'get on' verbal cue, repeat this. As a last resort you may have to walk over to the dummy, which should prompt him to follow. Then walk back to your starting position, recalling him with the dummy if necessary.
4. Offer lots of praise if he successfully follows your direction and returns the dummy (if he seems uncertain what to do > issue the hand signal, verbal cue and whistle signal again > If he goes in the wrong direction blow the stop whistle and if necessary walk him back to the starting spot and repeat the command).
5. Once he successfully returns the dummy, walk him back to his original start position and repeat steps (2) to (4) to retrieve the second dummy.

Repeat this several times during this session and for as many sessions as it takes until he is reliably executing the exercise. Also vary the order you send him and the distances you throw each time. Sometimes send him several times in the same direction by throwing the retrieved dummy out to the same side.

10) The 'go back'

The 'go back' is used if you have already issued the 'send back' (retrieve), but he hasn't gone far enough out/away. So you need to send him further out to search for the dummy. This situation is how you may have to direct him, if for example you were hunting and had shot a bird and you were now directing him to where you know the bird has fallen.

The procedure is simply to 'stop' him where he is > then issue a 'go back' command.

Please note it will be necessary to use a slip lead to quickly release him after you have walked him at heel.

Again choose an open field in a safe area that is relatively flat and does not have too much grass growth.

1. Begin by walking your dog to a part of a field, in a safe area, that is relatively close to a fence or hedge > heel him around so that you both have your backs to the fence/hedge > blow the stop/sit whistle > ask him to stay.
2. With your dog seated at your side > throw a dummy in front of you both about 3ft (1 meter approx) away. Make sure he remains seated throughout and doesn't suddenly

Advanced Cockapoo Training

chase after the dummy. If he makes a move for the dummy, again blow the stop whistle and start again.

3. Now walk him at heel, passed the dummy, about 10ft (3 meters approx) or so away from the dummy so that you both have your backs to it.
4. Stop and again get him to 'sit' and 'stay' > release his leash or take the slip lead off while you walk on a further 10ft (3 meters approx) or so away from your dog > turn around facing him. He should now be facing you with his back to the dummy. Again if he tries to follow you, as soon as you become aware of this, blow the stop whistle. If necessary, walk him back to the start position and issue the 'stay' command. Then walk to your last position 3 meters away from the dog.
5. After a short pause issue the 'go back' command > For this you sweep your arm from its resting position, in an arc in front of you, into the air, pointing to the sky, palm facing forward. Now slightly motioning towards the dummy > give the verbal command 'go back' or 'back'.
6. Hopefully he will understand that he should turn around > run towards the dummy and retrieve this back to you.
7. Again offer lots of praise when he does.

Repeat this as often as necessary until he is successfully completing the 'go back'. Eventually increase the distance by walking further away once he is successful at a short distance. Also practice in different terrain with more dense cover.

If he fails to understand, it may be necessary to walk/lure him towards the dummy. Again repeat the verbal command and hand signal as you do. Once he runs towards it, go back to your position so that he can return it to you.

11) Three Dummy Retrieve

As the name suggests, the three dummy retrieve will involve a left, right and go back dummy retrieve, all previously learned.

Please note that the exercise will be described here, but because each separate element has been detailed previously, you are asked to refer back to those, which are:

» The two dummy send back or Two dummy retrieve with Left, right and away hand signals, with the two toot whistle cue

» The 'go back'

1. For simplicity I would proceed as for the 'go back' steps (1) to (4). Get to step (4) of the go back and issue the 'stop', 'sit' and 'stay'. Now before you carry on walking for another 10ft (3 meters approx), throw one dummy to your left and one to your right. All the while ensuring your dog does not move. Now walk away from your dog for another 10ft (3 meters approx) > turn around and face him.
2. So now you should be facing him. There should be a dummy behind him, one to his right and another to his left.
3. You are then advised to send him in the direction of the last placed dummy, either left or right. Remember to use your left or right hand signal, two short pips/toots on the whistle 'pip, pip', and the verbal cue 'get on'.
4. Once he retrieves this dummy back to you > walk him back to his start position > then walk back to where you were stood > send him for the second dummy again remembering to use the same 3 cues or signals > then repeat for the third behind him > again, remember to use the hand signal for the 'send back' and the verbal cue 'go back' or 'back'.

5. Again repeat this several times during this session and for as many sessions as it takes until he is reliably executing the exercise. Also vary the order you send him and the distances you throw each time. Sometimes send him several times in the same direction by throwing the retrieved dummy out to the same side.

Once you need to increase the distances of each dummy beyond throwing distance either use a dummy launcher or walk so far and throw the dummy to increase the distance.

12) The Initial Blind Retrieve

As the name indicates, this is a retrieve that the dog should have no idea where the dummy is. This will closely resemble a typical scenario if he is having to search for a shot bird in the field. As previously mentioned he is therefore reliant on you giving him directions. For this reason dummies have to be placed without the dog seeing them. However, for the purposes of this preliminary exercise he will see where the object is thrown. The field that you choose should have grass that is cut relatively short. Ideally the dog should be able to see the dummy, or at least it should not take much searching to find. The idea is that he gets used to the mechanics of the exercise rather than whether it is an actual blind retrieve or not.

Initially it is best to send him on this 'blind retrieve', but in approximately the same spot as he picked the first up. If you have been sending him to the same area with previous retrieves he will expect to see a dummy and shouldn't therefore have to search very far.

You are advised to use a friend to help with this as he can stand at some distance away from you.

1. Ask your friend to stand relatively close to a fence or hedge, at a distance around 50ft (15 meters approx) away from you and your dog.

2. So wherever you are in relation to your friend, walk with your dog at heel to a central part of a field in a safe area, again around 50ft away from your friend, both of you facing him > blow the stop/sit whistle > ask your dog to stay.

3. Your friend should then throw a dummy either to the left or right. Again your dog will be able to see where the dummy has dropped > pause a few seconds then issue the 'send back' command; sweeping your hand pointing towards the dummy, bending at the knee if necessary, give the verbal command 'get on'. You are not using the two toot whistle command here as you are not strictly speaking sending him left or right, but sending him in a straight line.

4. The dog should run out towards the dummy > pick the dummy up > retrieve this back to you > as he is on his way back, your friend should throw another dummy in approximately the same place as the first. This time the dog will not see the dummy being thrown (this therefore provides a 'blind retrieve' to a certain degree).

5. Again as soon as he gets back to you, take the dummy > give him a treat/offer lots of praise.

6. Now get him seated by your side again > blow the stop/sit whistle > ask him to stay > pause a few seconds then issue the 'send back' command; sweeping your hand pointing in the same direction towards the second dummy > bending at the knee if necessary > give the verbal command 'get on'.

7. Again as soon as he gets back to you, take the dummy > give him a treat/offer lots of praise

8. Repeat this several times > once he is successful and reliable at this dis-

tance start to increase the distance in 10ft increments.

If at any point he struggles with finding the dummy, picking up or retrieving, simply shorten the distance. Always assume that you have moved on too fast and never blame or punish the dog.

13) ACTUAL BLIND RETRIEVES

All of the previous lessons learned so far will be needed for the 'actual blind retrieve'.

A few preliminaries will be necessary before you start:

The choice of terrain is important as it does not want to be too over grown nor cut like a golf course putting green. It will also be a good idea to plant or have someone plant several dummies before you introduce the dog to the area. You shouldn't bury them or make them difficult to find, but just out of obvious sight. Make sure these are sufficiently placed far enough apart, perhaps around 50ft (15 meters approx).

Also be aware of the direction of the wind when sending your dog out. Young dogs in general do better 'hunting' to a back wind (the wind blowing behind them) than running into a head wind. So adjust your positions according to you sending him away from a head wind. Quartering allows a dog to find scents, whereby a head wind will generally favour an experienced dog more, but a puppy may find scents difficult to pick up.

So again for the initial purposes of the blind retrieve it is easier to send him off down wind. As he gets more experienced picking up wind scents, introduce him to head winds on a calm day. Gradually increase the level of difficulty with greater wind strengths.

Important note:

Your dog will be introduced to a new command at this point, known as the 'Hi Lost'. 'Hi Lost' is the verbal command to let your dog know that he is close to the dummy. So if the dog is close to where the dummy is, you say 'Hi lost' to indicate to him that he needs to hunt/search in that area.

Some trainers also like to use a whistle command. There is no set command to use, but as long as it is different from any other, you can of course make your own up. For example, this could be one long drawn out blow of several seconds duration. As long as it is distinguishable from the short sharp stop pip, the several short pips to recall and the two short directional pips when quartering. At first he may not be able to make the connection that you saying 'Hi Lost' means that if he searches where he is, he will quickly find the dummy. However, he will soon catch on once he starts finding the dummies soon after you say 'Hi lost'.

When you eventually send your dog to search, do not be tempted to control or direct the dog too much. Instead allow him to hunt freely, but intervene with stops, left/right hand signals etc if he gets totally lost.

1. Assuming that several dummies have been planted > Lead him to the approximate area where the first dummy has been placed about 20ft (6 meters approx) away from the dummy.
2. Make sure that he will be downwind of the dummy before you send him off.
3. Blow the stop/sit whistle, with hand signal > ask him to stay > he should stay seated by your side both of you facing towards the approximate direction of the dummy.
4. Now Send him off > sweep your hand pointing towards but not directly at the dummy > bending at the knee if necessary > give the verbal command 'go back', or 'back'.
5. He should run out, and hopefully not run straight up to the dummy, but begin to search back and forth > Give no other direction and allow him to hunt for himself.
6. If he veers off out of the area > issue the stop command, which hopefully he will stop and sit, looking towards you >

This is were you start to have fun with the exercise. Bearing in mind you know where the dummy is, you now need to give your dog directions to help him find it.

You are now therefore using everything you have previously learned as follows:

» The stop whistle

» The left and right directions, using the verbal cue word 'get on'

» The whistle signal, two short pips/toots on the whistle 'pip, pip'. To send him left or right.

» The go back command; verbal cue words 'go back' with hand signal (sweeping your arm in the air, pointing to the sky, palm facing forward > slightly motioning towards the dummy).

» The 'hi lost' verbal cue to indicate that he should hunt in that area.

» The 'recall'; four short peeps of the whistle.

By way of an example, the following will illustrate a possible scenario:
1. You send your dog off issuing the commands for a normal 'send back' retrieve.
2. He starts hunting around for 20 or 30 seconds but seems to be getting lost.
3. You know the dummy is further away than he is currently searching so > blow the stop whistle and he should stop and look to you for directions > issue the 'go back' or 'back' command.
4. As soon as he has gone far enough > blow the stop whistle > use the cue word 'hi lost', to get him hunting in that area again.
5. He searches but starts moving away to your right of the dummy > blow the stop whistle again > as soon as he stops and looks at you > thrust your left arm, parallel to the ground, blow two short pips/toots on the whistle, use the verbal cue 'get on', to send him to his right.
6. He then goes too far over to your left > blow the stop whistle > as soon as he stops and looks to you > thrust your right arm, parallel to the ground, two toots, verbal 'get on', to send him to his left.
7. As he goes left he catches a scent and wanders away from the dummy > you again blow the stop whistle > now blow the 'recall' whistle, to bring him back in towards you and the dummy > again blow the stop whistle once he is back in the general vicinity > give the 'hi lost' verbal cue > and continue in this way until he finds the dummy and returns it to you.

This will hopefully give you some idea of how you should proceed until he eventually finds the dummy and returns it back to you. Once he does, send him out to the approximate area of the second dummy and continue as per the example, once again depending on how you need to direct him.

14) Steadiness

'Steadiness' is a very important aspect of a Gundogs training. It does not necessarily come naturally to them and so has to be trained.

The dog that hunts, flushes game and generally does its own thing, will be to say the least, untrained and therefore a nuisance on a shooting field. Furthermore, a dog that doesn't possess self control and steadiness will pretty quickly be disqualified from a field trial or working test. As you can imagine this will also pose problems for the family wishing to have a well behaved dog. In addition, the

Advanced Cockapoo Training

dog will be a danger to itself if it suddenly take off onto a busy road in pursuit of a rabbit or squirrel etc.

A major objective of all Gundogs is to indicate game (pointing, sitting etc) that they discover in undergrowth, but only 'flushing' on command. If the 'stop command' has been thoroughly learned by the dog then you should never experience him rushing off, flushing game and generally ignoring your commands for him to stop.

The following exercises will provide a good grounding in improving 'steadiness' already achieved with previous exercises.

Most of the exercises that involve him waiting until you ask him to move, are basically exercises in steadiness.

Practice steadiness as follows: You will preferably need 2 or 3 dummies for this exercise

1. Have your dog sit and stay and then walk back several meters.
2. Throw a dummy to the side of the dog about 2 meters away from him. If you notice him twitch as if he is about to go and pick the dummy up > immediately issue the 'stop command' a single short whistle blast. Repeat the 'stop command' as many times as it is necessary whilst he sits patiently. If necessary you may have to walk him back to the starting positions.
3. If he successfully leaves the dummy and stays where he is, walk over to him and give him lots of praise.
4. Now repeat steps (1) to (3), but this time, after you have thrown the first dummy, throw another to the other side or over his head. Again, repeat the 'stop command' if necessary.
5. Wait a few seconds and then walk back to him again offering lots of praise.

It is important with this exercise that you do not let your dog retrieve the dummy. This is something that you should do as it shows the dog, that he does not always pick the dummy up, but only when instructed to do so.

You may also need to initially use the stay command, if he attempts to come to you. But the 'stop command' should be used when you want him to leave the object.

Steadying to a thrown dummy whilst out on walks

The idea here is to present distractions to the dog. Your objective is to attempt to control him reacting to the stimuli.

1. In the first instance have your dog on a leash and walk him to heel. Also have a dummy or two to hand.
2. At any random moment throw a dummy out in front of you and at the same time issue the stop command with whistle; again a single short whistle blast.
3. Ask your dog to stay whilst you walk over > pick the dummy up > and walk back to your dog > picking up the leash.
4. Provided he has remained seated, give him lots of praise.
5. Repeat the exercise several more times each session
6. Steadying to a thrown dummy whilst hunting
7. Start by walking to heel with an extendable leash or long training leash then allow your dog to wander off in front sniffing for scents etc (technically he is hunting).
8. As he looks up throw a dummy again out in front as far as you can throw it > again issue the stop command.
9. Ask your dog to stay whilst you pick the dummy up as before and return to the dog.
10. Offer lots of praise if he has successfully remained in place throughout.
11. Repeat several more times each time.
12. An extension to the above two exercises is if you can acquire a dead game bird, feathers intact or a rabbit etc.

13. Following the same procedure as the previous two exercises replace the dummy with the game.

To add a level of difficulty if you have a starter pistol or dummy launcher either shoot the pistol as you throw the dummy or fire a dummy from the launcher. (Please note that this assumes he has already been successfully exposed to gunshot)

Steadiness to live animals

Having access to what is known as a rabbit pen will be a big advantage to test his steadiness to live animals. It may be necessary to contact your local gundog club who should have details of trainers or individuals who may allow you access, even if you have to pay for its use.

In this case you should take the dog into a rabbit pen but keep him on a training lead, in case he should decide to give chase. You do not want him to catch or kill the animal but simply to control his prey instinct or impulse to chase.

Alternatively take him to an area where you know rabbits, squirrels, game birds etc are likely to be. Perhaps whilst out on a normal walk at a local park or a country walk.

1. Proceed as before with an extendable leash or normal training lead and allow him to freely hunt.
2. Watch for his reaction to having seen or scented a game animal > Anticipate him making a sudden movement at which point you should immediately issue the stop whistle and stay command.
3. Give him lots of praise if he does as you ask and does not give chase. Obviously ignore and do not acknowledge any impulse to chase.
4. Continue and repeat (1) to (3) during the session and repeat when ever you get the chance.

Once you are confident that he is reliable with a leash, attempt (1) to (3) without the leash. It is vital that this is only done in an area that is safe such as a fenced enclosed field or similar well away from traffic, in case his prey instinct takes over and he exits the field.

You may have to repeat this a number of times until he is reliably ignoring the impulse to give chase.

15) INTRODUCTION TO WATER

Most gundogs, are naturally drawn to water and introducing them to water should be part of a young puppies socialisation. However until they gain confidence swimming, they should be introduced gradually and always supervised. Any traumatic events can lead to him fearing water and refusing to enter.

At first, choose a stream, pond or lake with a gradual slope into the water. As to how far you should allow him to paddle, think in terms of how far you can wade out in a pair of rubber boots, or fishing waders if you have them. If in doubt buy and fit him with a doggy life-jacket for extra safety. Again for extra safety, attach a training lead to the life-jacket so that if he does swim out you can pull him back in before he gets into difficulty.

Incidentally, do beware of blue green algae commonly present in certain lakes, drains, streams, rivers or ponds, which is toxic and can cause death should the dog drink the water.

View the following links for further information:

https://www.gov.uk/government/publications/algal-blooms-advice-for-the-public-and-landowners

https://www.pets4homes.co.uk/pet-advice/blue-green-algae-and-its-risks-for-dogs.html

Alternatively, introduce him to a narrow, shallow stream that you can easily wade across with rubber boots. Certainly do not allow him access to fast flowing rivers or rivers with strong under currents. For the same reason, until your puppy gains strength and experience, avoid allowing him access to sea waters. Unless as before you supervise and the waters are calm and the beach is gradually sloping. Also consider fitting him with a life-jacket in these situations.

If he is reluctant to enter the water at first it is a good idea to entice him with toys, tennis balls or one of your dummies provided it is suitable for use in water.

Once he is confident entering water, you can try a short retrieve in the shallow end or across a shallow stream as follows:

1. Get him to sit and stay about 6ft (2 meters approx) near the edge of the pond, lake or stream.
2. Walk away from him towards the waters edge. You may have to issue the stay command to ensure he does not follow you.
3. Either cross the stream or wade into the pond/lake shallow end.
4. Now call him to you with the recall/come command; several short pips/toots.
5. When he gets to you offer lots of fuss and praise as usual.
6. If he has been entering the water previously he should have no hesitation. But if he does seem reluctant, encourage him by perhaps coming further towards him or use a food treat.
7. Now again get him to sit and stay about 6ft (2 meters approx) near the edge of the pond, lake or stream.
8. Again either cross the stream or wade into the pond/lake shallow end.
9. This time toss a floatable dummy into the water again in the shallow end 6ft (2 meters approx) away from you near the waters edge.
10. Give the retrieve command. You will have to point towards the dummy and give the verbal command 'go back', or 'back'. Hopefully, he will enter the water, grab the dummy and swim to you.
11. When he gets to you with the dummy offer lots of fuss and praise as usual
12. Again get him to sit and stay about 6ft (2 meters approx) near the edge of the pond, lake or stream, but this time you stand with him.
13. Toss a dummy into the water > issue the retrieve command > again, he should enter the water, grab the dummy, swim back to the bank, climb out and deliver the dummy to you. Make sure the bank is easy for him to climb out, otherwise you may have to lift him out. But eventually he will be able to do all of this himself.
14. When he gets to you with the dummy offer lots of fuss and praise as usual.

Once he gains confidence entering the water and as long as he is swimming confidently, increase the distances.

Again, please remember to fit a life-jacket to him when entering deeper waters.

16) How Gundogs hunt: The Hunting Chain

The following is intended to give you an idea of how dogs naturally follow a 'hunting chain'. You can therefore see how aspects of training a gundog are supposed to fit in to this natural inherent skill. Hunting is a natural instinctive behavior for all dogs to varying degrees depending on the breed. It is a primitive set of behaviors that have been hard wired into them from thousands of years ago.

The actual act of hunting involves a set of behaviors with logical links that follow each other to a natural conclusion which in the wild would be to kill and to eat in order to survive. In the wild the chain of events would involve; scenting > searching > seeing > stalking > pausing > pouncing > chasing > grabbing > killing > eating or carrying > guarding etc.

In order to be useful to humans, specific training involves utilising and harnessing those instincts but interrupting and controlling the chain of hunting, such as the kill and eat parts, to therefore help the hunter catch/shoot the prey.

A specific example involving a segment of the hunting chain involves the Pointing breeds. Selective breeding has ensured that their ability to stalk and pause has been exaggerated. In other words, hundreds of years of selective breeding has chosen to breed with only those dogs each time with the strongest natural inclination to 'point'. It is important to point out that pointing is a natural ability that the dog can either do or they can't. You can nurture and develop this trait, but you can't actually teach any dog to point.

The pointing dog would then typically be taught to 'drop' and then pounce or 'flush'.

Chasing and grabbing have been modified as part of the retrieve as the dog runs out and picks up shot prey, but obviously they are not expected to kill as the gun would carry out the kill.

So the trained gundog hunting chain becomes:

Scenting > searching > seeing > stalking > pointing (pausing) > dropping > flushing (pouncing) > game is shot > retrieve (chasing, grabbing, carrying).

The trained gundog hunting chain will not always, or be expected to follow through every single step to completion.

Usually at the point where the dog has located a bird or other game, and is 'pointing', we may interrupt them before they carry on. This could be to continue the hunting chain, recall or retrieve what is perhaps an injured previously shot bird.

From a control point of view, it is beneficial to us that we break the chain as it makes the hunt unpredictable to the dog. Otherwise they would anticipate what they do next, ignoring us, resulting in them hunting for themselves.

Dogs that are expected to flush such as Spaniels, follow a trained hunting chain that would proceed as follows:

You set them off; They quarter on the wind, picking up and following game scents as they go; They locate any game, usually in undergrowth; They flush the game when signalled to do so; The dog would simultaneously drop and wait whilst the hunter would shoot fleeing game.

If a bird or other game is shot the dog is sent out to retrieve using their sight, memory or direction from the handler of where they saw the bird drop. Utilising the wind to pick up scents. Or again looking to the handler for directions (as taught with the blind retrieve).

Finally retrieving the game by returning to the handler and delivering it to hand.

HPR's also flush but whereas the Spaniel works at close quarters to the handler, the HPR is expected to work at long distances out of gunshot range.

This is why they remain on 'point' (indicate the presence of game) so as to allow the hunter to get within shooting range.

They then flush in a similar way to the Spaniel.

You set them off; They quarter on the wind, picking up and following game scents as they go; They locate any game usually in undergrowth, freeze and point; They remain motionless/steady on point; They flush the game when signalled to do so; The dog would simultaneously drop and wait whilst the hunter would shoot fleeing game.

If a bird or other game is shot, the dog is sent out to retrieve using their sight and memory of where they saw the bird drop. Utilising the wind to pick up scents. Or looking to the handler for directions (blind retrieve).

Finally retrieving the game by returning to the handler and delivering it to hand.

Retrievers usually simply retrieve and their trained gundog hunting chain would proceed as follows:

You set them off; If a bird or other game is shot the dog is sent out to retrieve using their sight and memory of where they saw the bird drop. Utilizing the wind to pick up scents. Or looking to the handler for directions (blind retrieve).

Retrieving the game by returning to the handler and delivering it to hand.

You will notice that your dog gets more excited by certain aspects of the hunting chain, in other words they find these more rewarding and are therefore motivated to a greater extent. They may be equally motivated by all aspects, but take note if one or two stand out.

It is important to reinforce/reward these behaviors and mark them with a 'click' or verbal 'good'.

They may value all aspects of the hunt, but some dogs are not as keen on certain aspects as others. They may be highly motivated to hunt or search, but not so keen on retrieving.

This would be problematic if the dog was a retriever to start with and the reward for the other aspects of hunting is supposed to be the 'retrieve'.

Chasing may be more valuable to them than searching. Finding and following a scent may be what motivates them to start searching. Running or quartering may be highly motivating to them, more so than the flush.

It is therefore important to reward/reinforce what is most important to them and that they make the connection between this and the overall hunting chain. They will then hopefully be motivated by all aspects of the hunting chain.

Otherwise the dog may become bored and give up if they are constantly doing things they do not find particularly rewarding.

Some dogs lack the understanding, instinct or motivation to hunt and therefore need to be encouraged and taught certain aspects. They may not know that the scent that intrigues them is connected to the very game that gave off the scent. It could be that they have followed scents but never found live game at the end of it.

For this reason if you intend to hunt on the shooting field with live game, it is vital that the dog is exposed live game in the early learning stage. They need to actually find and flush live game, otherwise they will lack the motivation, not see the connection between hunting and finding the game and probably lose interest.

a) Scenting or Tracking

Scenting or tracking is a skill that utilises the dog's incredible sense of smell. However, the dog needs to be exposed to ground and air scents in order for this sense to develop.

Dogs will pick up scents from the ground via soil and vegetation which have been transmitted from game as they have passed through the area or left faeces and urine markings. Ground scent indicates that something has been there and might still be in the area.

Air scent however, is a stronger indicator of where the game is at the present time which is likely to be close by. Air scent is emitted from the body which is then picked up carried and distributed by the wind.

All Gundogs should be exposed to both in order to develop and perfect this skill for the dog.

You will notice that different gundog breeds rely on or specialize in scenting a particular way.

b) How Spaniels (flushing dogs) scent or track

Gundogs that are specialists at flushing such as Spaniels predominantly ground scent and occasionally take in air scent until they find ground scent. Once they have located ground scent they excitedly scan and run around the area, diving into undergrowth to flush game. They usually continue like this, flushing more game unless they are instructed to retrieve.

As they are expected to work at close quarters and as part of a team they have been specifically developed for this task.

They hunt by quartering (searching) across a downwind at close quarters, usually no more than 5 meters away, with their noses close to the ground. The close proximity is again to keep within gunshot range and to take into account a bird flying away, therefore increasing the distance from the gun.

c) How HPR (Hunt Point Retrieve) scent and track

The HPR are expected to work at greater distances and therefore cover much more ground than the Flushing dog.

They typically utilise air scent much more, and home in on ground scent occasionally. When they have located something, they stand on 'point'.

As they move whilst quartering, they will raise and lower their heads accordingly 'fishing' for scents.

Again pointing has been used in order to indicate game and as this is likely to be out of gunshot range, give the hunter chance to get within gunshot range.

d) How Retrievers scent and track

Retrievers are not usually expected to hunt the same way as the Flushing dogs or HPR's, but still need to use scent to locate fallen prey.

They will use air and ground scent to locate a bird killed at distance or an injured bird still moving at ground level.

17) Hunting/Quartering

a) What is 'Quartering'?

Your dog will not need to be taught to hunt as such because he instinctively engages in this activity anyway. What needs to be taught is a controlled hunting, known as quartering which benefits the handler. When their 'prey drive' takes over, an uncontrolled dog is oblivious to anything other than following the scent. It is therefore vital that he responds to your whistle commands and does not please himself. This is why it therefore has to be firmly ingrained from the early days of training.

Having said that, quartering only controls the dog in the sense of keeping him within a manageable range. Once the dog has located a scent, you cannot expect him to follow the text book zig zag quartering pattern, as the scent can take him anywhere. The best that quartering can do is to maximise the dogs chances of catching a scent by efficiently covering the area.

Again Quartering is something you will see the dog doing when scent tracking; running back and forth to pick up scents. However, trained quartering involves controlling the dog by sending him to your left or right and bringing him back in again. The dog literally runs back and forth, in front, but working away from the handler in a narrow zig zag, S shape pattern parallel or at right angles, usually towards a head wind (with the wind). It is important to emphasise 'narrow' because if the dog takes a wide zig zag he will miss too much ground that may be scent marked. A narrow line will give him more of an opportunity to pick up valuable scents.

b) How the dog quarters

An experienced dog will effectively quarter into a head wind, but usually at an angle to the wind. Moving towards a head wind allows the dog to pick up scents much easier as the scent is naturally carried toward them. When learning to hunt, once again a beginner dog is usually taught to quarter with the wind to their back for ease of picking up scents.

More experienced dogs able to distinguish scents better than a beginner dog will usually quarter at an approximate 45 degree angle to a head wind. At least one obvious advantage of this is that in a strong wind it is not as severe as a head on wind. This is known as quartering with a 'cheek wind'.

The hunter then follows within a short distance if a flushing dog is used, or a greater distance if pointers or HPR's are used.

Tail wind quartering

Despite the name, this still involves the dog quartering into a head wind.

If circumstances dictate that you cannot quarter as normal into a head wind, quartering with a tail wind is adopted.

» Here you start with you and the dog with your backs to the wind.

Advanced Cockapoo Training

» You then send the dog out in a straight line ahead of you.

» The dog then begins to quarter back as normal into a head wind.

» You then move to the point the dog started quartering from and repeat the process.

» It basically involves the dog quartering toward you rather than away from you.

Side wind quartering

» In this case you stand with the wind blowing across your left hand side.

» You send the dog to your right and the dog begins quartering towards the wind so that as he zig zags, he comes towards, then away from you.

» You and the dog then move forward and start the pattern again quartering the new section and so on.

» The above, are all options for quartering under different circumstances.

The important point to note, is that the experienced dog always quarters into the wind and therefore has a greater chance of picking up any scents. Quartering should therefore not merely involve following a zig zag pattern for the sake of it, but should always take into consideration the direction of the wind.

Problems can arise when organised shoots have a line of beaters who are instructed to beat a line regardless of the wind direction. This is fine if they happen to move into a wind and the dog can quarter as normal.

Quartering distances for Spaniels and HPR

The mechanics of quartering are more or less the same regardless of the type of Gundog. However, it is important to be aware of how the different gundog breeds hunt, and how this affects the way different breeds quarter. Basically Spaniels typically flush game within shooting range and therefore at close quarters to the handler. HPR and other pointing breeds however are expected to quarter at much farther distances. Spaniels basically quarter > find game at distances less than 40 meters > sit, which is similarly indicating it has found something > then flush on command. The HPR will quarter > find game, quite possibly at distances of around 100 meters or more > and point > wait for the handler > then flush when prompted by the handler.

Opinions differ as to the ideal quartering distance for normal hunting/shooting with a HPR. However, a distance of around 80 meters (260ft approx) either side, and around 40 meters (130ft approx) ahead is typical.

However, to give you some idea of how field trials and tests criteria can differ please view the following PDF link from the Kennel Club UK
https://www.thekennelclub.org.uk/media/609878/pointing_test_guidelines_2014.pdf

Basically their criteria stipulates that a dog should quarter into a head wind side to side at 'beats' of at least 100 meters.

Spaniels on the other hand are expected to keep within a certain distance or radius, which for shooting purposes has to be within shooting range. Incidentally an optimum shooting range will differ depending on a number of variables. These variables can include; the type of bird, how fast they fly, whether they fly high or away, the type of gun used, the skill and experience of the person etc. Around 100ft (30 meters approx) is considered to be an average realistic shooting distance, although farther away can still be achieved. However, you need to bear in mind that the the dog needs to be closer to you than this because once the bird is flushed, it does not give you much time to take a shot, before it is out of shooting range. So the dog should be quartering between 10 meters (around 33ft) approx and a maximum of 20 meters (around 66ft) approx. Hopefully this will give you some idea of how close you need to keep your dog in relation to where you are standing.

An obvious advantage that you have training a Spaniel to quarter as opposed to the HPR is that the Spaniel is easier to train, control and motivate. HPR's can easily go wrong the farther away from you they get. If they are not picking up scents, they can become easily bored quartering a pattern, or decide to flush and give chase rather than point and wait. Of course this is more likely to happen with young dogs still learning rather than trained adults.

c) Teaching Hunting/(Quartering)

To a certain extent the skills of quartering will already have been introduced when he is taught to retrieve. This will have included hand signals and sending him away.

Once again, it is good practice to be aware of the wind direction. Remember in the initial stages, always begin with the dog coming away from a head wind. As he becomes more experienced practice again moving towards a head wind. This ensures that he picks up oncoming scents that will trigger his desire to hunt.

1. Begin this exercise with a retractable or long training lead attached.
2. Stand facing a head wind and call your dog to you > blow the one toot stop sit whistle and use the hand signal hand parallel to the ground at chest height for sit > He should now be sat facing you, his back to the wind > attach the training leash > make sure that you have 3 meters approximately of slack > give him the 'stay' command
3. Now walk away from him about 8 feet (2.5 meters approx) away. Ensure again that you are facing a head wind and your dog has his back to it.
4. Now start walking across wind, left or right away from him > he should follow, but if not recall him by issuing the verbal command 'here' > immediately follow the verbal command with two short toots of the whistle (this isn't the actual recall as such, but moving him left or right, hence the two toots rather than several)> at the same time thrust your arm parallel to the ground in the direction you are heading.
5. He will hopefully follow your direction and should pass you heading the same way, but ahead of you.
6. Let him continue until he has nearly taken most of the slack of the training leash > blow the stop whistle > now repeat from (2) but in the opposite direction and continue like this, all the while moving in a forward direction.
7. He should ideally be following the typical zig zag quartering pattern.
8. If he picks up a scent, let him follow this for a short while > then blow the stop whistle > using your hand signal, direct him in the opposite direction, walking away from him as before.
9. Once he has got the hang of this > repeat the exercise extending the distance and the amount of slack on the training leash each time.
10. After a lot of repetitions, and if you are confident he has got the hang of it, and you can stop him and redirect with the whistle, repeat the exercise without a leash.
11. So at this point you should be able to set him off in one direction > blow the stop whistle > direct him left or right using the hand signal, 'get on' verbal cue and the two toot/pip whistle command > allow him to continue in that direction > blow the stop whistle > direct him left or right

using the hand signal, 'get on' verbal cue and the two toot/pip whistle command >
12. Please note that it is important to keep the distances short initially for control purposes. He will obviously venture much further when 'quartering' but only once he is properly trained and under your control.
13. Repeat this routine for 5 to 10 minutes each day until he is reliably obeying the whistle, verbal and hand signals.

Alternative quartering exercise

If you have been using food in your training you may prefer to start with this exercise. You may also find that the he is struggling to grasp the previous exercise and wish to start with this one first, then move on without food

Begin this exercise in a room, your yard or garden where there are limited distractions.

1. As for previous exercises, prepare yourself with a piece of food in your dominant hand > your whistle should be around your neck for easy access > Pinch the treat between your thumb and forefinger.
2. Recall your dog, giving the recall whistle cue, several short pips (pip, pip, pip, pip)
3. Now about half way before he reaches you, throw the piece of food either left or right. As you throw the food, make this your left/right hand signal to send him left or right > at the same time blow the two toot whistle cue and give the verbal 'get on' command. He should chase the food.
4. As soon as he picks the food up that you have thrown and he has looked up and noticed you throw another piece of food in the opposite direction left or right. Again as you throw the food, make this your left/right hand signal to send him left or right > at the same time blow the two toot whistle cue and give the verbal 'get on' command. He should again chase after the food.
5. Repeat step (4) in the opposite direction and keep repeating this way for a few more minutes.

Once he seems to have got the hang of this, try continuing but without the food and just giving the right or left hand signal and issuing the verbal and whistle cues. Hopefully you can continue like this sending him back and forth in a quartering pattern.

As always, increase the distance gradually.

If you have problems with this at any point, take it a step back or back to small steps and build up again. Perhaps you will need to reintroduce food to maintain his interest and enthusiasm.

A few pointers to bear in mind.

Always build things up slowly, one step at a time before increasing the level of difficulty.

Gradually change the locations, distractions, distance, the direction you send him each time etc. This will keep things unpredictable and ensure the dog is paying attention and not simply going through the motions and anticipating.

Also bear in mind that when you are increasing the levels of difficulty, distractions, new location or introducing stimuli likely to trigger the prey drive, always use a long line for added safety and control in case they take off running.

Moving on

When first teaching a puppy to quarter we use their instinctive desire to want to be near us and follow us.

So we wander off, then move left, then right, then stopping and all the while the puppy is learning to follow a leader, a scent lead and ultimately to hunt.

If he picks up a scent and seems preoccupied, make a conscious effort to move purposely in the opposite direction in order to get him to follow. It is this type of movement/body language from you that will indicate to the dog that you have found a better area to 'hunt'. Ultimately we want him to trust us as part of the hunt. It is also advisable to direct him to areas where you know game resides as he will quickly trust your judgement and increase the likelihood of him following you.

Don't just purposely walk in the opposite direction, but change suddenly from left then to right and back on yourself again. Moving slowly towards (stalking) and stopping occasionally, (pointing), to observe areas also replicates the dogs natural behavior and hunting style.

Be aware of how your body indicates movement to the dog however slight this may be. You can subtly lean forward, left or right to indicate moving in those directions or remain stationary and lean back to indicate stopping. The dog will begin to associate this type of body language cues with hunting behaviors.

Don't forget that although you want him to enjoy scenting/tracking and pleasing himself, to a certain extent, you also need to maintain control.

18) Obstacle Training

Jumping obstacles

Please note, you are not advised to encourage your dog to jump obstacles until he has reached maturity in terms of muscle, ligament and bone growth. You should therefore not be in any rush to start any obstacle jumping until he is at least 9 months old preferably beyond a year old. Although he may be capable and willing much younger than this, he will be susceptible to muscle/ligament tears and potential bone breakages which can affect him for the rest of his life.

As part of his socialisation period he will probably have become accustomed to climbing steps and over a number of obstacles. This will build his confidence gradually. However these should always be supervised and never allow a young puppy to attempt jumping from high obstacles

If and when you do start training/jumping obstacles, as with all other training, start small and build up. In the real world once experienced he may be jumping 4ft high wire mesh fencing. Or perhaps dry stone walls or natural hedges. Please note, always be very careful to check fences for any barbed wire strands. Either avoid these or place a protective cover/sheet, perhaps your coat, over to protect your dog. You can buy special protectors for this purpose that are easy to carry.

Obstacles and training

You can make a suitable obstacle with a simple broom stick or other pole. You then use bricks, books, boxes or any stable containers that you can stack either end of the pole. Start the height at 6 inches or so and build up in 6 inch approx increments. Once you get to a certain height that he is tempted to crawl under, drape an old blanket or curtain over the pole to act as a barrier. Do not be tempted to increase the height before he is able and confidently jumping a particular height. It can take a few months or so before he is confidently jumping 3 or 4 feet in height. As always if he struggles to get over when you have increased to a certain height, go back a step.

As soon as he is jumping obstacles that you have set up at a similar height to those he will meet in the field, practice his jumping over field obstacles also. In other words actual wire fences, hedges, dry stone walls etc.

With wire mesh fencing it may be necessary to help him at first by placing his front feet onto the fence and lifting his back end as he climbs up and over. But some dogs use the wire holes to climb up and over without any help.

Once you have set up a suitable obstacle, proceed with training as follows:
1. Choose a cue word such as 'over' or 'get over' to use when you wish him to jump an obstacle.
2. Walk your dog about 6ft (approximately 2 meters) away from the obstacle > ask him to sit and stay.

Advanced Cockapoo Training

3. Walk over to the obstacle > issue the recall command and as he approaches > issue the 'over' command, encouraging him to jump over.
4. If he walks around you may need to lure him over with your hand or jump over yourself which he should hopefully follow.
5. As usual if he successfully jumps, give him lots of praise.
6. Repeat until he jumps the obstacle without you having to lead or lure him, but simply issue the 'over' command.
7. Next walk him about 6ft (approximately 2 meters) away from the obstacle > ask him to sit and stay, but you also stay by his side.
8. Throw a dummy over the obstacle and send him for a retrieve > If he seems reluctant to go you may have to wait by the obstacle and give the 'over' command again so that he gets used to jumping over to pick the dummy up and jump the obstacle again to retrieve back to you > As he jumps over, walk away from the obstacle so that he is encouraged to retrieve back to you > If when returning he goes around the obstacle, either make this wider or stay at the obstacle to encourage him back over until he is reliably jumping over.
9. Gradually increase the distance and height of the object until he is clearing heights similar to those he will normally face in the countryside. However, only start to increase the height when he is successfully and reliably jumping the obstacle each time without being lead or lured.

Again, if he successfully jumps the obstacle and retrieves back to you give him lots of praise.

Gradually increase the distance between you and the obstacle. You may have to get your dog to sit and stay as you walk over to the obstacle > throwing the dummy over > returning to the dog > then issue the retrieve command. Alternatively use a dummy launcher for longer distances

19) Field Trials and Working Tests

The following is a very brief introduction to field trials and working tests. If this is something you may be interested in, please have a look at the links that follow.

Field trials are set up to artificially imitate as closely as possible an actual shoot. In this respect a line of guns and dogs will 'walk up game' until birds are flushed and shot. A notable difference between the two is that a judge will be present and among other things, decide which dogs retrieve birds that have been shot. The rules and procedures followed do differ between the UK and US trials. Field trials involve certain rules for example KC registration in the UK is a requirement as well as being a member of a gundog club.

Working tests on the other hand, again emulate a shoot, but these tests do not involve the shooting and killing of live game. In this case dogs follow exercises similar to retrieves used to train them. So dummies are used for retrieves and typically include blind, marked as well as retrieves with 2 and 3 dummies.

Hunt Test Programmes

The following links will provide more information on the subject.

AKC

http://www.akc.org/events/hunting-tests/pointing-breeds/articles/get-started/

http://www.akc.org/events/hunting-tests/retrievers/

UKC

http://www.ukcdogs.com

Kennel Club (UK)

http://www.thekennelclub.org.uk/activities/field-trials-working-Gundogs/new-to-field-trials-Gundog-working-tests/

Gundog Club UK

http://www.theGundogclub.co.uk/?page_id=926
http://www.theGundogclub.co.uk/Training/awardsscheme/tests/spaniel/1beginner.htm

http://www.theGundogclub.co.uk/Training/awardsscheme/tests/retriever/beginner.htm

NAHRA

http://www.nahra.org/

NAVHDA

https://www.navhda.org/

6) ESSENTIAL EXERCISE

Dogs are generally considered to be similar to humans in their exercise requirements and can adapt to their circumstances. For example, the dog that is placed in quarantine will eventually leave, in a healthy condition, having spent several months in a pen with a run not much bigger than a small garden to exercise in. But their muscle tone will have deteriorated to a certain extent. Rescue dogs spending large parts of the day in kennels are in a similar position. A dog will nevertheless become healthier, fitter and with greater stamina levels, the more exercise it receives.

Having said that, dogs need daily active purposeful exercise, such as long walks, off lead runs, play activities and not just being turned out in a large yard or garden where they are likely to just wander about or lie down. Please do remember that although you will hear recommendations of certain breeds ideally needing a yard or garden, it is not the same thing as a purposeful walk or off lead run. A yard or garden is great if you intend to play fetch games, in an obvious safe area etc. Throwing a ball or stick has long been a popular alternative to help tire your dog out. Setting up an agility course, if your garden is large enough, with tunnels, ramps, platforms, short ladders, weave sticks etc, is a great way for you to interact and to tire a dog, preventing boredom. Indoor games such as hide and seek, scenting, tracking food, short retrieves etc are useful on days when the weather prevents normal exercise.

The exercising of your dog obviously gives you the perfect opportunity to exercise yourself. As a daily routine with the obligation to exercise your dog you are unlikely to fall into the trap of not following an exercise routine or a trip to the gym because you cannot be bothered today. Research your local area for suitable locations to exercise your dog. As well as the pavements in your immediate neighborhood these may also include; Local fields, wooded areas, dog parks, other local parks. Also check that it is permissible to exercise dogs in these areas.

Every Cockapoo dog needs daily walks, and will certainly not be happy at home all day. Remember that Gundogs and therefore the Cockapoo relation, were purposely bred for their stamina and ability to keep going all day if necessary. Unfortunately many pet owners fail to recognise the innate needs of such dogs to have a similar outlet, now that the average family home no longer requires them to flush and retrieve game birds.

The adult Cockapoo ideally needs a good long walk several times a day with the opportunity for off lead running. Otherwise he may develop problem behaviors. These gentle, sweet natured dogs are generally well behaved. However, excess energy build up can easily cause destructive or even aggressive behavior, to a certain extent.

Many dog behavior problems can be remedied very quickly when the daily walks are increased in time and intensity. Behavior can also change significantly when the dog's food is changed (food causing allergies or just poor food quality lacking necessary nutrients). But many of the most problematic behaviors stem from a lack of suitable exercise. Such behavioral problems can include: hyperactivity, excessive barking, digging, chewing, chasing, racing about the house, ripping things up, potentially knocking furniture or people over, causing an injury to either you or themselves.

Under exercised dogs are likely to become restless, tense, agitated, displaying heightened, aggressive behavior relating to food, toys, barking at the slightest thing etc. The thing to realise is that this is not the dogs fault, as they are reacting out of frustration to not having a suitable outlet for their pent up energy. In addition to behavioral problems, a lack of adequate exercise is also likely to result in him losing muscle tone, becoming lazy and possibly becoming overweight or obese, resulting in a gradual deterioration of health.

If you are out at work for a full day then why not consider a doggy day care or professional dog walker for your Cockapoo dog. The dog also cannot be expected to hold it in all day if they need to urinate or defecate. A good professional canine caretaker will wear your dog out and meet his care and social needs all at once.

Puppy exercise

Please be aware that Cockapoo puppies along with other puppy breeds, need to be broken in gently to exercise, as their bones are soft whilst they are still growing. Your regular, long walks will begin when your puppy is several months old.

Puppy exercise should involve gentle short walks; the UK Kennel club advises;

"Puppies need much less exercise than fully-grown dogs. If you over-exercise a growing puppy you can overtire it and damage its developing joints, causing early arthritis. A good rule of thumb is a ratio of five minutes exercise per month of age (up to twice a day) until the puppy is fully grown, i.e. 15 minutes (up to twice a day) when three months old, 20 minutes when four months old etc. Once they are fully grown, they can go out for much longer.

It is important that puppies and dogs go out for exercise every day in a safe and secure area, or they may become frustrated. Time spent in the garden (however large) is no substitute for exploring new environments and socialising with other dogs. (Make sure your puppy is trained to recall so that you are confident that he will return to you when called)".

See more at:
http://www.thekennelclub.org.uk

How much daily exercise is enough?

So are you aware of how much daily exercise this breed will need to keep him happy, healthy and burn off pent up energy?

Opinions differ but it is generally considered that at least an hour, preferably two, brisk walking per day, with some off lead running, is necessary for most gundogs. It is preferable that this is split into half an hour or so in the morning and the same in the evening.

Opinions differ, but an off lead run is considered more beneficial to them than a long walk.

A breed requiring a lot of exercise such as a Cockapoo needs an actual off lead run of over a mile per day, either free running in a field or park, or whilst jogging with yourself. This would probably be the equivalent of 1 ½ to 2 hours of brisk lead walking.

A 10 minute off lead run several times a day for pups and a 20 minute off lead run morning and evening for adults, should be included as part of their daily exercise. Jogging or running in a safe area will encourage the dog to follow you and to run harder than if you leave him to it.

Chapter Nine:

Cockapoo Behavior Problems

In this area of the book we will look at potential behavior problems that the Cockapoo may develop. Like people, dogs have their own specific personalities. The behavior that the Cockapoo displays is partly based on his nature, and mostly a result of the nurturing effect that life has bestowed on him so far. Most canine problems can be halted before they get too severe, or even modified into manageable acts. It is important to have an understanding of behavior before trying to make any changes.

Please Note: With the exception of food related problems and some physiological disorders, most of these behavior are simply a symptom of boredom, lack of mental stimulation and a lack of exercise. More often than not, when these matters are addressed, many behavior problems disappear.

Also please be aware that puppy mills and other bad breeding practices, have been known to breed dogs that have a number of serious issues. These include dogs that can be neurotic and aggressive with a tendency to bite, as well as a host of serious physical health issues.

As with physical health issues, the following behavioral disorders have been noted in some dogs of this breed. This may be of a relatively small frequency. You should therefore not be overly concerned about your dog developing a number of these conditions. Your dog may not be affected by any of them, but again, forewarned is forearmed.

1) Dealing with Common Behavior Problems

It is not fair to generalise, as two dogs of the same breed could be either high maintenance or no trouble at all. As previously noted however, if your dog doesn't get enough exercise or attention he is likely to develop problem behaviors which in serious cases may require professional training to correct.

What you first of all need to understand before you try to tackle any behavior problem, is that many behaviors that you might consider problematic are actually natural behaviors for your dog. For example, chewing is a very natural way for puppies to learn about their world. They also do it to ease the pain of teething or to alleviate boredom, tension or anxiety. When your puppy fulfils his need to chew by gnawing on an expensive pair of shoes, is when the behavior becomes a problem. The best way to deal with problem behaviors is not to teach your puppy to avoid the behavior altogether but to channel that behavior toward a more appropriate outlet. So in this case, it is a simple matter of providing plenty of chew toys, and not allowing him access to anything you do not wish chewed. Below you will find tips for dealing with some of the most common behavior problems potentially affecting this breed:

The following is presented in alphabetical order. It is not meant to indicate problems in any order of importance or severity.

a) Aggression

Aggression is one of, if not the most commonly reported disorders affecting dogs and their owners. In the U.S.A for example, it is

Cockapoo Behavior Problems

estimated that between 3 and 5 million dog bites are reported annually. Many of these affect children and are of a serious nature, in some cases fatal. Aggression between other dogs is also a common problem.

Aggression is a broad ranging problem and can include incidences relating to the following: resource guarding relating to food or general possessiveness; fear; defence; territorial; familiar and unfamiliar people; familiar and unfamiliar dogs; other causes of an idiopathic nature such as epilepsy.

Important note: Many 'minor' cases of aggression can be dealt with by following a program of behavior modification at home. However, for more serious cases it is highly recommended that you consult a dog behavior specialist, perhaps via your vet.

Aggression with other dogs

Main causes

Imposed restrictions such as fences, leashes or being chained up. This in turn prevents a dogs natural access to other dogs, in order to greet and socialise normally. This can typically occur during a puppies 12 to 16 week 'critical period'.

In some cases dogs are encouraged to be hostile and suspicious of strangers in an attempt to make them 'guard dogs' or 'watchdogs'. The dog that is chained up, becomes more aggressive. This is similar to the situation when out on lead walks as owners pull or jerk the dog away from another dog walker, further exacerbating the aggression.

Punishment or threat based training techniques can also exacerbate aggression. Conversely it can create submissive or fear responses.

Preventative measures

Correct and adequate socialisation is the most obvious remedy for this problem. Correctly socialised dogs are highly unlikely to experience problems. However, that is not to say that under socialised or hostile dogs will not attempt to attack your dog.

Controlling the problem

A dog that has a tendency for aggression towards other dogs, might not entirely lose the tendency. However, it is possible to modify and desensitise the behavior with the following techniques:

» A reliable well trained 'recall', is a very important factor here.

» Use of a training leash, around 5 meters to give him greater freedom.

» Try and maintain a slack leash by allowing him to safely wander, but train him to regularly come back to you. Gradually expose him to other dogs in order to condition him coming back to you, in preference to going to the other dog.

» Do not display hostility towards another dog that you may wish to usher away from your dog. This can often trigger aggression from your dog.

» As with any training, avoid acknowledging unacceptable behavior simply by ignoring the behavior.

» Castration in males can lessen aggressive tendencies but this is not 100%.

Aggression towards adults and children

IMPORTANT:

For obvious reasons of safety, if this is a problem, you should seek professional help. Your vet will be able to diagnose a possible medical cause that may require medication. Otherwise for behavior problems, help should come from either an experienced dog trainer or behaviorist.

Gundog types in general are not known for aggression towards people, but can become aggressive if mishandled.

A Note on Growling

It is important to know your own dog, where growling is concerned. Take a look at the scenario within which the growl occurs. Observe your dog's body language and the signs that show how he must be feeling, before deciding why your dog may be growling.

Generally in the dog world, growling is an early warning system that something is not right. The growl from an aggressive dog can be delivered seconds before a bite. If a dog growls at your approach or attention, then it is a request to be left alone. You should adhere to that, for the dog has very few methods of communicating his wishes.

Dog growling during play and tug games is actually common. So if your Cockapoo growls when he is playing, it is probably him expressing himself rather than a display of aggression. Although it can sound pretty fierce, play based growling is usually nothing to worry about.

B) ATTENTION SEEKING: WHINING, BEGGING, BARKING, PAWING ETC.

Unfortunately, in many cases this problem starts when the dog is a cute, adorable puppy. It is actually normal behavior for a young puppy to seek care and assurance from their adult carers, whether human or their mother.

However, it is important that the puppy learns to become an adult and not depend or rely on us to baby them.

It is easy to unwittingly teach a dog to seek attention with the following:

Constantly lifting the puppy up, cuddling and carrying him; Giving into him barking, whining, pawing etc, and attempting to pacify him by giving him a treat; Stroking him if he licks, paws or conducts any other unwanted behavior; Even pushing him down or away is giving him attention; During meal times, giving him food from the table when he sits and begs; Encouraging him to jump up and stroking him when he does.

Of course it is beneficial to you and your dog that you should stroke, cuddle, pet him etc. However, this has to be done on your terms. In other words only doing so if and when he is not pawing, barking, whining etc. This should hopefully reassure him that you will stroke him, but not when he whines, barks or paws.

Preventing the problem:

We unwittingly reinforce these unwanted behaviors by indulging and giving into the behavior, therefore reinforcing, rather than ignoring the behavior. If you do not mind these behaviors then fine, but otherwise it is not advisable to indulge the dog by stroking or praising him when he persistently carries out potentially annoying behaviors.

Make sure he is getting plenty of exercise and play time during the day. In other words, alleviating boredom and getting your attention.

It is very Important to avoid confusing the dog. The only realistic way to achieve this is for every person who comes into contact with the dog to stick to a few simple rules.

Do not feed your dog treats from the table. Even if this is very occasional, you are still encouraging or reinforcing him to continue begging.

Occasionally you may have to temporarily leave your dog in the yard or garden or a room in the house (of course this assumes you are also in the house). If he starts whining, barking or pawing at the door, only let him back in when he stops those behaviors.

He may come to you when you are busy doing something else, and start pawing, whining, jumping up or barking. Again, do not give into him, but simply ignore this by turning or walking away, perhaps into another room and close the door. Wait for a few seconds until your Cockapoo stops the attention seeking, then return to the room and pet him calmly. Repeat this sequence every time your dog whines, paws, barks at you will eventually learn that these behaviors do not earn him your attention.

If he seems to be relying on you, or pestering you all the time, another dog may be the answer or involve other people in walking him or playing games.

Do not be overly protective, keeping him away from situations that he needs to be exposed to. Give him the freedom to 'safely' explore and discover his surroundings. Socialisation should give him many opportunities to confront unusual situations.

c) Barking

Dogs can easily become victims of poisoning, from what you may consider as malicious neighbours who are annoyed with a dog that incessantly barks or comes into their garden digging up flower beds, harassing the cat, defecating etc. It is usually against council regulations to allow dog fouling and incessant barking. Obviously your neighbours have a right to enjoy their home environments in peace.

Dog barking can be a useful warning or deterrent for would be intruders, but can be problematic if this becomes habitual or excessive. Certain guard dog breeds are selected for the specific purpose of barking to warn off intruders. The unfortunate downside to this, is the dog that reacts and barks at the slightest thing and consequently cause problems with neighbours.

Please consider the problems you may encounter with neighbours and local councils if you live in a built up urban area or apartment block. You can control barking to an extent whilst you are home, but if the dog is on its own for large parts of the day, you will not know until you receive a complaint. Certain local authorities can impose warnings if complaints are made or even court orders enforcing action from the dog owner and fines or bans for non compliance.

Why dogs bark

A key reason dogs bark is through boredom. Please refer to the section on boredom that follows.

Dogs that habitually bark, do so for a variety of reasons such as fear; asking to be let inside the house; through separation anxiety when alone or because they derive pleasure from the act.

It is also thought that excessive barking is strongly linked with how reactive the dog is. Terriers are a typical example and again this is related to their excitability levels, activity or hyperactivity levels, snappy and affection seeking.

In most cases a breed that is relatively un-reactive is unlikely to bark. An exception to this is a low reactive breed such as a Beagle, a breed that is expected to bark as part of hunting, letting hunters on horseback know which direction the fox is heading.

Preventing a problem:

Once you have addressed possible problems associated with boredom, the following should help. You will often find that if you leave your dog out in a fenced yard or garden, he is likely to hear sounds that trigger him to bark. The obvious solution to this is to bring him back into the house.

The easiest way to teach your dog to stop barking if you are present, is actually to teach him to bark on command first.

For this you will need to have a friend stand outside your front door and to ring the doorbell.

Get your Cockapoo's attention and give him the cue word 'speak' > As soon as you give the command, have your friend ring the doorbell to get your dog to bark > When he barks, praise him excitedly and reward him with a treat.

After a few repetitions, your dog should start barking on command before the doorbell rings when you issue the 'speak' cue word.

Once your dog learns to respond to you by barking on command, you can then teach him a 'hush' command. Give your Cockapoo the 'speak' command and let him bark a few times before telling him 'hush'. When he stops barking, praise him excitedly and reward him with a treat.

Repeat this sequence several times until your Cockapoo gets the hang of barking when you say 'speak' and stopping when you say 'hush'. Cockapoos are an intelligent breed that will be eager to please, so this shouldn't take too many repetitions.

So to recap, first teach the dog to bark and add a command ('Speak/Bark') to it. Next, start to reinforce the short pauses between barks and add a command ('Hush/Quiet') to THEM. The dog will soon learn that the pauses are rewarded too. Therefore he is rewarded for being quiet as well as when he barks. It may seem odd that you are teaching the dog to bark, the very thing you are trying to avoid. This is merely for exercise or control purposes as you would otherwise have to wait for your dog to start barking before implementing a stop barking command.

The command word you use could also be 'quiet' or 'be quiet', rather than 'hush'. It is important that your timing is correct as you want him to know at what point he receives a treat for being quiet. Again, once he is barking on cue and being quiet on cue, stop rewarding him for barking. So you will no longer reward the barking, but you ARE rewarding him being 'quiet'. From now on, when he barks, issue the 'hush' cue and treat him when he immediately stops. Of course, it is unlikely that you will stop the natural impulse for him to bark, but at least now, you should be able to quickly stop him.

d) BITING (FEAR OR OTHERWISE)

Biting is an inherently natural thing for any dog to do. The Wolf for example, during the hunting process, has to bite in order to survive. This is most notable when either killing prey to eat, or attacking an 'enemy' Wolf straying into their territory. It is therefore unsurprising that the dog has inherited this tendency. Dogs naturally explore and investigate using their mouths. Movement can also trigger the game of chasing and biting.

Although the media reports many cases of dog bites, these are not always the so called dangerous dog breeds such as the Staffordshire/Pitbull types, Rottweilers etc. Smaller dog breeds including terriers, Sporting/Gundogs are also breeds that have been linked with dog bites. Arguably Cockapoos who can be indifferent to obedience training and children and if not properly handled have a predisposition to become hostile or even bite.

Also see sections (a), (f), (i), (q), (r), (s), (v)

Preventative measures

Bite inhibition is something that the puppy has to learn. This is not to be confused with teething which generally involves biting on relatively hard objects to relieve the discomfort of teething.

As previously noted elsewhere, providing plenty of chew toys and restricting access to any item likely to be chewed, is the first step.

Be aware that a playful puppy or dog may react to your movements or clothing likely to move; loose clothing and shoelaces are a prime target.

E) BOREDOM

Lack of exercise, mental stimulation, attention, being restricted to the house, yard or garden for extended periods, are all reasons dogs become bored. Signs that a dog is bored include, digging, attempting to jump your boundary fence, destroy furnishings and other items etc.

Feral or stray dogs have the freedom to roam and so are highly unlikely to develop symptoms of boredom. Obviously letting your dog roam the streets is not the answer. Dogs need similar mental and physical outlets to us, and to deny them this would be akin to being imprisoned, in solitary confinement.

Preventing the problem:

Provide opportunities for him to explore his environment out on walks and 'safe area' off lead runs on a daily basis.

Be prepared for him to keep stopping to sniff where other dogs have been and to scent mark. This is often more important to the dog. So it is very important that you allow him this time, and do not drag him away.

Be aware that his hunting instinct does not disappear just because he is well fed and not hungry. He will therefore be keen to follow the scent of another animal.

Allow him the opportunity to meet other dogs. It is important to note that unless another dog is hostile and dog aggressive, most dogs are generally well behaved when not restricted by a leash.

Human interaction is also very important. Leaving a dog home alone all day is never a good idea. If possible take the dog to work, or employ a dog sitter or ask a neighbour, friend or family member to keep him company and take him for walks etc.

Long leashes, between 3 and 5 meters in length, allow the dog to safely wander. You also minimise lead pulling. However, be careful near busy roads as your dog could easily wander into the road. Be careful with retractable leads as many have a breaking strain of 30 to 40kg. The pulling power of most dogs is considerably more than their actual weight. So if a dog suddenly lunges, perhaps having seen a cat, the retractable can easily snap.

f) Chasing

All dogs have a prey drive to varying degrees, which in some cases is very strong, in others hardly noticeable. Breeds such as the Terrier, Gundog, Hound etc have a strong instinctive prey drive that was particularly useful for hunting centuries ago and to a certain extent to this day.

However in most cases it can be a problematic trait as dogs chase cats, cyclists, rabbits, livestock etc. Dogs that have a strong tendency to chase need to be desensitised with lots of socialisation and exposure to such triggers. Training may also be necessary for them to resist the temptation to chase. As a last resort, the dog may have to be kept on a lead or kept away from situations and locations likely to trigger a chase.

Older dogs moving into a new home can also be a problem with small pets such as guinea pigs, cats, rabbits or even smaller dogs.

Most Sporting/Gundog types are inquisitive and will want to investigate anything unusual. If let off the lead this could well involve chasing after small animals or following scents.

It is important to be generally aware of certain consequences of chasing behavior that could affect any dog. Chasing wildlife, livestock or similar animals, can be a problem with most dog breeds. Just as other animals are easy targets, so are cars, pedestrians and bikes. Chasing behavior can also be a very dangerous game with potential fatal consequences. In the UK for example, a farmer is legally entitled to shoot a dog chasing his livestock.

The steps that we take to reform chasing behavior are similar to those which we use for social fear. It is a gradual process of teaching the dog to stay relaxed with the trigger at a distance. Eventually you build the dog's capacity to be near the trigger whilst he also stays relaxed and controlled.

It's important to focus on your dog's behavior carefully, and reinforce every time he looks towards you instead of at the trigger. If you can master this art alone, then your control over the behavior of your Cockapoo will improve dramatically.

The law and your dog

Included in the following resources you will find the sort of information that may be applicable to you, depending on your global location. The document includes keeping your dog on a leash under certain circumstances including country walks.

A short 16 page PDF document produced by The Kennel Club UK, will give you basic information regarding the law and your dog.

The Kennel Club UK
https://www.thekennelclub.org.uk/media/8277/law.pdf

Additionally do a Google search using a search term such as [the law and dogs], for more information. Obviously this is applicable if you are searching in the UK, simply add your location 'USA' etc for specific laws and legislations where you live.

Preventing the problem:

Again, socialisation and desensitising the dog from anything likely to trigger a chase response will probably be necessary. Ideally this should take place when still puppies, particularly during their critical period. Older dogs however, can be exposed in the same way, but results may take longer.

Once a dog has given chase, this becomes their reward or reinforcement and is often difficult to suppress or change. It therefore becomes necessary to use training and control measures.

Fortunately much of gundog training is designed to suppress the natural instinct to give chase. A reliable 'stop' and 'recall' command is very important preliminary requirement, as well as basic obedience of 'sit' and 'stay'. Once these training commands are reliable, you are then ready to start exposing your dog to situations likely to trigger a chase.

Whenever introducing your dog to unfamiliar animals, it is vital that you attach a long training leash of about 5 meters, in case he gives chase, possibly across a busy road.

If you are likely to exercise your dog in the countryside you should ideally introduce your dog to the type of farm animals or horses he is likely to encounter as follows:

Approach the animals at a distance with his training leash attached. Allow slack on the lead, but do not give him 2 or 3 meters incase he decides to chase. He could cause himself a neck injury if he comes to an abrupt halt.

1. Once you are reasonably close, provided he has not reacted by barking or lunging on the leash, get him to sit and stay for a few moments. Give him a treat and lots of praise occasionally to reward him for remaining calm.
2. Now move closer repeating (2). If at any point he loses control and attempts to chase, as (1), make sure he does not have too much slack. He should pull up short after a few feet anyway, at which point ask him to sit.
3. If you have taught him the 'stop' command, blow the stop whistle if his body language suggests he is about to give chase. You can also use the verbal cue, 'no' or 'ah ah' at the same time.
4. Once he is again calm, continue to slowly move forward. It is important that you praise and reward him when he is calm, and don't give in to him chasing.

You should be able to use the same procedure if chasing cyclists or joggers is a problem. In this case I would firstly advise asking a friend to cycle or jog by. Again, begin at a distance and gradually move closer. Reward him when he remains calm, and ensure you hold his leash securely so he cannot suddenly take off. Other domestic animals such as cats can be dealt with in a similar way.

g) Chewing

The simplest way of preventing your Cockapoo from chewing items you do not want chewed, is to make sure that he has plenty of chew toys available. Many dogs also chew on items out of boredom, so ensuring that your Cockapoo gets enough exercise and play time, will also help to prevent him from chewing on things around the house. If chewing does become a problem all you need to do is replace the item your dog is chewing on with one of his toys (swapping). Ideally you would have taken care of such items in your initial puppy proofing stage. However, we can't always be present or be sure which items he will chew and which he will ignore. You are therefore better off keeping every potential chewable item that you wish to keep intact, out of his reach.

If after this you still find your Cockapoo has found something you had forgotten about and is chewing on it, do not make a fuss about this, or show displeasure, but simply say 'NO' or 'leave', and take the object away. Immediately replace the object with your dog's favourite toy, then praise him when he starts chewing on it. Eventually your Cockapoo will learn what he is and is not allowed to chew on around the house.

H) Destructiveness

Unfortunately many dogs have been euthanised due to a lack of understanding as to why they are chewing or destroying household furnishings. Again this is a symptom of insufficient exercise, lack of mental stimulation and general boredom. The dogs are not necessarily being delinquents, they are merely acting out of frustration at not having an outlet for pent up energy.

Tug of war games are often encouraged as a good game to play with our dogs. However, it is also thought that this encourages destructive activities such as tugging or ripping curtains, washing hanging out to dry and other hanging objects.

Preventing the problem:

In the first instance make sure that the dog is getting enough exercise, mental stimulation with games and general attention. Additionally refer to the advice for the boredom problem.

Ensure he has a large array of chew and other toys to keep him preoccupied.

Avoid games which encourage the behavior such as tug of war. Retrieving is an excellent alternative that will burn off energy as well as mentally stimulate him. Throwing a stick or ball has a similar effect. You could also try activities such as 'scent work'. These activities are also ideal for dog owners whose mobility may be an issue.

Again referring back to proofing your house. If you have to leave him unattended for however short a time, it may be necessary to restrict access to rooms such as your lounge where he may be tempted to destroy your sofa etc.

I) Dominance

The general perception of gundog breeds, is that they were selectively bred to work with and tolerate other dogs. Typically these other dogs may not have been part of that particular dogs social group. However, this is a generalisation and individual cases can result in dogs that do not necessarily fit that mould. It is therefore possible that dominance, possessiveness and aggression can occur with any individual dog within a breed group.

Dominance/Status

In most cases a dog will be a member of a number of social groups. A first group will no doubt include humans within the immediate family and then a wider circle of friends and neighbours. A second group may possibly include other dogs living in the household.

A hierarchy or pecking order will typically occur when two or more dogs share the same household. A puppy will probably be submissive or subordinate to an adult. However, once the puppy matures and gains strength the status can easily change. Two or more adults may live harmoniously without conflict, or a dominance, submissive 'game playing' may take place.

What is important in these situations is that we remain in control of any potential conflicts. Such conflicts can easily escalate into aggressive behavior which could be dangerous to the dogs as well as human family members.

Preventing the problem:

Preventing a competitive environment is important here. If it is possible to leave toys, gnarl bones lying around, have plenty spread over a wide area. This will avoid a central focus for one dog to guard and create a potential conflict.

Also become the controller of the resources. It will therefore be necessary to allow play time with toys. However, if confrontations occur, remove all of them until things have calmed down. The dogs should hopefully learn that the toys are a reward for good behavior and unacceptable behavior results in their removal.

The dogs as a group may well establish a 'pecking order' between themselves. However, it is important to not favour any in particular to prevent any jealousies occurring.

Teaching cooperation and group harmony:

Each dog should already be well experienced with the 'recall' and 'sit'
1. Call the dogs together and ask them for a 'sit' and 'stay' > Once they are all sat facing you, randomly and quickly give each one a piece of food.
2. Walk away > 'recall' them > ask for a 'sit' and 'stay' > once they all comply > give each a piece of food.
3. Repeat this several times and on a regular basis. If at any point they attempt to jostle, compete or show any aggression towards the other, ignore the behavior and walk away. Then repeat the steps until they harmoniously obey the command and patiently wait for each other to receive a food treat.

Try and keep them all together so that they work as a unit and see the benefit of each others company. This will teach the dog that cooperation will get a reward, competing with each other will not.

Dominance aggression

IMPORTANT: In severe aggressive cases it is important to consult with a professional behaviorist/trainer. Quite often the context of the situation can be too specific to make a general 'one solution fits all cases'.

Modification of mild cases would normally involve a variety of solutions. For example if any kind of handling elicits a growl, it would be necessary to gradually introduce the dog, probably giving treats to make the experience pleasant for the dog. If the dog attempts to guard or possess a particular toy, the couch, access to these should be denied.

This type of aggression occurs when, for example two dogs are in conflict for the control of a resource. It can also occur if a dogs perceived social status is challenged. As well as other dogs, this aggressive response can be directed towards humans. This is often more noticeable towards immediate family members rather than strangers. Dogs can challenge human members of the family, such as when the dog is asked to move from the couch.

In such cases it is important that the owner of the dog becomes the keeper or controller of the resources. It may be necessary to teach the dog to regularly give up or swap their toys or other objects the dog may wish to guard. The dog also needs to regularly comply with the basic control commands 'sit', 'come', 'stay', 'stop', 'heel', 'down' etc.

The aggression can range from subtle posturing, growling to full on biting. The occurrence of this type of behavior is usually from one year old as the dog starts to mature, but it can occur sooner. The behavior can occur with either sex whether neutered or not, but commonly occurs with un-neutered males.

Dominance and possessiveness

The extent to which a dog will react to an item he wishes to possess, depends on the value they place on the item. It can also depend on how the dog views the 'status' of the other dog or human, as to whether he will challenge them. In the same respect a dog may react depending on historical experiences of previous conflicts.

At its very basic level, food is seen as valuable in order to survive. But the same instinct to posses does not necessarily apply to all elements necessary for survival. Water is probably more important for their survival as they can survive without food much longer than water. However, dogs rarely if ever fight over water. But dogs can become obsessive about items such as toys, balls, nylon gnarl bones, a favourite bed, couch or other sleeping area etc.

If the dog feels one of their valuable resources is about to be taken away, they may threaten and possibly attack. You will typically see the dog stiffen, growl, snarl, bare their teeth, snap, bite etc.

Preventing the problem:

It is important to never use physical reprimands, shout or otherwise raise your voice, as it is likely to worsen the situation. For example, the dog may growl before you physically remove him from the sofa. However, next time the dog may have learned that growling does not work so they may snarl or snap.

It is easier to condition a puppy to relinquish or swap an item. Than it is for an adult. This is best approached by getting him used to early retrieves. That is, he willingly gives up an item in exchange for lots of praise or food.

Getting him off the sofa:

Teaching a dog to come away from a sofa is best achieved by encouraging him with food.

1. With a piece of food in your hand, place this to your dogs nose, but not allowing him to take it.
2. Now lure him by gradually pulling your hand away from his nose towards the floor. If he seems reluctant, try his favourite toy or other item. If he is particularly reluctant you could also try placing a piece of food on the sofa for him to take. Once he has taken this, place another piece on the floor, which hopefully he will jump down to take.
3. The moment he jumps down use the command word 'down'. You could use 'off' if 'down' confuses him, and he lies down on the sofa > give him lots of praise when he jumps down.

It may also be necessary to place an object on the sofa so that he cannot jump straight back on again.
4. Practice this as often as necessary, with food at first and then just using the 'down'/'off', and perhaps luring with your hand, but without food.

Once you have a controlled response from him, it is your choice whether you occasionally allow him back on the sofa. As long as you can easily get him off if you have to.

Getting him to give up an item (swapping):

This can be carried out a number of ways. Usually swapping is used to take an item off him, such as a shoe, and replace this with a toy or gnarl bone.

This is best approached by first of all having a toy, chew or gnarl bone to hand and a piece of food.

1. Offer the item (toy, gnarl bone) to him, which hopefully he will take, but keep hold of the item.
2. Now with the food in the other hand, present this to him and at the same time use the word 'leave' or 'give'.
3. As soon as the dog releases the item, give him the food and offer lots of praise.
4. Practice this a number of times so that the dog is conditioned to handing over items they are in possession of. Gradually phase out giving food and offer praise only.

Swapping an item the dog already has:

This assumes that the dog already has an item that he is playing with or chewing on.

1. Take another item, toy or gnarl bone in one hand and show this to him. He may immediately drop the item he has and take the item you are offering.
2. If not, as you show the toy, slowly move your hand towards the shoe or other item the dog has. Avoid

any sudden movements as this may encourage him to snap.
3. Gently take hold of the item and use the word 'leave' or 'give'. Hopefully he will let go of that and take the item you are offering. If not, try the previous exercise with food.

Regularly practice this exercise so that he gets used to relinquishing items and does not become possessive.

Possessiveness around food:

Be very careful with possession problems relating to food. You are advised to consult a professional behaviorist/trainer with any kind of aggressive response from the dog.

However, in mild cases you can try the following:

A similar exercise is described in the section on resource guarding.
1. At feeding time, take his food bowl with food and hold this high enough so the dog cannot take it, usually just above the dogs nose level.
2. Take a few pieces of food from the bowl and offer this to him. Be careful that he doesn't snatch. Now take the bowl away from his nose, possibly standing up for a few seconds.
3. Return the bowl to him but place this at his nose level, again so that he cannot immediately help himself. Once again offer a few pieces then take it away for a few seconds.
4. Now return the bowl to him, but just below his nose level. Do not allow him to help himself, but feed a few pieces as before, them remove the bowl for a few seconds.
5. Continue repeating this in 3 to 6 inch increments, gradually getting lower to the ground. Eventually you should be able to place the bowl on the ground.

By this point your dog should be conditioned to accepting you as part of his feeding, and not wish to possess or guard the food.

You can also practice adding pieces of meat as the dog is eating. They will therefore be further encouraged that your visit has a positive outcome.

You should be cautious about proceeding like this with an adult, possibly rescue dog. It is often useful to practice feeding the dog on neutral ground where he would not normally be fed. This can be your yard or garden. Do not place all of his food in his bowl, but spread or scatter this around the yard or garden. For the purposes of this exercise it is advisable to use a basic dry kibble food.

As the dog is eating, approach him and offer pieces of cooked meat. Again the idea is that he gets used to your presence as part of feeding. Also with the food spread out, he does not have a single focus point to guard, which he would have with a food bowl.

Practice this each day during feeding times, until he is relaxed with your presence. Gradually scatter the food in a smaller area until you can place it in a small pile. You should then be able to put the entire meal in his bowl.

If you have two dogs that resource guard, quite often the most straightforward solution is to feed them separately, perhaps in separate rooms.

j) Escaping and Roaming

Escaping can take the form of digging under the boundary fence, or attempting to jump or climb over.

It is an offence in certain countries to let a dog roam the streets. In such cases a dog must be kept on a lead in designated areas, but in particular on public highways where dogs could be a hazard to motorists. But some owners still allow their dogs to roam the streets, harassing people or other animals.

Once again, this can occur simply because the dog is; under exercised, under stimulated and generally bored. It also relates to his innate desire to investigate and explore his surrounding area. It generally involves him wishing to be free from the confinement of his immediate, less stimulating surroundings. A

Cockapoo Behavior Problems

common reason why dogs escape and roam also occurs when a bitch is in season. A dog will instinctively wish to escape and pursue a bitch in season. But bitches are also known to escape for the same reason, in order to fulfil an instinctive urge to mate.

Preventing the problem:

In the first instance the fence should be at least 6ft to 8ft high. It may also be necessary to modify the base, by placing paving slabs around the perimeter to prevent him from immediately digging under the fence. In extreme cases you could also try digging a trench of approximately 1 to 2ft deep and sinking a wire mesh or similar barrier. In other words, even if he attempts to dig out he will be prevented by the barrier.

k) Fussy/picky eaters

If your adult or puppy seems off their food for no apparent reason, you should consult with your vet. The vet can then diagnose whether or not there is a medical reason for this.

However, if the puppy does not appear ill, it is worth noting that a major reason for this problem, is 'over feeding' the dog or puppy. Most dogs will eat as much daily nutrients and calories as his body needs, then stop. If you continue presenting him with more than he needs, this may then result in him, either showing a disinterest or picking and choosing what he eats, or attempting to bury or hide food.

If you are having problems with your puppies picky eating, consider the following:

» At 8 weeks of age, a puppy can be fed 3 meals per day. Unless of course the breeder has fed perhaps 4 times per day with a specific diet. In which case, you need to stick to that for a few weeks then aim to reduce this to 3 per day.

» At 12 weeks old a puppy can realistically be fed twice per day. At 4 months of age, this can further be reduced to a single meal per day. Although many dog owners prefer to feed two meals.

» You should however, proceed with caution. The puppy is still growing and underfeeding can be as detrimental as overfeeding, potentially causing problems of stunted growth through malnutrition etc.

Basically feeding is simply a matter of providing the correct amount per day, divided by the number of meals per day.

With the correct amount in his food bowl, place this down on the floor for him to start eating. If he does not finish it, then leave it with him for approximately 10 minutes. After which time, take this away, refrigerate if necessary and provide this next time. Have to hand his full ration for next time, but be prepared to let him finish the food he previously left. You can then add half of the new ration, again if he finishes this, add the rest. Make sure you are providing enough for his current weight.

A mistake some people make is to tempt the dog with a different food. Again, if your dog generally has a healthy appetite and suddenly stops eating for no apparent reason for a couple of days, you can assume there is a problem and you should consult with a vet.

Feeding can be a bit of a juggling act based on a number of variables including: metabolic rate; activity level; the richness of the food etc. Unless you make a scientific analysis of these variables each day you are unlikely to get it exactly right each time. It is therefore easier to take into consideration what he normally eats, then expect him to want slightly more or less each time.

l) Gluttony

Some dogs will happily leave food when they are full and not return to eat until they feel hungry again. However, a gluttonous dog, will tend to gorge themselves regardless. Gluttony can be a similar condition to scavenging, if a dog has been conditioned to never know when their next meal is coming from, it can become mentally ingrained to eat as much as possible, whenever possible.

If your dog is given palatable food that he particularly likes, he will perhaps eat more than he needs if an unlimited supply is presented to him. This in turn can easily lead to obesity, if he is not burning off those extra calories through exercise or other activities. This is why it is important to match his intake with his ideal weight, factoring in his activity level. Obesity is a serious problem in terms of shortening a dogs life and potentially causing illnesses such as heart disease, diabetes and even cancer.

With some dogs, even though they may be obese, begging and gluttony can be habit forming. However, if a dog looks underweight, it will be necessary to rule out a possible medical problem such as a parasite infestation, before drawing any conclusions. It will also be necessary to confirm the nutritional value of the food and determine whether or not the dog may be suffering a nutritional deficiency.

Increased appetite can be caused by any one of a number of physiological conditions including: Cushing's disease, hyperthyroidism, diabetes, intestinal worms, an overgrowth of bacteria etc. Ultimately many of these conditions lead to an inefficiency in digesting food or absorbing nutrients.

Research has also taken place, leading scientists to believe that there is a genetic connection, (a gene known as POMC), with appetite and obesity in certain breeds such as the Labrador.

Preventing the problem:

You may wish to consult with your vet or a canine nutritionist to establish what calories and dietary needs your dog needs every day.

Stick to a feeding schedule including the same diet, in the correct quantity. Also feed at the same times per day, so that your dog gets used to only eating at certain times. In addition, get into the habit allowing him time to eat, but as soon as he walks away, leave the dish down 5 or 10 minutes, then take it away until the next day.

Do not be tempted to chop and change foods or tempt him with treats all of the time, unless of course he earns them. Also remember that it is important to cut down and phase out food treats, beyond initial training.

If the reason is psychological, it may be because something has changed in the household, initiating an anxious response. This could include a new dog, which perhaps makes him eat more, particularly if he feels his food resource is threatened.

If there have been no obvious changes in the household recently, then the most likely cause of your dog's increased hunger is a physical problem. This may also be the case if there have been changes, but the methods above show no results after a week or two.

M) HOWLING

Some dogs howl for a variety of reasons such as when hearing sirens or perhaps as part of being left home alone.

Although it is common for Wolves to howl, it is less common in dogs. It is commonly thought Wolves howl in order to resume contact when separated from other members of the pack. The reason dogs howl is not as clear cut, however it can occur when they are isolated. There does seem to be a connection with separation anxiety. But again, howling often occurs if the dog hears an unusual sound. In some cases sound frequencies not apparent to humans can trigger howling.

There isn't a great deal you can do if your dog suddenly starts howling at passing fire engines or ambulances. However, if you are present then the easiest solution is to interrupt the howling by calling your dog or issuing a 'no' or 'ah ah'. Please see the section on separation anxiety if you suspect this may be a symptom once you leave the house.

N) Hypersexual

This generally involves some sort of sexual behavior such as mounting. The behavior is often seen in dominant male dogs, but bitches to a certain extent are also known to mount other dogs. Intact females in season can often demonstrate mounting, and be mounted by other females. Obviously the pheromone which bitches give off when in season will play havoc with males.

Mounting of humans often occurs if a dog is an only dog within the family. Neutering does not necessarily correct this behavior as established mounting behavior can become a habit, rather than hormonal.

Preventing the problem:

It is advisable to keep dogs away from bitches in season. However, this is not always possible as the scent can carry and cause problems with howling, escaping, loss of appetite etc.

The action of mounting is similar to jumping up. It is therefore advisable to use the solution to the jumping up problem. It is also advisable to anticipate mounting and use commands such as 'sit', 'down', 'stay' etc.

If the dog should attempt to mount you or someone else, again use the control commands of 'sit', 'down', 'stay' etc. You can also simply turn or walk away.

As always, the unwanted behavior should be ignored. Similarly the dog should be praised when they stop the unwanted behavior and comply with one of the commands.

Diversion tactics are also useful, such as engaging the dog in a trick, game or retrieve.

It is also important that the scent of a bitch in season, does not find its way into your house or on your clothes. Disinfect household areas and wash clothes if this is the case.

Destruction of furnishings and other items can often relate to these items having scents on them. However, this could also relate to the dogs frustration due to boredom and lack of exercise and attention. Getting angry with the dog when this happens is not the answer. This actually gives the dog attention for the wrong reasons, as they are likely to repeat the destructive behavior in order to get the attention they crave.

O) Hyperactive; Overly enthusiastic; excitable

Excitable behavior is often evident when you are about to go on a walk. The dog begins to bark excitedly, spin in circles, rush back and forth etc.

Preventing the problem:

Quite often, high energy, easily bored breeds display this type of behavior. So first and foremost, enough exercise and mental stimulation is a necessary requirement.

Socialisation is vital as it is necessary to desensitise the dog from triggers that he is unfamiliar with and likely to overly stimulate him.

As you can imagine, any stimulating game is also likely to trigger excitability. Games of tug or teasing fetch games etc, can also easily trigger excitability.

It may be necessary to remain relaxed and calm when interacting with him. Also control commands such as 'sit', 'stay', 'stop' etc are important to pacify him if things start to get out of hand.

However, be aware that any kind of restless behavior may also be due to pain or discomfort. In this case you should not hesitate in getting him checked out with your vet.

P) Jumping up

The first thing to note is that jumping up is something we humans inadvertently teach and encourage a puppy to do. This occurs in the early days of bonding and playing with a small puppy. As the puppy grows in size and strength the puppy obviously continues the behavior. It also becomes an appropriate (to the dog) means of greeting you after an absence. It is also their way of expressing how happy and excited they are at the prospect of being fed or going for a walk. Children quite often trigger and encourage this excitability with their actions.

When your Cockapoo is a cute and cuddly puppy it can be tempting to reward him with pets and cuddles when he crawls into your lap or jumps up at your legs. When your Cockapoo grows up, he expects you to react in the same way to this behavior because you have reinforced it.

Preventing the problem:

Don't be tempted to push the dog away as this just becomes a good game for the dog. Pushing the dog away also becomes a means of getting attention. Cruel, physical deterrents should also be avoided at all costs. In the past, techniques were used such as kneeing or punching the dogs chest; hitting their nose; squeezing the front paws; standing on their feet; squirting water at them etc. The dog would also invariably be shouted at.

Quite often when a dog jumps up, many people instinctively hold out their hands to stop the dog. The best approach is to get into the habit of turning your back, the moment he jumps up. He may try again, but will soon realise, the only way you acknowledge him is when he greets you without jumping up.

With this in mind it is better to prevent this, or teach this not to occur when your dog is still a young puppy. Of course for someone acquiring an older dog, this is never possible.

For a young puppy it is simply a matter of ignoring the jumping behavior and obviously not encouraging it.

Teaching the 'sit', 'stand', 'down' and 'stay' as soon as possible, teaches the puppy the correct, well behaved manner of greeting you. By asking for these commands you can then legitimately give him a treat as a reward.

However, very early conditioning can be achieved by pre-empting your puppy approaching you. Before he gets chance to jump up, have a treat in your hand and hold this to his nose as he gets close enough. This will act as a focus, so be careful not to raise your hand, encouraging him to jump up. Once you get him to remain calm and not jumping up, you can then give him the treat.

If jumping up at doors is a problem, it may be necessary to have an internal baby gate or similar barrier to discourage him from immediately jumping at the door.

Jumping up on other people:

To teach your Cockapoo not to jump up on other people, you may need to enlist the help of a friend.

1. Have your friend stand outside the front door to your house and get them to ring the doorbell. This should get your Cockapoo excited.
2. After ringing the doorbell, have your friend enter the house. When your Cockapoo jumps up, your friend should place their hands behind their back and ignore the dog for a few seconds before turning around and leaving again.
3. After a few repetitions of this, have your friend give your Cockapoo the 'Sit' command. If he complies, allow your friend to calmly pet the dog for a few seconds before leaving again.

Repeat this sequence several times until your Cockapoo remains calm when the doorbell rings. It may take quite a few repetitions to recondition your dog against jumping up, but with consistency you can make it happen.

Q) MOUTHING

Mouthing is a common means by which puppies explore their environment. It is part of the rough and tumble of play. However, it becomes a problem if the puppy plays a little too rough and the mouthing turns into a nip or a bite. Pups learn bite inhibition from the mother and litter-mates when they mouth a little too keenly and consequently gets reprimanded. It is also important that human play interaction can unwittingly encourage the same mouthing problem.

The problem is worse if the puppy becomes the adult who has not learned bite inhibition. As you can imagine, the adult dog is a lot stronger and capable of inflicting serious damage. Play mouthing can easily lead to aggressive biting. You should consult a qualified professional canine behaviorist if you suspect any kind of aggression problem.

In less serious cases you can manage this by not engaging or encouraging the dog if he starts chewing your hand fingers and generally play mouthing.

Preventing the problem:

As with other problems that need a verbal correction, you can simply raise your voice and give a sharp 'ah ah', 'No' or 'ouch'. Do not be tempted to tap the dog on the nose or use any other physical reprimand.

Ignoring the behavior is also advised. You simply disengage from the play, stand up and either turn away or walk away. If he is persistent and follows you, it may be necessary to leave the room, and perhaps employ a baby gate so that he can see you, but cannot physically touch you. If he starts to bark or whine, again do not give into this until he stops, when you can re-engage with him.

It is also useful to practice swapping, that is substituting your hand for one of his toys.

Basic obedience commands of 'sit', 'leave' 'stay' etc also calm things down. These should as always be rewarded so that he learns to differentiate between when he gets rewarded for good behavior, a 'sit' and ignored for unacceptable behavior, you ignoring him, or verbally letting him know it is not acceptable.

Also use these simple procedures if he mouths your feet or legs.

Engaging in play activities is a very important aspect of bonding, so it is not advisable to stop engaging with him. But he needs to be able to play in a gentle manner and remain well behaved by applying the previous techniques or similar ones.

r) Neurotic and aggressive

A common reason for neurotic behavior again relates to general boredom, lack of exercise, lack of mental stimulation etc.

Neurotic behaviors can include: being preoccupied with imaginary objects; compulsive, excessive barking for no obvious reason; obsessive pacing of boundaries; pica (eating and swallowing non food objects); chasing his tail; constant licking and chewing of body parts (self mutilation); destruction; aggression.

Preventing the problem:

If there is a boredom issue due to lack of exercise etc, you should deal with this regardless (see the section on boredom). Quite often dogs in prolonged confinement have to make work for themselves such as pacing of whirling, tail chasing.

However, it is also important to consult with your vet to rule out any medical reason as to why the behavior may be occurring. This could be a brain injury, brain tumour, genetic, food sensitivity, a chemical imbalance such as endocrine etc.

s) Overprotective

This is a form of aggressive behavior relating to the dogs perceived territory. It can involve the dog being hostile to guests and other visitors to your house, leaving the owner concerned about a potential dog bite or attack.

It is also a leadership issue, which means that the dog may feel the need to take charge of a situation, if he does not feel that you are there to take charge. Dogs like to feel safe and secure in their environment and rely on a leader to provide this. It is therefore up to us humans to be in charge.

Some dogs can be clever at manipulating their owner. You will typically see this when the dog barks for you to open a door, get out of bed to let him out in the morning (unless of course he is generally desperate to relieve himself), stroke him etc. You will also typically find that he will obey you if and when he feels like it. Under these circumstances he may perceive himself as being in charge, the leader.

Preventing the problem:

A good place to start in order to avoid this, is to routinely issue basic commands.

You should also only reward him when you have asked for a particular command. This will mean that if he initiates a sit or performs any other taught command, he should not be rewarded. Again YOU have not asked for it. It is therefore necessary to ignore this unwanted manipulative behavior, otherwise you will be reinforcing him leading you into giving him a reward.

You also need to be aware of what triggers him into taking charge. This can be if someone knocks at the door or rings the doorbell; he hears your front gate open, or a visitor walk down your pathway.

Preferably you need to act as soon as you hear one of the triggers. You ideally want to avoid him reacting by jumping up or starting to bark, otherwise it will be difficult to stop him as it quickly escalates into a barking frenzy. You therefore need to redirect this, take charge and get him to 'sit', 'come', 'stay', 'wait' or whatever. You could also try redirecting the behavior at this point, by engaging him in a game of fetch or throwing one of his toys.

Be aware that overprotective dogs can often favour a particular member of the family who perhaps gives the dog a lot more attention. This can then lead the dog to be protective of that person. It is therefore very important that in order to avoid any conflicts, all family members should take a relatively equal role in handling the dog. This will entail each family member being involved in training and issuing him with basic obedience commands in order to earn praise or treats.

It is also worth noting, that dogs who display aggressive tendencies such as snarling or growling, often react positively (tail wagging, relaxed etc) when you react in a humorous way towards him. This can involve laughing, or generally behaving in a lighthearted, jovial manner towards him, similar to how you might talk to a baby. Physical punishments and threats will only promote an aggressive response from the dog. Only positive reinforcements (non physical) methods should ever be used.

Caution: In serious cases of aggression, or if you are in any doubt about the seriousness of a case, you are advised to consult with a professional behaviorist/trainer.

T) PICA

Pica is a condition whereby a dog craves and ingests non-food objects. The condition may relate to an underlying medical cause or a behavioral issue. If diagnosis relates to a medical issue then it is a simple matter of treating the medical cause. If a behavioral problem is indicated, it may be necessary to modify the dogs' behavior.

Symptoms

Items that the dog may eat, is not limited and can include soil, rocks, plastic, rubber, chemicals such as soap etc. The gastrointestinal tract is principally affected, should an item be swallowed, beyond chewing. Symptoms largely depend upon the substance. If this is relatively toxic there may be a general lethargic, weakened state. Other symptoms may include vomiting, diarrhoea etc.

Causes

Again, pica can be caused by either a behavioral issue, or any of a number of medical conditions.

Medical issues can include: neurological, thyroid, bowel disease, parasites of the intestine, anaemia, malnutrition, hunger, a vitamin deficiency.

Overfeeding and underfeeding can also be a reason. The diet in all cases should produce firm stools and certainly not loose or soft. If not, the diet may be at fault and will need changing.

Diagnosis

Initial investigations by your vet will establish whether there is a behavioral or medical reason. In addition to a physical examination it will be necessary to provide information about the dogs environment, diet, appetite etc. The vet will of course treat an underlying medical issue. They should also

Cockapoo Behavior Problems

be able to advise you of your best course of action, if pica occurs because of a behavioral condition.

u) Pulling on the lead

Leash pulling or straining should never be a problem if you have followed the basic obedience techniques of 'heel', 'recall' and 'stop'.

Without this control, a dog will resort to its instinctive desire to sniff, scent mark, hunt, chase etc. The problem arises when we attach a lead and expect a dog to do the preceding at our pace, not theirs. We are unlikely to be able to go fast enough for the dog.

Once we lose control of the dog, it becomes a problem taking them out in public. This in turn leads to the dog not having a sufficient outlet to burn off pent up energy, because it is not getting sufficient exercise. The dog is largely kept indoors or the yard, boredom sets in, destructive behavior ensues and a whole vicious circle can occur.

As heeling is best taught off lead as well as on, what we often find is that the dog responds much better if he feels he is not restrained by a short leash. In public areas therefore it is beneficial to utilise a long training leash of about 5 to 10 meters. You can then allow him the freedom he desires. It also allows you plenty of time to practice recalling him if he decides to take off.

v) Resource guarding, objects, people and places

Again the thing to realise here is that guarding food is a natural survival instinct for all dogs. However, it can be a potentially serious problem if the dog snaps at or bites anyone coming too close.

Resource guarding is something that any dog can develop, but it is usually as a result of a past learning experience. A dog that has been truly hungry for instance is likely to develop resource guarding of food which may settle when the dog feels secure.

When a dog is scared of losing a resource he may be reactive to anyone who approaches the resource. He may growl or even bite. To then approach the dog and focus on the resource, is doing nothing more than intensifying the fear. Therefore, the dog is likely to be more aggressive, not less.

When resource guarding is based on fear, confrontation is the last thing that will end the behavior. Fear aggression is actually a major reason for a dog to bite.

Preventing a problem:

A puppy is easy to condition or train to accept us near the food bowl. Unfortunately an adult, possibly rescue dog will be more difficult to cure.

An adult dog:

If you have an adult rescue dog and this is a problem, you are advised to consult with a dog trainer/behaviorist. In relatively safe cases, it is possible to condition him to you being associated with feeding. This is easily done by scattering some pieces of kibble in an approximate 6 feet circle. By doing this you are diffusing the focal point of a food dish to a much wider area. You should next proceed with caution. As he is eating, walk into this area and drop small pieces of a favourite food, cooked meat or cheese etc. It is important to condition him to your presence like this, so don't get too close at first.

It is then a question of repeating this on a regular basis, at the same time reduce the area you scatter the food. Eventually you will be able to simply place the food in the bowl, whilst you are close by. Again, never take anything for granted.

It may also be necessary to change his normal feeding location, perhaps to a part of your yard or garden. This will be important if he is associating a particular room with feeding.

A puppy

A puppy however, can be taught from day one to accept you feeding him from the bowl.

It is a simple matter of feeding him from the dog bowl.

Once he is used to this, place a bowl of dry kibble down, then allow the dog to eat.

Now with some small pieces of cooked meat, start to periodically drop these in whilst he is eating. This should indicate to the puppy that you are providing him with something even better. He will therefore welcome you around the food bowl. Remember to offer lots of praise and encouragement.

w) SCAVENGING FOR FOOD

Scavenging and stealing food are similar problems. This is relative to opportunism, which is a natural trait all dogs are capable of. The dog may scent something edible on an off lead run, or he may raid a garbage bin that he believes contains something edible.

Preventing the problem:

For off lead opportunism, you will have to rely on a good 'stop' and 'recall', or get to him as soon as you can. Around the house it will be necessary to purchase child or dog proof bins that are lockable or not easily opened.

You will also have no doubt taught your dog the 'leave' command or a variation of it. You can therefore put this to good use in all situations where you catch him in the act.

x) STEALING FOOD

Once again, the simple fact of the matter is that dogs are opportunists who instinctively take whatever is presented to them. What we may call theft, is a survival mechanism to the dog. If a dog is hungry, he will not be concerned about morality, right and wrong, guilt or remorse.

Preventing the problem:

As with many problem behaviors, it is a question of pre-empting the dogs likelihood to take the opportunity that is presented. So in the same way that you should not leave items lying around for the dog to find and chew, you should not leave food within reaching distance.

y) SEPARATION ANXIETY

The strong bonding and desire to please people is an overriding reason the Sporting/Gundog types have been so successful in the field and family home. This lack of independence and the desire to be with you most of the time however can cause a number of problems such as separation anxiety. The dog can become needy to the extent that he looks for attention for example by following family members around the house. For this reason a Sporting/Gundog is not an ideal choice for families who are away from home for large parts of the day or do not have alternatives such as pet sitters/walkers.

Separation anxiety typically occurs when a dog fears being alone to the point of becoming severely stressed or distressed.

It is currently thought to be for one of an unknown number of reasons. There are two types of separation anxiety, amid other undefined reasons for the disorder. These are fear of unexpected noises or over attachment to the owner.

It is often suggested that two dogs will provide a good human substitute and alleviate the problem of separation anxiety. However, it is debatable, and some would argue that there is no evidence that two dogs together will still not suffer separation anxiety. Having said that, dogs do become attached to each other and when separated, display signs of distress such as pining, howling, whining etc. So I would say that two dogs together do add mutual comfort to a certain extent. But two or more dogs can still display a type of anxiety which seems to be linked specifically with the absence of human presence from the home. As every dog is an individual, so is their experience when suffering from separation anxiety.

Some suffer greatly and become destructive to themselves and their surroundings. Others simply become sad and depressed when left alone. They leave no trace of the stress, thus leaving owners unaware that anxiety occurred at all during the dog's alone time.

The actual anxiety becomes a phobia and can become so severe that the dog develops serious stress related behaviors causing poor health, self-harm and obsessive worrying about being left alone.

Preventing the problem:

To prevent separation anxiety in your own dog you have a number of options. The best one, if you are leaving your dog regularly, is to employ a willing neighbour or relative to periodically check in on your dog. Alternatively, consider employing a doggy day caretaker or similar canine professional. This usually takes the form of a canine crèche area or similar and is wonderful for meeting the dog's mental and physical needs alongside ensuring the dog is not alone regularly for long periods of time.

A dog walker is the minimum provision that a full time, at home dog, should have when everyone is out at work all day.

Once again, the other possibility here is having two dogs. Companionship can make all the difference, whereby the dogs keep each other company and entertained. However, this doesn't always work and some dogs can still become overwhelmed with separation anxiety, resulting in the aforementioned negative behaviors.

If separation anxiety becomes a real problem, a local dog behaviorist may be the answer. They can observe your dog and create a modification program to try and alleviate his stressed reaction to being alone. This can work really well when carried out carefully.

z) Soiling in the house

As long as the recommendations in the chapter on toilet training have been applied, you should not experience further problems.

However, problems can and do occur even after successful toilet training. If a problem does occur at any time it is first of all necessary to establish whether this is due to a behavioral or physical problem. Usually if an adult suddenly starts soiling in the house, there would generally be a physical cause, such as cancer or urinary infection, bladder stone, hormones etc. The problem may also relate to a problem with diarrhoea, possibly due to food poisoning or a bacterial/viral intestine infection. In all cases it would require a consultation with a vet to diagnose the possible condition and medically treat the problem.

If you have acquired an adult, possibly rescue dog, you may experience soiling in the house simply because the dog has not been taught otherwise. If this is the case it will require that you start from the beginning of the chapter on toilet training him as if he were a puppy.

Submissive urination

As the name suggests, the dog will lie on his side and literally wet (pee) himself. In some cases the dog may defecate or empty the anal glands. This is a fear response designed to prevent aggression or to give in to the perceived dominance of another dog, or in some cases a person. This can typically occur if the dog has been harshly treated during training or otherwise. It is therefore common in rescue dogs. It can become a habitual trigger to defuse an anticipated attack. It is a typical response of timid, shy, anxious sensitive breeds.

Preventing the problem:

Harsh punishment based methods should never be used.

It is important to treat any urination the same as any other toilet accident by not acknowledging it and simply cleaning the mess up.

We may wish to reassure a dog who is acting submissively by patting them. However, it is advisable to refrain from this as the dog can easily view this as a dominant, aggressive act on your part. Similarly avoid standing or looming over the dog as again this can be perceived as a threat. It is therefore better to crouch down, approach him sideways on and avoid eye contact, when moving towards him.

Be aware of the dog displaying avoidance behavior such as cowering, and be careful not to inadvertently acknowledge this. The 'recall' command is a very useful technique in this respect as it requires that the dog is encouraged to come back to you, resulting in a food reward and lots of praise. Other basic commands will also build his confidence as you reward and praise him.

It may also be necessary to involve other family members or friends if other people evoke a submissive response.

Early socialisation is very important to prevent this problem. The dog should therefore be exposed to many positive experiences in order to build his confidence.

Excitement based urination:

Initial greeting can also initiate urination due to excitement. This usually occurs if the adult or puppy is expected to spend prolonged periods of time on their own. They then become excited when you return and in some, not all cases, urinate in the process.

In such cases you may have to ignore the puppy, not engaging with him for a few minutes. This will allow him to calm down in his own time and negate his need to urinate.

You can also train him to greet you with greater control using a few pieces of food.

If your front door is your first point of contact with the puppy, upon returning, have to hand a couple of pieces of food.

1. As you open the door, as soon as the puppy jumps up or rushes over, make sure that the first thing the puppy greets is your hand with the food in it.
2. Hold this to his nose and ask for a 'sit' or 'stand' to establish control. If he at any point urinates then do not acknowledge this, and certainly do not give him the food treat.
3. Simply step back > then come forward again with the treat to his nose > ask for the 'sit' or 'stand'. Once again provided he does not urinate, give him the treat and offer lots of praise.

Practice like this until he greets you each time without urinating. You can then ask for a 'sit' or 'stand' as soon as you greet him each day.

Tips to help the situation:

» His overexcitement will diminish if he has regular contact throughout the day. So if you are away for extended periods, arrange for someone to visit every hour or so.

» Ensure that he gets regular walks, safe off lead runs and play time each day.

» Do not encourage the puppy if he is already excited. It is best to remain calm and still until he calms down. Touching or stroking him is also likely to excite him more.

» As with any toilet accident, do not make a fuss or get angry, and certainly do not physically punish him. Simply clean up the mess and things will soon settle down.

Fears and Phobias

Whether they have lived in a safe home since puppy-hood, or were raised in a different environment, any dog can develop fear behaviors. Fireworks, thunder, travel, other animals and people are some examples of why your dog can become afraid.

A dog that is fearful has a very distinct body language. He will tuck his tail below his hind quarters and cower. He may try to leave the situation and look away from the frightening stimulus. It is vital that a scared dog is never cornered.

A scared or worried dog will often display calming signals. Some calming signals include yawning; a stressed dog will yawn frequently.

The yawning response is often mistaken for tiredness by an uninformed human. However, once you know what to look for, it is easily recognisable. Licking his lips; a calming signal and stress response, can take the form of a single nose lick or more. Sniffing the ground is a 'leave me alone, I am invisible' plea.

Your job as the owner of a fearful dog is to neither ignore nor encourage the fear. Be aware of the situations in which your dog feels threatened and gently build him up by gradually exposing him to the trigger and desensitising him. Introduce new and worrying situations gradually, and amalgamate them with rewards such as playing with a toy or receiving a treat for relaxed behavior.

A very important point is to never over sympathise with your dog as this can reinforce the fear. If he gets too much attention when he is afraid, he will either repeat the behavior for the attention, or even worse think that the stimulus is a threat which you too recognise. If he sees that the stimulus doesn't concern you, then your dog will learn that it shouldn't concern him either.

A scared dog should never be cornered or forced to accept attention. If he is, then he will become more scared, growl and possibly even snap. It is better to help him relax around people without them paying him any attention, than to push him into a negative reaction.

If the fear has an environmental cause, for instance fireworks, then it is worth trying a natural remedy to appease your dog's fear. Rescue remedy which can be bought in most chemists/drug stores, is suitable for short-term treatment of a worried dog. Your vet may also be able to suggest something to get your dog through difficult times such as on bonfire night or New Year's Eve, when there are a lot of fireworks.

Chapter Ten:

Week by Week Puppy development & care guide: 8 weeks old to 1 year and beyond

This chapter intends to summarise and show you week by week what you can expect in the general caring of your Cockapoo.

Learning and development stages

The general behaviour of any puppy in the very early stages of development, focuses on them learning through play and interaction. Additionally behaviour intended to gain attention, cleaning, grooming, nutrition and warmth etc, initially from the mother via yelping, whining, nuzzling etc. With the exception of a few involuntary movements, they are mostly reacting to a stimulus that makes them uncomfortable or restless.

Three weeks of age until approximately 12 weeks of age is the most impressionable stage when a puppy forms lasting impressions of its environment including people and other dogs. Reputable breeders recognise this period as essential in terms of socialisation. Conversely puppy farms disregard the importance of this, confining the mother and puppies in cramped spaces or cages. Consequently the puppies never receive the socialisation and the opportunity to form relationships which is essential to avoid the risk of starting life with fear related and other behaviour problems. Many behaviourists assert that such dogs although improving significantly once they are able to live with a loving family in an optimum social environment, never fully lose the handicap of a lack of early socialisation. It cannot be said often enough, early socialisation must involve many and varied experiences with lots of different dogs, people of all ages, animate and inanimate objects etc.

The juvenile period ranges from twelve weeks to six months whereby previously learned behaviours become more fixed. The juvenile period is arguably an optimum stage whereby good behaviour can be encouraged and undesirable behaviour can be changed. After the juvenile period, the dog progresses to adulthood where behavioural changes become more difficult.

Puppy life stages

Birth to 2 weeks (neonatal)

At this stage the puppies are completely dependent on the mother for food, warmth, protection, safety, care, hygiene, grooming etc. They can feel, taste, suckle and nuzzle but their ability to regulate their own temperature, to hear or see are not developed. They will learn to cope with mild stresses such as when the mother temporarily leaves them alone and exposed to lower temperatures. It is also beneficial to introduce them to human contact by regular handling.

2 to 4 weeks (Transitional period)

At this point their senses develop with eyes and ears opening and they begin to respond to the consequent external stimuli of light and movement. Awareness of their mother, litter mates, human contact and general environment becomes stronger. Their physicality and motor skills develop and strengthen as well as the mother initiating weaning with her regurgitating food for them to eat. They begin to explore, play, interact, learn and remember via interaction with their mother and litter mates. This is one of a number of vital periods that must be experienced with the mother and litter mates. The breeder should be introducing them to new stimuli such as new scents, playing surfaces, obstacles etc. The puppies should also be regularly handled, examined, massaged, stroked, groomed etc, through additional human contact.

4 to 16 weeks old (socialisation)

At 4 weeks and beyond all gundog types, will benefit from the introduction of loud, potentially disturbing noises which they would have to become accustomed to if hunting with gunshot. There is therefore no need to worry about accidental banging and clattering noises going on around them. At this stage puppies are ready for complex learning experiences with sufficiently developed senses. Learning about bite inhibition and compromising with their mother and litter mates will occur. It is very important that they are exposed to as much human contact as possible. It is usually recommended after their final vaccination shots that they start being introduced to the local environment. This will include short walks and runs, opportunities to retrieve objects, obstacles to climb, concrete steps etc,

Birth to maturity life-cycle

At Birth: The puppy is born deaf, blind and toothless, but with limited senses of taste, scent and touch, which allow the puppy to detect the mother and to suckle.

At 7 days: By approximately the end of the first week, the puppy will be spending most of its time sleeping. Approximately 10% will be spent suckling. The pup has very little limb strength and is relatively helpless. The mother carries out the ancestral throwback trait of licking the anus and genitals to stimulate defecation and urination. This act is considered a survival instinct against predators who would otherwise pick up the scent of a litter.

At 14 days: The front leg strength develops and whereas previously the puppy would only be able to crawl, they now begin to sit up. Between 7 and 10 days the eyes begin to open, but vision is limited. Approximately 10 to 15 days the puppy will be able to see. At around 14 days the ear canal opens and the puppy is able to hear. Also around this time, the first adult roundworms will be passed.

At 21 days: Strength and reflexes in the rear end at around 21 days, enable the puppy to stand and start moving about on all fours. The primary milk teeth generally appear between 14 and 21 days. At approximately 18 days the puppy will begin to make play movements and vocalise with barks/yelps. By 21 days they are able to urinate and defecate unaided.

At 28 days: At approximately 28 days they should have full vision, be playing with litter mates, be walking and running, be eating from a dish. The mother at this point spends less time with the puppies. She will however, be on hand to break up fights, console injured pups and correct excessive biting (bite inhibition). Weaning usually starts around 4 weeks and should be a gradual process over a couple of weeks, fully weaned by about 7 weeks.
http://pets.webmd.com/dogs/weaning-puppies-what-do

At 42 days: Development of coordination, balance, reflexes, strength and confidence will continue. As they gain confidence, they begin to explore more. At approximately 35 days the hearing will be more acute and they will be actively playing with toys. By about 40 days they will be playing more constructively, with mouth and paw skills developing.

At 56 days (7 to 8 week period): By now, the breeder should have socialised the puppy to a vast amount of household experiences and noises. This includes household appliances, exposure to children and different adults, regular handling, grooming etc. By 8 weeks the nervous system has matured, and with early socialisation and weaning completed, they are now able to go to new homes.

At 126 days (8 to 18 weeks): Voluntary control of defecation and urination will start around 10 to 12 weeks of age. This is important to note as success with toilet training will be possible, but any prolonged crate training before 12 weeks will be difficult to achieve. By 4 to 6 months of age however, they should have full voluntary control. Continuing with socialisation is very important from 8 weeks.

At 4 to 6 months: With correct adequate socialisation, having being completed previously, particularly during the 'critical period' (up to 16 weeks of age), the puppy will continue to grow in confidence and independence and be now testing his limits of permitted behaviour.

12 months: At one year old, the young dog is not physically or mentally mature. However, they are considered an adult in terms of height and sexual maturity. From this age they gradually gain muscle mass and so broaden out proportionally.

18 months to 2 years: During this time they become more emotionally mature

The following check list should ideally be consulted a week before your puppies arrival. It is then hoped to give you an action plan to follow for each day.

WEEK 1: (8 WEEKS OLD)

Important check list of things to do during the week:

» Make sure you have his food available and familiarise yourself with how much he needs per meal

» Work out the times you will feed him such as 7 – 8am, 11am - 12 noon, 3 – 4pm, and 7 – 8pm.

» Ensure his bed is in place and that you have his water bowl ready and filled with water. Again please remember to keep this topped up with fresh, clean water at all times.

- » Have news paper or puppy pads ready for his toilet training routine

- » Have scales ready to weigh him

- » Make sure he is eating his meals and check that his faeces look normal; reasonably solid, no runny diarrhoea or unusual discharge

- » Check whether he needs flea and worming treatment. Make a note on your calendar if you haven't already

- » Check the dates for his initial vaccination shots if these have not already been initiated by the breeder

- » Start brushing/combing him at least once or twice per week

- » Allow for some play time/exercise in the yard, garden or room in the house

The first day home

You should hopefully have prepared everything necessary for his arrival, so that you can simply and safely introduce him to his new home.

As soon as you arrive home, take the puppy into your back yard/garden and allow him to wander about and to hopefully do his toilet business. Give him at least 5 minutes or so, then pick him up and take him back inside the house.

Take him to his bed area and again allow him to explore, settle and sleep if he wants

Weighing the puppy. Although it is not vital, it is a good idea to start weighing your puppy as soon as you can, and keep a record of this. He will be naturally growing and this will be quite rapid initially. You will need to ensure that he is gaining weight on a weekly basis and contact your vet if you notice a lack a growth or any other abnormalities.

From day one and the first week you should simply allow the puppy the freedom to settle in and bond with the family. Most puppies will want to be with you and therefore follow you everywhere. It is a good idea to have his bed where ever you are likely to spend most of the day, assuming that you or someone else will be at home most of the day.

Your puppy should be fit and healthy when you pick him up, but keep an eye on him in case he suddenly develops an illness. Obviously if this is the case, contact your vet without delay. For peace of mind some dog owners prefer to make an appointment as soon as possible anyway to let the vet check them over.

Training

You should ideally familiarise yourself with the Initial Obedience Training chapter. Although you will be busy bonding with your puppy the first week, you should be getting him used to initial 'recall' and 'retrieve' etc.

Housebreaking routine

Consult the previous chapter on toilet training, but this will provide a general summary of what to expect.

Toilet training involves taking the puppy, or encouraging him outside as often as possible. This is usually after he has had a drink, eaten, having woken from a sleep, first thing in the morning, last thing at night and any time you notice him sniffing the ground, circling etc. In most cases however, it is necessary to build in a routine of taking him out up to every hour, but more usually every half hour. If he has a toilet accidents before the hour, reduce this to every half or three quarters of an hour. Remember to praise him and offer a treat every time he successfully does his toilet business outside in the yard/garden. Under no circumstance punish or shout at him for any accident inside the house. This will only frighten him and possibly induce a phobia relating to doing his toilet business. Ignore the accident, clean up the mess and be more vigilant next time.

Feeding

Puppies usually require their daily food intake split into four equal meals. It is best to keep to a regular routine morning, noon, tea time and early evening. Hopefully you have purchased the food recommended by the breeder, even if they provide a few days supply.

Fleas

Again you should have enquired with your vet as to the best flea treatment for your puppy. Unless the breeder has already administered flea treatment treat as soon as possible.

You should find that if you stick to a regular flea treatment you should be able to keep fleas under control. However at any other time be aware if you notice any of the following:

If you notice any obvious scratching, check the coat for fleas, bites, black specks which could be an indication of flea droppings.

Exercise at 8 weeks old

Obviously the puppy is still growing and his joints and bones will be vulnerable to injury or breakages. It is therefore important to restrict exercise, play time and general physical activity.

Socialisation

Unfamiliar surroundings

This initial period will be a big upheaval for a young puppy newly separated from his mother, litter mates and his old surroundings. Do not worry too much if he appears nervous or anxious. Simply give him lots of fuss and attention and again if he wants to hide in his crate or elsewhere don't worry as he is just attempting to cope with the situation. It is all perfectly natural and he will soon adjust and settle.

Important check list of things to do during the week:

» Remember to have his food available and how much he needs per meal

» Stick to the times you are intending to feed. Again for example 7 – 8am, 11am - 12 noon, 3 – 4pm, and 7 – 8pm.

» His bed will already be in place, but again please remember to keep his water bowl topped up with fresh, clean water at all times.

» Have news paper or puppy pads ready for his toilet training routine

» Have scales ready to weigh him

» Familiarise yourself with the procedure for giving him a health check and carry this out. A health check basically involves feeling and massaging his body checking for abnormal lumps etc. It also involves checking his back side for any discharges, similarly his eyes and nose. You will also need to check inside his mouth for bleeding gums or any other abnormality.

» Have his collar and leash to hand ready to introduce this as part of his leash walking

» Make sure he is eating his meals and check that his faeces look normal; reasonably solid, no runny diarrhoea or unusual discharge

» Remember to brush/comb him at least once or twice per week

» Allow for some play time/exercise in the yard, garden or room in the

WEEK 2: (9 WEEKS OLD)

house

You should notice by week two a much more happy confident puppy. His routine should remain much the same as week 1, feeding, toilet training etc.

Taking his weight

You will probably notice a change in his growth by the second week. Again weigh him on the first day of week two and write this down, making a comparison with day one of week one.

IMPORTANT: 8 to 16 weeks of age (the critical period)

Please refer back to the chapter on socialisation and his vaccinations.

Socialisation is very important during this period in order for him to develop into a happy, confident, un-fearful young dog. It is during this period that he should be introduced to as many experiences as possible. This should include different sights, sounds, smells, people and age groups, different animals, varied environments (quiet countryside, noisy pedestrian areas etc).

It is important to be with him at all times to offer lots of encouragement, praise and a treat, particularly if he reacts calmly and without fear.

There are no breed specific guarantees regarding whether they will act fearful, or confident and friendly. It is very much down to the individual.

Weekly routine health check

Similarly to weighing your puppy on a weekly basis, it is also a very good idea to get into the habit of giving them a check up yourself.

You are obviously looking for any signs of illness or abnormal swellings on the body.

Lightly stroke/massage each part of his body in turn starting around their head; look in his ears, eyes, nostrils; lift his lips and check his teeth and gums; check each leg, paws, pads; run your hands along their back, sides, tummy; finally check their tail, lifting this to check the anus and genitals.

Training

You should ideally have already familiarised yourself with the Initial Obedience Training chapter. As well as the collar and leash information you should start introducing him to early recall and retrieve around the house. There is also nothing to stop you introducing the basics of 'sit', 'down', 'stay' etc.

Introducing the collar and leash

In addition, check the chapter on Initial Obedience Training:

Some people introduce the collar and lead from week 1 at 8 weeks old. It is not vital, but it is advisable to start his introduction by week 2, 9 weeks of age. Most puppies react to a collar as it is uncomfortable when they are not used to it.

1. On a daily basis, put the collar on for short periods of time and allow him to wander around the house, yard or garden.
2. Ignore any protestations and after five or ten minutes remove the collar, enthusiastically praise him and offer a treat.
3. Repeat this a number of times throughout the day
4. Always try to be present as you do not want him getting snagged or caught on something, potentially choking him
5. Now attach a lead to the collar and let the puppy wander around, trailing the lead.
6. Move in opposite directions and call him to you with a 'this way', 'here' or 'come'. This is his first introduction to the 'recall'.
7. When he comes to you offer lots of praise and a treat.

Initial walk with leash

Following on from the previous, you now want to offer some sort of resistance. He will need to get used to walking on the lead when you take him for his walks.

1. As before with his collar and lead attached let him wander.
2. Recall him to you > when he comes back, say 'good boy' > and this time pick the lead up.
3. Let him try and wander but stand still without saying anything.
4. He is bound to try pulling away > Again stand firm and say 'this way' or 'here' > Do not try and pull him away, but wait for him to move towards you > when he does, say 'good boy' and then start walking away.
5. Hopefully he will follow and go as far as you can before he pulls back on the leash.
6. If he does, again stand firm saying 'this way' or 'here'.
7. Again when he comes to you, say 'good boy' and walk as far as you can.
8. Once you have done this several times offer lots of praise and a treat
9. Remove the leash and let him freely wander again

Socialisation and fear

There are bound to be noises, people, animals or other situations and objects that may cause some fear during his socialisation period. You should never punish, scold or attempt to correct his reaction. A useful tip is to anticipate a fear response and immediately distract the puppy by moving away and calling him to you, in other words distract him. Then immediately praise and reward with a treat. He will soon associate being rewarded with coming to you and not the fearful trigger.

During this socialisation it is important to let him freely explore your house, garden, yard and eventually beyond this. It is also important to stay close by to monitor his reactions and again keep him safe.

Other considerations

He needs to get into a routine of sleeping at set times

Don't forget to practice his Weekly routine health check

Make sure he is eating his meals and check that his faeces look normal; reasonably solid, no runny diarrhoea or unusual discharge

WEEK 3: (10 WEEKS OLD)

Important check list of things to do during the week:

» Remember his food routine from the previous weeks. Stick to the times as per previous weeks.

» Please remember to keep his water bowl topped up with fresh, clean water at all times.

» Have news paper or puppy pads ready for his toilet training routine.

» Have scales ready to weigh him and keep a record of the measurement.

» Remember to give him a health check.

» Continue his collar and leash training.

» Make sure he is eating his meals and check that his faeces look normal; reasonably solid, no runny diarrhoea or unusual discharge.

Chew toys should ideally be available from week 1. However, you may notice him becoming more troubled by teething at this time, so make sure he has plenty of suitable chew toys.

» Remember to brush/comb him at least once or twice per week.

» Allow for some play time/exercise in the yard, garden or room in the house.

Teething/chewing

You will hopefully have purchased a number of chew toys for your puppy before he arrived. The desire to chew can occur early on and indeed bite inhibition is something the mother and other litter mates will kerb whilst still part of the litter.

Similarly to an adult baby, teething can be troublesome for a young puppy. They will need to alleviate the pain and discomfort of teething by chewing on hard objects. In the absence of hard chew toys, the puppy will seek out alternatives such as shoes, furniture etc. You are therefore strongly advised to ensure the puppy has a number of chew toys for this purpose. However, be aware that even with a supply of chew toys they can become bored and generally do not discriminate when looking for things to chew. So if you wish to keep expensive shoes etc intact, make sure you keep these out of reach.

Bite inhibition

Although biting will have been discouraged in the litter this will not stop some puppies from playfully attempting to chew your hand. Bite inhibition should be discouraged from day one. It is therefore important to pull your hand away and vocalise with a firm 'No', to let the puppy know they should not do this. Do not be tempted to hit the puppy, not even a tap.

Energy

Again not unlike children, a puppy at this age will be full of energy and excitability. They have a tendency to madly rush about to the point of exhaustion, at which point they will wish to sleep until the next burst. During periods of excitement they can suddenly relieve themselves, so again be vigilant of this. If you notice him suddenly squat, don't shout but give a firm 'No', pick him up and take him into the yard/garden, allowing him to do his toilet business there.

Dominant behaviour

Around this time it is not uncommon for the puppy to start feeling his feet and gain in confidence. He may therefore show signs of dominance by barking, growling, snarling and other behaviour designed to get your attention. In this case it is best to simply ignore the behaviour and walk away. Don't be tempted to indulge him or otherwise acknowledge this.

Check list reminders

You will hopefully have been instructed from the breeder of any vaccinations or parasite treatments already carried out. It is advisable to write any vaccination or treatment dates on a wall calendar that you can quickly refer to and take the appropriate action.

Taking his weight

Don't forget to weigh him again on the first day of week three and again write this down, making a comparison with day one of week three.

WEEK 4: (11 WEEKS OLD)

Refer to the information to follow regarding his food routine. Basically you have been feeding 4 meals per day, now is a good time to reduce this to 3, but increase the amount for each portion.

The new feeding times will reflect the fact that he now has three meals spread throughout the day. So for example the first one can be between 7 and 8am, then between 1 and 2pm and a final meal between 7 and 8 pm. You may have to be flexible on those timings, depending on your availability and lifestyle. However, try and be as near to that sort of schedule as you can.

» Always remember to keep his water bowl topped up with fresh, clean water at all times.

- » Have news paper or puppy pads ready for his toilet training routine.

- » Have scales ready to weigh him, again making a note and comparing the previous week.

- » Don't forget his health check.

- » Continue his collar and leash training.

- » Make sure he is eating his meals and check that his faeces look normal; reasonably solid, no runny diarrhoea or unusual discharge.

- » Make sure he has plenty of suitable chew toys available.

- » Remember to brush/comb him at least once or twice per week.

- » Allow for some play time/exercise in the yard, garden or room in the house.

Growth and development

The puppy is still growing and developing and in order to avoid muscle, bone or ligament injury it is best to prevent him from becoming overexcited. It is normal around this age for him to start losing milk teeth so do not be alarmed if you notice a small tooth on his bedding or the floor.

Socialisation and behaviour

His socialisation around the house should continue. It is important to continue your normal household routine; vacuuming, switching on appliances etc. It depends on the personality of the puppy and he may be either indifferent or fearful to anything unusual. It is also important to keep him exposed to anything that makes him anxious as he needs to become 'desensitised' to fearful triggers. This certainly does not mean that you should literally take hold of him and make him face it. This is likely to terrify him and potentially have a long term psychological effect. It is therefore best to remain calm and reassure him but don't give in to this fear and attempt to protect or hide him away from it. Generally encourage him towards the thing he fears, all the while saying, 'come on', 'its alright', or words to that effect.

Play

The puppy will be naturally playful, but any play sessions with the family or other dogs should be monitored. You do not want things to get too rough or boisterous, and again be aware of biting which again should be corrected with a firm 'No'.

Toilet training

He should be getting used to the house-training routine by now. But do not neglect taking him out first thing in the morning, last thing at night, after each meal, having woken from sleep or any time he looks as if he is about to do his toilet business.

Planning a socialisation programme

For obvious reasons it is generally considered to be inadvisable to expose a puppy to potentially life threatening diseases until he has completed his final vaccinations. It is also generally considered that a puppy should be sufficiently socialised before the end of their 'critical period' usually at 12 to 16 weeks of age. Again refer to the chapter on socialisation.

Feeding

As you will be reducing his meals from 4 to 3 per day, be aware that an upset tummy can occur as a result of any changes of diet. Hopefully this will not happen if you change the times you feed which again ideally should be early morning, mid day, early evening.

Leash training and socialisation

This follows on from the leash training started during the previous week. Ideally you should be aiming to have your puppy leash trained for when he can safely socialise out and about. Again, it is important that he is comfortable being led on his lead without pulling. So it is advisable to carry on practicing leash walking around the yard/garden in order to make the transition as smooth as possible, in preparation for this. It is not vital that he is walking at 'heel' which will be covered later, but comfortable being led and not pulling or holding back.

WEEK 5: (12 WEEKS OLD)

- Make sure you are sticking to his 3 meals per day, and ensure his bowel movements are normal and regular

- Stick to the feeding times as per previous weeks. Always remember that it is better if your puppy keeps to a routine.

- Always remember to keep his water bowl topped up with fresh, clean water at all times.

- Have news paper or puppy pads ready for his toilet training routine.

- Have scales ready to weigh him.

- Don't forget his health check.

- Continue his collar and leash training.

- Make sure he is eating his meals and check that his faeces look normal; reasonably solid, no runny diarrhoea or unusual discharge.

- Make sure he has plenty of suitable chew toys available.

- Remember to brush/comb him at least once or twice per week.

- Allow for some play time/exercise in the yard, garden or room in the house.

Leash walking

If your puppy has completed his vaccination shots (this will only apply if you are following a UK, schedule. However, for the US or anywhere else, bear this information in mind for when your puppy finishes his schedule at approximately 16 weeks of age) and your vet has advised you that he is now safe to interact with other dogs, then start taking him out walking either around your neighbouring area or perhaps a dog park or local field. Again refer to the socialisation chapter for specific information.

His bones and ligaments are now stronger and he will have movement similar to a grown adult. However, as he is still growing and developing, walking should be restricted to 2 or 3 short walks and the odd romp in the garden, but nothing overly energetic. As a rule of thumb the larger the dog breed, the less exercise they will need or should have. If you go to an open space, be sure to attach a long training lead or attach a long retractable lead in case he goes running off.

Tooth loss

Again, you may notice milk teeth loss as the new teeth emerge, which is normal between the ages of 12 and 16 weeks old.

Socialisation and anxiety

As you may now be introducing new and potentially frightening experiences, be mindful that he is likely to act fearful. Again it is best to remain calm and reassuring, but do not make a fuss or attempt to hide him. If you are walking near busy roads, vehicles will seem large, added to this the noise and fast movement, it may take some getting used to.

It is important at this stage to put the socialisation action plan into motion. The same old people and locations are not adequate for this. New locations, sights, sounds, objects; people of all ages, shapes, sizes, personalities etc.

Training

At this age, a big obstacle is holding the puppies attention for longer than 10 minutes. They have a limited attention span and tendency to become easily bored at this age, concentrate training sessions to short 5 or 10 minutes gradually pushing this to 15 minutes at a time.

Bonding

He should be closer to everyone now and will be keen to please you and start behaving appropriately.

Home alone

We also cover this to a certain extent in the section on crate training.

Some trainers advise training the puppy to be home alone for short periods each day after the first week at 9 weeks old. However, it is advisable, in order to avoid separation anxiety, to start this no later than 12 weeks of age.

It is normal for any dog to pine or fret if they have been used to human company to suddenly be left on their own. They have no idea if or when you will be coming back. For this reason get him used to you leaving for short periods.

Set this up as follows:

1. It is best to confine him to the one room they sleep in along with his bed and his crate if you are using one. Again, the crate covered in a blanket with the door left open can offer a comforting retreat. Also leave toys and an item or items of clothing with your scent on. It is also a good idea to have the radio switched on as the music and talking, will be a distraction from the silence. Do not forget to leave water and perhaps a few treats.
2. Start by saying something like ' I won't be long' then closing the door for 10 seconds.
3. Provided he does not whine or bark, open the door again giving him lots of praise and offer a treat. If at any point he starts to whine or bark, only go back into the room once he stops. Otherwise it will become a habit that if he whines or barks you will return, and he may continue this if left for any length of time
4. Now repeat (2) and (3), but increase the time to 20 seconds then 30, then 40 and so on. Once you reach a minute, increase the time by minutes, so 1 minute, then 2 then 3 etc.

This training may sound long winded, but the repetition of this routine will soon accustom him to expecting you to return once you leave.

Nail clipping

Once your dog is regularly walking on pavements or running about a concrete yard his nails will probably not need clipping. You should still check them in case they become overgrown, particularly if you hear a scraping or tapping sound.

WEEK 6: (13 WEEKS OLD)

Keep following the checklist routine for the previous weeks. It will not be listed from now on, unless you are reminded about changing a specific aspect such as cutting his feeding down.

General condition

Weighing your puppy in the initial stages can be a useful indication that he is gaining weight. However, it is also a good idea to make visual and physical checks. As part of the weekly health check, take note of the puppy's body shape. It is obviously important that he is neither over nor underweight. Common sense will no doubt tell you whether he looks too thin with an obvious visible rib cage or obese, no ribs showing and obviously fat or barrel shaped.

A useful link showing illustrations from underweight to obese can be found at the following:

https://www.purina.co.uk/dogs/health-and-nutrition/exercise-and-weight-management/dog-body-condition-tool

It is therefore important that he receives a correct calorie intake and increase or decrease his food intake accordingly. Also, relate this to any increase in exercise and other activity likely to burn more calories.

Be aware that an underweight condition may be as a result of worms or other internal parasite. If after a couple of weeks, an increase or decrease in food intake does not show improvement then it is important to consult your vet for a check up.

Growing confidence

At this stage in his socialisation development, providing he has not experienced anything fearful or traumatic, most puppies will be confident expanding their experiences.

Mentally, he should be getting stronger and be in need of more mental stimulation either training or social experiences. At this age he is also likely to start pushing boundaries. Your usual well behaved puppy may start to misbehave. This can manifest in him wilfully ignoring you as he starts to please himself.

Regular routines

Once again, dogs like to know where they stand and therefore respond well to routines. These should include the following:

» Times of day when they know you will not be in the house, in order to avoid separation anxiety.

» Regular feeding times.

» Times when they know it is time for them to sleep when you go to bed.

» Exercise, play time and training times at approximately the same time per day.

Limits

As well as keeping to routines and letting him know where he stands you should also be very careful how you reward behaviours. During formal training you usually reward behaviour you want repeated and ignore behaviour you don't want repeating.

Problems can occur when you are playing and generally giving him attention. As puppies you will feel the need to encourage them by petting, stroking and saying 'good boy' etc. But if they start to misbehave, chew your hand or whatever, it is important to stop this. Encouraging the behaviour is obviously seen as rewarding to the puppy and they will continue.

Obedience training

Basic training, 'sit', 'stay' etc, should be improving by now providing you are continuing this on a daily basis. Regular repetition is a must, in order to keep him focused, reliable and well behaved.

Motivation

By regularly interacting with your dog through play and general interaction, you will soon find out what his is motivated by. This is very important in terms of rewards for training and general obedience. He will either be motivated by playing a certain game, being allowed to play with a favourite toy, or like most dogs, by food, and in some cases a favourite food.

Bite inhibition

Play mouthing or biting is inevitable for most puppies to varying degrees whilst they are teething. This is another area where you need to be very careful not to reward such

127

behaviour. You either need to stand up and walk away, or give a firm 'No', certainly no praising or trying to make a game of it.

WEEK 7: (14 WEEKS OLD)

As usual, make sure you are following the checklist of routines to carry out each week.

Although these may happen sooner or later, as he grows in size and confidence, you may experience the following behaviours:

Jumping up

Ignoring this behaviour by turning away as he jumps up usually has the desired effect of not rewarding the behaviour or acknowledging it as acceptable. If you can anticipate him jumping up, move toward him invading his space and taking away his momentum.

Manic exuberance

Over excitement is a problem that is started as a puppy, but can easily continue into adulthood. This usually happens when the dog anticipates a walk, or game etc. Again it is best to ignore the behaviour and not continue until they are calm. Please be aware that you are not ignoring him if you maintain eye contact with him. Therefore to make the ignoring more effective always break eye contact.

New socialisation experiences

Please note: if you are based anywhere where he will still be undergoing his vaccinations, socialisation may have only taken place under strict conditions. It is a risk to expose your puppy to infected areas until after his 16 week vaccination program is complete.

For anywhere else, the following may apply.

When exposing your puppy to any new experiences always remember to put him on a lead. It is unlikely you will have reliable control over his actions until he has desensitised from stimuli likely to cause either a fight (curiosity) or flight response.

WEEK 8: (15 WEEKS OLD)

As usual, make sure you are following the checklist of routines to carry out each week.

Growth and development

Up until 15 weeks of age you will have gradually noticed your puppy getting bigger and stronger in terms of bone and muscle growth. After 15 weeks you will probably notice things starting to slow down. His calorie intake and therefore food needs will also reach a plateau.

However it should be noted that he may still eat everything put in front of him. You should therefore be careful not to over feed, as he probably does not need as much food as he is willing and able to eat. Obviously cut down his daily food intake if he starts to look overweight.

Children and puppy play

Allowing children to interact with puppies from day one is usually recommended as long as this is always supervised. Usually by 15 weeks of age he has learned or is learning bite inhibition and that biting or nipping is not acceptable. However, if a puppy gets too excited during play nipping, play biting or mouthing can still occur.

If this happens as always give a firm 'No', end the game by ignoring him or walking away until he has calmed down. These are all procedures that should be practiced by you and your children.

Testing your leadership

As your puppy begins to gain confidence he may test your authority and leadership. This can happen sooner or later but is common around this age. It is always wise to assert your authority by being firm and letting him remember that you control the resources; food, attention, play toys etc. This is not about you been a dictator, but about retaining good manners and behaviour. He should also realise that any misbehaviour will result in you taking these resources away. Again it is simply a question of rewarding acceptable behaviour and ignoring anything unacceptable.

Resource guarding

This again is about you controlling the resources. It can occur over anything the dog wishes to possess and in extreme cases involves food which can lead to serious fights. If however your puppy takes a fancy to your best pair of shoes it is best to practice 'swapping'. Again, this is simply distracting him with one of his toys which hopefully he takes once he drops your shoes or other item. Never physically punish 'bad behaviour' but practice ignoring it.

Avoiding destructive behaviour

As a reminder, the biggest reasons for bad or destructive behaviour is a lack of general attention, exercise and mental stimulation.

On a daily basis it is therefore your responsibility to provide the following:

Sufficient exercise, preferably off lead running in a safe area; Walking several times per day; Taking time each day to play games of tug, fetch etc; Training; Agility and tricks; A varied assortment of soft, hard and puzzle toys (the previous activities should also provide much needed mental stimulation)

WEEK 9: (16 WEEKS OLD)

Make sure you are following the checklist of routines to carry out each week.

Weight

If you have been weighing your puppy on a weekly basis you may realise that at 16 weeks he is approximately half of his expected adult weight.

Bladder-control and house-training

As a young puppy he will have found it difficult to hold his bladder for more than an hour. At this age he should be able to hold it without needing to urinate between 3 and 5 hours. However, it is important to not get complacent as accidents are likely to happen if you do not take note of when he last did his toilet business and when he is likely to need to go again. As a matter of routine, plan to let him out for 5 minutes or so at least every 3 hours.

Continued socialisation

If you are in the U.S.A or other locations with a vaccination schedule up to 16 weeks of age, you may be safe to continue socialisation anywhere. However, as always check with your vet beforehand.

Similarly to the previous week and since you started socialising, endeavour to expose him to new experiences.

Household pets

If you have other pets, you may suddenly notice that the puppy at this age reacts differently towards them. This is generally as their senses and perceptions become more acute. What he may have ignored before may suddenly be an object of interest. This is important for breeds with a strong prey instinct. Pet cats, guinea pigs, rabbits etc may suddenly be vulnerable to an attack or an episode of chasing. He may of course react with fear or friendliness toward them. However, to be safe, carefully monitor his behaviour and supervise any interactions or let him observe whilst the pet is caged. Or in the case of a cat, the cat has an obvious escape route.

Dominant behaviour

Touched on previously, this is a trait which can occur by now. Unlike other unwanted behaviour this is best not ignored, but tell him 'No' if he starts to show any wilfulness or dominance towards anyone.

Grooming

As a reminder, in many cases extensive trimming, bathing etc is only required occasionally, every one to two months or so. However, on a daily basis it is a good idea to at least give a good brush and comb to prevent a build up of mats or loose hair, and to generally keep the coat healthy. It is also a good idea to coincide this with his weekly health check. Don't forget to check for signs of fleas or droppings, perhaps using a fine flea comb.

House proof evaluation

It is also important as the puppy grows to go over the routine you initially did before his arrival. Things that were safely out of his reach as a small puppy may now be reachable and may need moving or readjusting. As he is no doubt stronger and more active he could also potentially bump into objects that a young puppy would be unable to do, smashing or knocking them over. Food or harmful substances again should be kept out of reach.

WEEK 10: (17 WEEKS OLD)

Make sure you are following the checklist of routines to carry out each week.

Teething

At around this time his new teeth will begin to emerge. His gums will become irritable during this process and he will seek out opportunities to chew on hard objects. It will therefore be necessary to ensure he has a variety of chew toys hard and soft.

Exercise

You will no doubt notice he is more energetic at this stage

Confidence and curiosity

As his confidence grows, so will his desire to explore his surroundings. It is important to keep him safe and anticipate potential hazards when out in public. If in doubt keep him on a long training lead that you can easily follow and catch if he takes off and fails to respond.

Fear and socialising

Once again increase his exposure to new experiences. Be mindful that he may become fearful and as usual it is best to not give into this by being overly protective. This increased fear aspect may be more prevalent in puppies that have just started properly socialising after their final vaccination jab at 16 weeks old.

Housetraining

Even though his housetraining will be relatively reliable by now, do not take it for granted that accidents will never happen. Keep a routine of letting him out at regular intervals of at least 2 to 3 hours or so. Once again, accidents should never be punished.

Mental stimulation

He will respond and benefit well from you engaging him in one or two new mental stimulation games.

There are a number of useful books on the subject. Without wishing to recommend any in particular I would suggest doing a search on Amazon for search terms [dog tricks] or [dog games].

Obedience training

Hopefully you will be continuing with new training or revising skills already covered.

Food intake

Again, it is important to physically appraise your puppy and make sure he's neither too fat nor too thin.

WEEK 11: (18 WEEKS OLD)

Make sure you are following the checklist of routines to carry out each week.

Once again the puppy will require fewer calories than before and it is not unusual for him to start leaving part of his meal. In this respect it is not necessarily an indication that he is ill. You should therefore not worry unduly. Unless of course you suspect an illness, in which case do not hesitate to consult your vet for a check up.

However, muscle growth is a significant factor at this stage. It is therefore important that your puppy is receiving sufficient levels of protein in the form of good quality food.

Male puppies

At this stage males are beginning to sexually develop, with an increase in testosterone and consequent sexual behaviour.

Separation anxiety

Many people do not like the idea of crate training. However it is important that puppies are trained as early as possible to sleep remotely from you in some respect (this was covered in WEEK 5, but you can start this earlier). This may be utilising a crate or it could be confining him to the kitchen or other room. He needs to feel comfortable sleeping or generally being alone otherwise he may develop fear responses such as separation anxiety if he is not with you all the time.

Individual character

The puppy will have matured mentally at this stage and will be displaying more of his natural adult personality.

Independence

In the same way that children gradually gain independence from their parents, so the puppy will begin to venture and be keen to meet new potential playmates. This will usually take place where other dog walkers frequent such as parks, local recreation fields or pavement walking. This will be a strong temptation for any dog to rush off to greet other dogs. Do not therefore trust him off lead until you have trained a reliable recall.

Changing his collar

You may find at this stage that he has outgrown his collar; in which case it is advisable to take him to your local pet store and get them to size him for a new one.

WEEK 12: (19 WEEKS OLD)

Make sure you are following the checklist of routines to carry out each week.

In a similar way to previous weeks, growth and weight gain will be slowing down as he reaches maturity.

Adult coat

During puppyhood his coat will have been softer and by this age you may see signs of his adult coat coming through. Continue with regular grooming

Pecking order

His natural adolescence will see him pushing boundaries whether this is with you or other pets.

Growth and fear

In a similar way to human teenagers, growth can involve anxieties, fear and aggression. If this happens with your dog, accept this as a phase that he is likely to grow out of.

Feeding

At this stage it is a good idea to review his diet. He will have been on a diet suitable for a growing puppy. But again although muscle growth will continue to a certain extent, as his growth generally slows, he will need less protein than before.

Exercise

As with all exercise up to this point, long extended walks of three miles or more should be avoided. He will be getting stronger muscle and bone wise but is still vulnerable to injury. In this respect keep walks short and frequent.

Try and make sure that he has the opportunity to socialise and play with other dogs. You may wish to organise a group of other dog owners, join an organised group or simply meet other dog owners at a park etc.

Give him plenty of opportunities to meet dogs of different ages. In particular older dogs who will teach him appropriate behaviour and what he can and can't get away with.

WEEK 13: (20 WEEKS OLD)

Make sure you are following the checklist of routines to carry out each week.

If you have been weighing him on a regular basis, the weight that he will be at this stage should be approximately three quarters of his adult weight. His height should also be approximately three quarters of his adult height.

Teething

His gums will probably still be sore as his adult teeth are still emerging. It is important to note that certain dry dog food may be uncomfortable to eat as the hardness may jar on his sore gums. If you notice he seems off his food, try softer foods such as cooked chicken until this period subsides.

Sexual development

You should expect him to reach sexual maturity now or in the next week or so. Although his toilet training will for the most part be reliable, you will need to be aware that 'marking' behaviour in your house is a possibility, mostly by males. It will therefore be necessary to be vigilant to prevent this from becoming habitual.

Training

Basic commands should be solid and reliable by this point if you have been regularly practicing. You may have also started on some of the more advanced techniques.

If you have taught him routines beyond the basics, be aware that these need to be maintained with regular practice otherwise you may find he quickly forgets. As with all other aspects of maturity he will soon be mentally mature, but will not be as flexible at learning new information as he once was as a young puppy.

Continued socialisation

Again, if you have been following a socialisation plan you will be looking to add new experiences and solidify older ones.

Feeding

Up until this point you will have been feeding 3 meals per day. As his growth is slowing and he advances towards adulthood plan to cut his meals to two per day. Remember that when you reduced the number of meals from 4 to 3, it was necessary to make sure each meal is increased to keep the overall daily allowance in line with the recommended amount for his age and weight.

Cutting his meals down to 2 per day, also makes it much easier if your lifestyle dictates that you will not be around mid day as you can now feed morning and evening. If you stick to these routine times, he will invariably be ready to eat at these times.

Exercise

Remember to avoid boredom and behaviour problems by providing regular exercise and mental stimulation games.

WEEK 14: (21 WEEKS OLD)

Make sure you are following the checklist of routines to carry out each week.

He is now nearing 6 months of age and is nearing his physical and mental peak. If you have a bitch you may find she has her first season around now. Be aware that discharges (blood or otherwise) are possible, so be prepared to clean any mess up or confine her to any area that is easy to clean. Remember to not allow contact with intact males if she comes into season.

Dogs are also likely to exhibit mounting behaviour as part of their growing sexual maturity. In this respect they are capable of fathering a litter of puppies.

Again, be vigilant about catching them scent marking.

WEEK 15: (22 WEEKS OLD)

Make sure you are following the checklist of routines to carry out each week.

Bathing and teeth cleaning

Regular grooming is something you will have been doing on a regular basis since he arrived. However, bathing and teeth cleaning may not have been actioned as yet.

Intermediate training

Again, if you have not continued training him beyond basic obedience, you may wish to consider intermediate to advance training now. Many owners do not train their dog beyond basic obedience. This is fine but the puppy will benefit a great deal from further training procedures that will keep him mentally stimulated.

Having said that, please be aware that too much physical and mental stimulation can do more harm than good if he is not getting sufficient rest and sleep as well.

WEEK 16: (23 WEEKS OLD)

Make sure you are following the checklist of routines to carry out each week.

By this stage things will hopefully be going smoothly in terms of training, feeding and all other routines.

WEEK 17: (24 WEEKS OLD)

Make sure you are following the checklist of routines to carry out each week.

You may notice at this point or sooner his nails start to appear thicker and harder as his adult nails emerge. Nail clipping is something you have been doing or at least keeping an eye on as part of his regular checks and grooming. Be aware that they will be harder to cut.

Shedding

This depends on the breed but many breeds shed or 'blow' their coat twice per year. This is not dependent on seasonal changes as such but sunlight seems to play a part in the release of melatonin from the pineal gland, which causes shedding. Shedding can also occur as a result of artificial heat and light, an allergic reaction etc.

WEEK 18: (25 WEEKS OLD)

Make sure you are following the checklist of routines to carry out each week.

As he nears the six month mark he is still growing and maturing, but he will probably be at a size similar to his eventual adult size.

Problem behaviours

The ironical thing about problem behaviours is they are only a problem to us. To a dog the following are perfectly natural. However, as previously noted they are all also usually a symptom of boredom, lack of exercise or in some cases maturity, as follows:

Chewing; Digging; Resource guarding; Biting; Growling; Dominance; Fighting; Scent marking; Sexual behaviour; Roaming; Barking; Howling

It is obviously important to control or discourage these and should therefore be tackled before they get out of hand.

WEEK 19: (26 WEEKS OLD)

Make sure you are following the checklist of routines to carry out each week.

Again check your puppies general appearance and weight, ensuring they are not overweight through over feeding.

Tooth brushing

It is a good idea to start brushing their teeth as soon as possible for their oral health as well as getting him used to the routine. In the early stages his gums will have been benefiting more so as his baby teeth give way to adult teeth. Up to approximately 7 months of age his adult teeth will have come through. If you haven't already started this, it is now recommended that regular tooth brushing takes place. It is also recommended that you make available dental chews, and or raw meaty bones (never cooked bones, likely to splinter) will be an important routine, to clean the teeth and gums.

Scavenging

A natural behaviour for dogs is scavenging and begging, which you may encounter around this time.

It is important to discourage this by not randomly giving them food other than their meals or treats for good behaviour.

Adulthood and dominance

Group hierarchy is natural for dogs as they reach adulthood and sexual maturity. They may form 'pecking orders' with other dogs, but in the absence of firm leadership from you, may also attempt to dominate you or other family members, if you let them.

The opposite of this is submissive behaviour. This is a fundamental reason why traditional dog training involving 'alpha rolls' and other techniques are a bad idea for many dogs. A lot of dogs can become fearful and lack confidence if they are subjected to such harsh training methods.

Keeping calm

During his transition towards adulthood you may find that certain socialisation encounters, make him fearful and consequently stressed. It is very important to remember to deal with these as noted before, by firstly identifying the trigger/problem and then gradually desensitising him.

WHAT TO EXPECT DURING THE NEXT 3 MONTHS (6 TO 9 MONTHS)

Although chewing is associated with teething, if a dog has a predisposition towards chewing, this will continue regardless. However, many dogs do exercise the need to chew around this age, specifically in conjunction with them acquiring their adult teeth. For this reason it is always important to provide chew toys as well as keep chewable valuables, shoes etc, out of reach.

Growth

Slow gradual growth will now continue towards adulthood. In most cases a six month old puppy will be approximately at their expected adult size. However, depending on the breed and the individual, adulthood usually occurs around 9 months, but can be another 6 months beyond this. His senses will also be much more acute around this age.

Hormonal issues

You may have already encountered issues associated with hormonal increases such as sexual behaviour, general aggression, resource guarding or aggression towards other dogs. It usually passes without issue, but if you get recurring problems then you may need to consider neutering. If so you are advised to consult with your vet as to your puppies suitability.

Feeding

Once again, continue to regularly check your dogs weight against the ideal weight. Also visually check for obesity or being underweight. Again, if when you feel along the rib cage you cannot feel his ribs, chances are he is overweight through over feeding.

House training

Hopefully you have been keeping to a routine of regularly letting him outside to do his toilet business. In addition, provided you have been vigilant, watching for signs of him needing to go, you should be encountering few if any 'accidents'. It is worth noting however that at this age most puppies are able, or potentially capable to hold their bladder for between 6 and 8 hours. Technically speaking he can now hold his bladder overnight, but this does not mean you will not come down to a pool of urine. It all depends if he has a drink overnight, or whether he urinated before you retire to bed.

WHAT TO EXPECT DURING THE NEXT 3 MONTHS (9 – 12 MONTHS)

Despite him nearing maturity, he is still likely to retain his puppy exuberance.

Chasing

The chase prey instinct, if this occurs, should be channelled into acceptable alternatives such as chasing balls or other toys. Although with perseverance, a reliable recall can be achieved. You do however, have to be prepared for unpredictability. Prevention is therefore often the only reliable solution to chase behaviour. In areas where rabbits, squirrels and other wildlife frequent, keep him on a long line leash unless it is safe from road traffic or other hazards, let him off leash.

Infections and disease

Ear and skin disorders are common until he has a strong, developed immune system. Parasites can take their toll in terms of weakening the immune system which is why you should treat for worms and fleas etc on a regular basis. As part of his regular health check you should also check the ears for mites or infection, and the skin for disorders.

Injury, strains and sprains

As he matures and grows in strength and confidence, so will the risk of injury. Obviously injuries can occur at any age, but will be more so the stronger and more active he becomes. Ligaments, joints and muscles are therefore susceptible to tears, strains, sprains and breakages. Do not hesitate to consult your vet if such injuries occur during any kind of activity.

1 YEAR AND BEYOND

Do not confuse muscle gain with obesity. Having reached one year he will have attained an adult physicality but may still bulk out muscle wise up to 18 months of age.

Routines which you have been following must be maintained at all times.

Be careful not to over feed, or to leave him with ad lib food and expect him to eat only as much as he needs. Some dogs are good at eating only their daily needs but others can be greedy which results in obesity issues.

Hopefully you have read this far and have found the contents useful, informative and inspiring. There is a lot to consider when buying any dog, and consequently to appreciate their needs. Hopefully this book reflects that. For the most part, dogs that are properly looked after with love, care and respect, will repay you with unconditional love and devotion, many times over.

The intention of the book was not to overwhelm you the reader and put you off committing to being the guardian of this fantastic Cockapoo breed. The intention was simply to give you as broad an appreciation as possible of his training needs, so that you are fully prepared and equipped to properly look after and appreciate your new friend.

As you will realise, having read the various chapters, keeping a dog happy does not necessarily come without its problems. However, with correct awareness and training, many potential problems can be avoided. The health and welfare of your new Cockapoo should go without saying, so please do everything you can to provide healthy food and a safe warm environment. In essence, it doesn't take a lot to keep your dog happy and healthy.

At the very least you should be providing the following:

(i) A warm safe habitat. (ii) Healthy food and fresh water, daily. (iii) Routine health procedures such as worming, flea treatment and veterinary check-ups. (iv) Basic training and regular daily exercise. (v) As much love and attention as you can provide.

Thank you for reading and allowing me to assist you in being a loving, caring guardian for your new friend.

Printed in Great Britain
by Amazon